D0219357

The Cambridge Introduction to
Travel Writing

Critics have long struggled to find a suitable category for travelogues. From its ancient origins to the present day, the travel narrative has borrowed elements from various genres – from epic poetry to literary reportage – in order to evoke distant cultures and exotic locales, and sometimes those closer to hand. Tim Youngs argues in this lucid and detailed Introduction that travel writing redefines the myriad genres it comprises and is best understood on its own terms. To this end, Youngs surveys some of the most celebrated travel literature from the medieval period until the present, exploring themes such as the quest motif, the traveller's inner journey, postcolonial travel and issues of gender and sexuality. The text culminates in a chapter on twenty-first-century travel writing and offers predictions about future trends in the genre, making this Introduction an ideal guide for today's students, teachers and travel writing enthusiasts.

Tim Youngs is Professor of English and Travel Studies at Nottingham Trent University. His publications include the forthcoming *Beastly Journeys: Travel and Transformation at the Fin de Siècle* (2013), and he is the co-editor of *The Cambridge Companion to Travel Writing* (2002). In 1997, he founded *Studies in Travel Writing* and continues to serve as the journal's editor.

The Cambridge Introduction to

Travel Writing

TIM YOUNGS

Nottingham Trent University

CAMBRIDGE
UNIVERSITY PRESS

32 Avenue of the Americas, New York NY 10013-2473, USA

Cambridge University Press is part of the University of Cambridge.

It furthers the University's mission by disseminating knowledge in the pursuit of education, learning, and research at the highest international levels of excellence.

www.cambridge.org
Information on this title: www.cambridge.org/9780521697392

© Tim Youngs 2013

This publication is in copyright. Subject to statutory exception and to the provisions of relevant collective licensing agreements, no reproduction of any part may take place without the written permission of Cambridge University Press.

First published 2013
Reprinted 2014

A catalog record for this publication is available from the British Library.

Library of Congress Cataloging in Publication data
Youngs, Tim, 1961–
The Cambridge introduction to travel writing / Tim Youngs.
pages cm
Includes bibliographical references and index.
ISBN 978-0-521-87447-2 (hardback) – ISBN 978-0-521-69739-2 (paperback)
1. Travelers' writings, English – History and criticism. 2. Travelers' writings, American – History and criticism. 3. Travelers' writings – History and criticism. 4. Travel in literature. 5. Travel writing – History. 6. Voyages and travels – Historiography. I. Title.
PR756.T72Y68 2013
820.9′32–dc23 2012019950

ISBN 978-0-521-87447-2 Hardback
ISBN 978-0-521-69739-2 Paperback

Cambridge University Press has no responsibility for the persistence or accuracy of URLs for external or third-party Internet Web sites referred to in this publication, and does not guarantee that any content on such Web sites is, or will remain, accurate or appropriate.

To Peter Hulme for leading the way

Contents

Figures

Acknowledgements

This book results from a quarter of a century's work on travel writing. A disadvantage of this fact is that I am conscious, on completion, of all the reading I have not been able to fit into it, and of all the reading yet to be done. There is always more to do, especially in a field as dynamic as this one. A happier outcome is the opportunity to acknowledge, if insufficiently, the number of debts I have incurred. Any list would be incomplete, so, with apologies to those whom I have overlooked (and with the usual but sincere caveat that all weaknesses and mistakes are my own), I am grateful to the following who have variously provided encouragement, support, hospitality and ideas: to Nottingham Trent University for my career so far; to Tara Books for permission to reproduce images and text from Bhajju Shyam, *The London Jungle Book* (London: Tara Publishing in association with the Museum of London, 2004); to the anonymous readers of the proposal for and submission of this work; to Susan Bassnett, Françoise Besson, Dinah Birch, Peter Bishop, William Blazek, Jan Borm, Roy Bridges, Peter Brooker, Adam Burbage, Robert Burroughs, Mary Baine Campbell, Steve Clark, Ben Colbert, Patrick Crowley, William Dalrymple, Robyn Davidson, Jean-Yves Le Disez, Stephen Donovan, Jacqueline Dutton, R. J. (Dick) Ellis, Charles Forsdick, Indira Ghose, Pere Gifra-Adroher, Jayati Gupta, Betty Hagglund, Martin Hargreaves, Glenn Hooper, Peter Hulme, John Hutnyk, Alison and Andrew and Sarah Johnson, Anna Johnston, Emilia Ljungberg, John Lucas, Gesa Mackenthun, Tilar Mazzeo, Nivedita Misra, Sharon Ouditt, Alasdair Pettinger, Russ Pottle, Silvia Ross, Anka Ryall, Ray Ryan, Dinah Roma Sianturi, Paul Smethurst, Stan Smith, Juan Pablo Spicer-Escalante, Lee Sterrenburg, Claire Thomas, Carl Thompson, John Tomlinson, Gary Totten, Sam Ward, Richard White, Gregory Woods, Tom Wright, Gary Younge, Waldemar Zacharasiewicz, Carl Thompson's and my Travel Writing students at Nottingham Trent University (especially those who graduated in 2011) and my postgraduate travel students, completed and current. The book serves as an inadequate memorial to Sarmukh Singh Sikand and Sohindar Kaur Sikand, both of whom passed away during the time I was writing it, and whose journeys made possible this final acknowledgement: above all, and always, to Gurminder and Natty, with love, gratitude and admiration.

Chapter 1

Introduction: Defining the terms

a genre in which I don't believe.
Jonathan Raban[1]

What is travel writing?

Travel writing, one may argue, is the most socially important of all literary genres. It records our temporal and spatial progress. It throws light on how we define ourselves and on how we identify others. Its construction of our sense of 'me' and 'you', 'us' and 'them', operates on individual and national levels and in the realms of psychology, society and economics. The processes of affiliation and differentiation at play within it can work to forge alliances, precipitate crises and provoke wars. Travelling is something we all do, on different scales, in one form or another. We all have stories of travel and they are of more than personal consequence.

Travel narratives, both oral and written, have been around for millennia. Yet their longevity has made it no easier for critics to agree on how to define or classify them. No discussion of travel writing seems complete without critics remarking on the difficulty of determining their object of study. Carl Thompson remarks that the term 'encompasses a bewildering diversity of forms, modes and itineraries'.[2] For Patrick Holland and Graham Huggan, the genre is 'notoriously refractory to definition'.[3] Michael Kowaleski refers to its 'dauntingly heterogeneous character', and notes that it 'borrows freely from the memoir, journalism, letters, guidebooks, confessional narrative, and, *most important*, fiction'.[4] Charles Forsdick describes 'the generic indeterminacy of the travelogue, a literary form situated somewhere between scientific observation and fiction, while simultaneously problematizing any clear-cut distinction of those two poles'.[5] Barbara Korte finds that 'the travelogue is a genre not easily demarcated'.[6] This is in part because, 'As far as its theme and content matter are concerned, the travel account has not emerged as a genre hermetically sealed off from other kinds of writing.'[7] Jonathan Raban, in a comment quoted so often that any discussion of the character of travel writing seems incomplete without it, suggests that, 'As a literary form, travel writing is a notoriously raffish open house where very different genres are likely to end up in the same bed. It accommodates the private diary, the essay, the short story, the prose poem, the rough note and polished table talk with indiscriminate hospitality.'[8] In a less-often cited extension to his metaphor, Raban alleges that 'critics, with some justification, have usually regarded it [the travel book] as a resort of easy virtue'; he even charges that travel writing is located in 'literature's red-light establishment'.[9]

When Peter Hulme and I edited *The Cambridge Companion to Travel Writing* (2002), our task was complicated by our first having to define the object it was meant to accompany.[10] I am now faced with the challenge of making a *Cambridge Introduction to Travel Writing* introduce this stubbornly indefinable form that some critics argue does not constitute a genre at all and that languishes in a house of ill repute. It is difficult to know where to begin.

One step is to identify the importance of the concept of genre. It is not merely a descriptive label but a way of making sense of the structures by which we describe our surroundings and perceive meaning in them. In John Frow's words, 'genres actively generate and shape knowledge of the world'; they 'create effects of reality and truth, authority and plausibility, which are central to the different ways the world is understood in the writing of history or of philosophy or of science, or in painting, or in everyday talk'.[11] They, or what Frow calls 'generically shaped knowledges', are also 'bound up with the exercise of power, where power is understood as being exercised in discourse, as well as elsewhere, but is never simply external to discourse'.[12] We shall turn to the specific relationship between travel and power shortly. When we have arrived at a definition of travel writing, we should bear in mind Frow's assumption that 'all texts are strongly shaped by their relation to one or more genres, which in turn they may modify'.[13] Fittingly, given that our subject is mobility, genres are not fixed but dynamic. As Frow puts it:

> [B]ecause the range of possible uses is always open-ended, genre classifications are necessarily unstable and unpredictable. And this is so above all because texts do not simply have uses which are mapped out in advance by the genre: they are themselves *uses of genre*, performances of or allusions to the norms and conventions which form them and which they may, in turn, transform.[14]

Just as Frow acknowledges that his book on genres itself has a 'generic shape, that of the "introductory guide"'[15] so does this *Cambridge Introduction to Travel Writing*, which fits both into the series that gives it its name and into the genre of introductory works on travel writing. The latter have themselves set up their own pattern and expectations, as Dinah Roma Sianturi shrewdly notes:

> Recent travel theory books are often introduced in a growing standardized manner. It begins with a reminder of how there has been a resurgence in critical attention to travel writing over the past decades alongside commentaries on how the belated recognition of the travel writing genre has been on account of its "heterogenous nature." It crosses boundaries and unsettles the conventions of other disciplines. It is both fact and fiction. It was for a long time viewed [as] amateurish and sub-literary until finally the introduction touches on its so called "imperial origins." And it is here [that] the arguments begin to tread on sensitive grounds.
>
> The key question that confronts contemporary travel theory involves the very question that launched a long standing investigation [of] the genre. Can it divest itself of its imperial origins? Can it, despite being reminded of its violent beginnings, move forward and achieve discursive maturity?[16]

Sianturi shrewdly maps the contours of such discussions. This introductory chapter has inevitably been informed by and follows many of them. Whether and how it deviates from these, and, if it does, what effect the detour will have on future examples will become more apparent later.

The guiding principle of this book is that travel writing consists of predominantly factual, first-person prose accounts of travels that have been undertaken by the author-narrator. It includes discussion of works that some may regard as genres in their own right, such as ethnographies, maritime narratives, memoirs, road and aviation literature, travel journalism and war reporting, but it distinguishes these from other types of narrative in which travel is narrated by a third party or is imagined. Comparison with these latter narratives aids a clearer understanding of the relationship between forms. The boundary between them is not fixed. The way that texts are read changes over the years. Our understanding of genres is historically as well as textually determined. For example, Herman Melville's *Typee* (1846) was received as a truthful example of the kind of shipwreck narrative on which it was modelled until the author's reputation as a novelist became better known and the work's complex interplay of autobiography, fiction and literary influences was better understood. Likewise, and more famously, Jonathan Swift's *Gulliver's Travels* – or, to give it its proper title, *Travels into Several Remote Nations of the World* by Lemuel Gulliver (1726) – presents itself as a travel narrative but is now known as a humorous work of fiction with political and moral intent; its satire on travel narratives takes second place. Neither *Gulliver's Travels* nor *Typee* would be considered travel writing any longer, but their form illustrates how fiction has borrowed from travel texts. The borrowing happens the other way, too. Travel writers draw on the techniques of fiction to tell their stories. Plot, characterisation and dialogue all play their part.[17] Whereas some travel writers insist on absolute verisimilitude, others readily admit to the manipulation and invention of detail.

Travel and movement (metaphorical or actual) are so fundamental to literary writing in general that, as Peter Hulme puts it, 'There is almost no statuesque literature'.[18] The prevalence of literary journeys – noted also by Casey Blanton, who observes that 'the journey pattern is one of the most persistent forms of all narratives'[19] – leads Hulme to argue that an exclusive definition of literature and of travel writing is required. For texts to count as travel writing, Hulme believes, their authors must have travelled to the places they describe. There is, he insists, an ethical dimension to their claims to have made the journeys they recount. If the claim is later found to be false, the author's work 'is discredited' and the text moves out of the category of travel writing into another such as the imaginary voyage.[20] Hulme's distinction is an appealingly straightforward one. Yet, for other critics, it is complicated by the existence of close overlaps between fictional and factual accounts of travel. Each borrows from the other, employing similar narrative structures and literary techniques.[21] As Kowaleski observes, not only are 'travel writing's affiliations with other kinds of factual writing … both complex and abiding', but 'travel accounts have historically formed one of the main sources for the novel and travel writers continue to utilize fictional devices such as an episodic structure, picaresque motifs, and (most significantly) the foregrounding of a narrator'.[22]

Indeed, some works of literature may even shift from one category to another. I have mentioned the examples of *Gulliver's Travels* and *Typee*, to which another famous addition would be Daniel Defoe's *Robinson Crusoe* (1719). Put one way, such cases do nothing to undermine Hulme's case: they simply show that works of imaginative fiction employ some of the methods of travel writing in order to establish and maintain the pretence that the journeys undertaken by their protagonists actually took place. Knowing at the time or later that Lemuel Gulliver, Robinson Crusoe and Tommo are fictional creations, even if their adventures are based on those of real people (Crusoe's on Alexander Selkirk and Tommo's on those of Melville himself), is sufficient to disqualify them as travel writing, according to Hulme's criterion. The status of most texts can readily be judged by that test. Nonetheless, it is difficult to overlook the mutual influence of fictional and factual accounts of travel. An examination of the strategies of both kinds of narrative will show that they have much in common, whether they observe Hulme's rule or not. Even Korte's delineation of the 'basic understanding' of the travelogue's 'characteristic features' that 'has evolved over the centuries' does not distinguish between fictional and factual treatments of travel:

> [A]ccounts of travel depict a journey in its course of events and thus constitute narrative texts (usually composed in prose). They claim – and their readers believe – that the journey recorded actually took place, and that it is presented by the traveller him or herself. Within this basic frame of definition, accounts of travel manifest themselves in a broad formal spectrum, giving expression to a great variety of travel experience.[23]

Korte goes on to note that, 'As far as the text and its narrative techniques are concerned, there appears to be *no essential distinction between the travel account proper and purely fictional forms of travel literature*'. Defining travel writing by its authenticity, by the criterion that the journey that is narrated did actually take place, depends, Korte remarks, on an assumption that 'can only be tested *beyond the text itself*'.[24]

Some theorists will agree with Korte and regard appeals to biography an irrelevant distraction. Others will consider the requirement that travel writing record actual journeys a reasonable test. Texts are not read in a vacuum. Korte's point, however, is that both authentic and fictional works employ similar literary devices to achieve their effects. In Korte's words, 'The actual experience of a journey is reconstructed, and *therefore fictionalized*, in the moment of being told'.[25] Her statement that 'reports of travel necessarily *re-create* the experience of the journey on which they are based'[26] superficially resembles what Hulme tells his students: 'All travel writing – because it is writing – is *made* in the sense of being constructed, but travel writing cannot be *made up* without losing its designation'.[27] Yet Hulme is adamant that 'travel writing is certainly literature, but it is never fiction'.[28]

Mindful of dissenting voices, the focus of this *Cambridge Introduction to Travel Writing* is on travel writing as Hulme defines it. It will follow Hulme's premise that travel writing must relate a journey that has been made by its author. Discussion of iconic figures such as Mandeville and Marco Polo, about whom there is still uncertainty and argument, inevitably involves caveats. Some prominent examples of fictional travels are noted, but the emphasis is on texts that narrate real rather than imagined journeys, although there is some consideration of how travel writing and other types of literature (factual and fictional) are interlinked, sharing motifs, themes, settings and techniques.

The distinction between travel writing and other forms of literature that deal in part with movement should not, however, lead to an assumption that travel writing itself is homogeneous. The opposite is true. Not only is it the case that 'travel writing employs a range of concepts of otherness',[29] but, as Korte reminds us: 'Works of "non-fiction" also treat the journey in various forms'.[30] Guidebooks, manuals, itineraries, reports and other factual accounts have their own characteristics and these may differ by, among other factors, period or location. For Korte, the 'particular attraction' of travel writing 'lies in its very heterogeneity in matters of form and content'.[31] It is that quality, along with travel writing's long history, that has contributed to the problems of definition. The genres from which travel narratives borrow, or of which they are composed, stand in their own right: the scientific report, the diary, autobiography, correspondence, the novel, journalism and so on.

The presence in travel writing of features associated with other literary forms leads many critics to regard it as lacking an identity of its own. Holland and Huggan refer to it as 'this most hybrid and unassimilable of literary genres'.[32] For them, 'Travel writing … is hard to define, not least because it is a hybrid genre that straddles categories and disciplines'.[33] Korte writes of its 'generic hybridity and flexibility'.[34] To Jan Borm, 'it is not a genre, but a collective term for a variety of texts both predominantly fictional and non-fictional whose main theme is travel'.[35] More specifically, Jill Steward writes of 'the fluidity of the boundaries between [travel] literature and journalism'.[36] A near-consensus has developed that travel writing is a mixed form that feeds off other genres. There are other points of view. A rare dissenting voice is that of Guillaume Thouroude, who cautions that 'it is misleading to consider travel writing as a quintessentially hybrid genre *as opposed to* other presumably "pure" genres'.[37] Thouroude mounts the very interesting argument that:

> As a work, or as a group of works (i.e. a genre), it is obvious that no strict limitations can be accepted when categorising travel writing and its forms, and that hybridity is constitutive of it. But a shift in theoretical perspective, which allows us to regard travel narratives as a generic category (mode), leads us to question this hybridity, and to detect a fundamental attitude connected to travel, displacement and territories in contemporary literature.[38]

Thouroude suggests that rather than view travel writing as hard to classify because of its generic admixture, we should accept that this is what actually characterises it. It is a genre whose intergeneric features constitute its identity. Adoption of this position would certainly save much critical agonising and reduce the number of circular discussions (like this one) about the make-up of travel writing.

Yet a further problem of definition lies in determining the point at which travel narratives become ones of sojourn or residence. Book titles may refer to a particular number of years, or, more rarely, weeks or months spent in a place, but there is no fixed period at which an account of a journey becomes one of settlement. In such cases it may be helpful to apply Kowaleski's statement that 'No matter how much "inside" description a traveler employs in evoking another culture and its people, a crucial element of all travel writing remains the author's "visitor" status. He or she remains, as the reader's surrogate, a cultural outsider who moves into, through and finally beyond the places and events encountered'.[39] Or we may decide that what makes the difference in such cases is the degree of openness shown by the traveller towards the host culture and the extent to which the visitor is assimilated by it, regardless of length of residence. It is easy to think of the monolingual, culturally unadventurous expatriate as remaining more of an outsider after decades of residence in his or her new country than the short-term visitor who speaks the host language and is familiar with its culture.

The study of travel writing

Popular with the reading public, travel writing has been taken seriously in universities only in the past three or four decades. Indeed, the public enthusiasm for travel writing may be a reason for the slowness of academics to give it the attention they bestow on other literary forms or historical documents. Korte is right to point out that 'literary studies have taken comparatively little interest in travel writing until fairly recently … unless it related to "recognized" works of literature'.[40] Kowaleski also hardly exaggerates when he complains that, 'There is a venerable tradition of condescending to travel books as a second-rate literary form'.[41] That condescension may be a cause of the denials from prominent authors of travel books that they are in fact travel writers. To name only two among many, Bruce Chatwin did not like the label and Jan Morris is reported as saying at the 25th Thomas Cook Travel Book Awards that 'I've never thought of myself as a travel writer. The term travel writing seems a bit demeaning'.[42]

Jonathan Raban has gone beyond the standard rejection of the label. One of the most novelistic of travel writers, Raban has stated that he does not believe in the distinction between fact and fiction. The travel book, he remarks, 'is a genre in which I don't believe. I just don't believe that it exists. It isn't as though I think I do something more than write travel books – it's just that I don't believe in the travel book as a legitimate form'.[43] Related to Raban's comment is the question of the veracity of the narrative. Even if the text recounts a journey that did take place, there are disagreements over the degree to which it may be embellished. One prolific British travel writer, Geoffrey Moorhouse, acknowledges that 'the travel narrative is indeed in a rather special category of literature: it can include topographical description, history, autobiography, reminiscence about almost anything under the sun that you think your readers will tolerate as having some relevance to your journey or your disquisition on a particular place'. As far as Moorhouse is concerned, however, this variety should not extend to invention. What Moorhouse describes as the 'almost all-embracing freedom' of the range of elements, 'should only be enjoyed … within a very exacting discipline. And that is to tell the truth. Why? Simply because *that*, I think, is what your readers expect you to be doing when they read your account of some distant place and your experiences on the way'.[44] The expectation voiced by Moorhouse is similar to William Dalrymple's idea of a compact between author and readers that places a responsibility on travel writers not to breach the trust invested in them. Dalrymple draws parallels with the obligation on journalists to tell the truth.[45] Significantly, Moorhouse and Dalrymple, like many travel writers, also practise journalism. For such figures, any alteration of experience for the sake of the story must be minimal. Moorhouse reports that the furthest he has gone in his travel books is 'to edit some conversations which, if repeated verbatim, would have bored *me* stiff, let alone my readers. Beyond that I have always found I cannot go, because I would feel uncomfortable about the deception'.[46] (Of course, the excision of boring detail is itself an editorial compromising of reality.) Moorhouse does admit, however, when recalling an earlier book whose self-exposure now makes him feel awkward, that 'I can see how it is that most authors may prefer to write themselves into fictions, so that while telling the sometimes painful or embarrassing truth about themselves, they can nevertheless enjoy the illusion of concealment'.[47] We shall return later in this volume to the distance between author, narrator and protagonist, a matter essential to an understanding of travel texts as constructions – as *made*, in Hulme's terms.

Some travel writers, on the other hand, are more comfortable than Moorhouse and Dalrymple with embroidering. In the late 1990s, Dea Birkett and Sara Wheeler proclaimed: 'Travel writing has made a new departure. A generation of writers who push the limits of the genre has emerged from the old adventure school. … Travel writers have become more literary and less literal. This fusion of biography, memoir and fiction – let's call it New Travel Writing – is among the richest literature around'.[48] In this new travel writing, what matters is 'not *what* we see, but *how* we see'.[49] The aphorism 'more literary and less literal' may be catchy and the coinage of the new neat, but these stereotype both the old and the new, exaggerating the dominance of types in each. There are plenty of counter-examples in the new and in what came before it.

It is in part because of the new – or newly designated – women's and postcolonial travel writing in particular that the study of travel writing has become more established since the 1980s. True, some literary scholars contend that scrutiny of the genre is more the responsibility of cultural than of literary studies, believing its interest to be primarily sociological and its aesthetic value less than that of the novel, poetry and drama. That perception owes much to the fact that the new academic interest in travel writing can be dated, like many developments in colonial and postcolonial literary studies, to the publication in 1978 of Edward Said's *Orientalism*. Said's text generated a wave of studies that looked at the ways in which travel writing, particularly of the nineteenth century, represented other cultures. Whereas Said's focus was on the Middle East, his identification of the connections between travel, representation and empire continue to influence countless works on travel to other areas of the world. Perhaps Said's major contribution in this context has been to show that travel writing does not consist simply of individual or disinterested factual accounts. Rather, travellers have already been influenced, before they travel, by previous cultural representations that they have encountered. Thus, they never look on places anew or completely independently but perceive them instead through an accretion of others' accounts. Said's influence, and that of postcolonialism, is evident in Blanton's prefatory remark that her method of proceeding in her survey of travel writing became easier once she understood 'that travel books are vehicles whose main purpose is to introduce us to the other, and that typically they dramatiz[e] an engagement between self and world'.[50]

Postcolonial theory's recognition of the connections between travel, empire, capitalism and racial ideologies gave an important impetus to travel studies. It broke the illusion that travel texts are ideologically neutral and objective, but it also had the unfortunate effect of making travel writing seem essentially a conservative genre, complicit with the forces of patriarchy and imperialism. Debbie Lisle, for example, writes that 'colonial relations are constitutive of both the historical development of the genre *and* its general poetics'.[51] That is a partial view, ignoring a range of travel texts that do not fit the pattern. For one thing, there are works of domestic travel that do not venture beyond the borders of the nation in which they are produced (although in some cases, processes similar to those witnessed in overseas travel texts are evident, especially in the construction of class and gender).[52] These often raise challenging questions about economic structures, political governance and social arrangements. For another, there are works that are radical in their politics – challenging capitalist and colonial expansion – and radical in their aesthetics, too.[53] Such texts have received far too little notice. Lack of awareness of them produces a skewed sense of the genre.

Postcolonial and other theories demonstrate that 'The biggest fiction … is travel writing's own claim to being an objective genre. What does anyone really know about a foreign place that isn't partly his or her own creation? We're always choosing what we see, what we don't see, and whom we meet; we're always inventing our destinations'.[54] All sorts of factors contribute to that lack of objectivity and to the invention of the places we visit. In addition to the processes noted by Said that involve our prior exposure to cultural representations, there are also psychological, technological, aesthetic and material aspects. These obstacles to a neutral, direct experience of a destination are reinforced by the existence of many other points of intervention between the acts of travel, writing, publication and reading. Scholars such as Roy Bridges and Ian MacLaren have examined and attempted to classify the different stages of written account, from fieldnotes through written-up journals, to edited copy and the finished, published work. Travel writers such as Robyn Davidson have talked about the gap between the journey and its narrative; between the travelling self, the narrated self and the author.[55] Commercial considerations also come into play alongside generic convention: writers generally want to sell their work and publishers need to sell books. Hence, for example, the proliferation of titles that follow a popular formula (e.g., Tony Hawkes's gimmicky *Round Ireland with a Fridge* [1998] or the 'footsteps' motif).

Travel also entails cultural and linguistic translation. These displace meanings from their original context into another. Not only is accuracy at stake, but also the process of transference that heightens the sense of movement, of contingency. Michael Cronin and Loredana Polezzi are among the translation and comparative literature scholars who have written about these issues specifically in relation to travel writing.[56] Like travel itself, translation can produce violence or cooperation, conflict or exchange. It also leads to the creation of an intermediate ground on which newly formed meanings find their own space. Translators and travellers may be seen as liminal figures moving between cultures, not quite or wholly belonging to any one exclusively. The subject of translation and travel will be discussed further in Chapter 11.

One of the questions running through this book, then, is: what happens between the experience of travel and the perception, representation and the reception of it? Key to this is the 'foregrounding of the narrator', which Blanton regards as 'central to an understanding of the travel book'.[57] Once we attend to that, we will be able to move towards a greater appreciation of the literariness as distinct from – or even as opposed to – the documentary function of travel writing.

In recent years, much work has been done on the rediscovery of the travels of non-Europeans; of accounts from the so-called periphery to the centre. This new body of scholarship serves to remind us that travel is not singular in direction or in perspective: people journeyed from India, Africa and other colonised regions, as well as between and within them. They wrote about their travels in ways that sometimes mirror the accounts of Britons overseas. Britons themselves emigrated and made return visits.[58] Studies have also shown encounters from a reverse perspective: indigenous peoples discovering strangers arriving in their countries. This work informs Chapter 8, but its influence also runs throughout the volume.

Omissions and caveats

Many travel books, especially in the eighteenth and nineteenth centuries, begin with an apology for their inadequacy. In homage to that tradition, I remark here that an introduction such as this one can only ever be that: an *introduction*. It cannot possibly be comprehensive. My concentration on travel literature excludes oral narratives of travel and omits the unwritten stories of the impoverished and the persecuted whose journeys have a grim economic or political necessity.[59] Even within the strict criteria I have applied, travel texts of many areas, periods, types and by important individuals will escape mention. One should not infer from their exclusion that they do not matter. They do. But an introduction cannot be an encyclopaedia. Even from within the English-language tradition alone – the main focus of this volume – there are unavoidably many notable writers and works not featured here. My principle has been to combine range with focus and to include some lesser-known authors in order to challenge some of the assumptions often made about the genre. If the gaps weaken the book, they nevertheless underline its motivation: to show that this poor cousin of literary genres, as it is often regarded, is rich, complex, flexible and worthy of endless study. After a quarter of a century devoted to its study, I remain more conscious than when I began of examples that remain out of my reach. Appropriately, travel writing is not a static object. William Dalrymple has described it as 'a very popular form still, because it … has the ability to reinvent itself for each period'.[60]

Furthermore, like all literature and all criticism, this *Introduction to Travel Writing* must be read in its context and seen to be of its moment. Modern-day theorists run the risk of appearing self-congratulatory in their critiques of colonial texts and of critics less enlightened than themselves, as though they have themselves attained a peak of critical acuity and cultural sensitivity. Caren Kaplan is right when she points out that 'the "travel" of theories and theorists [has not] been fully considered as part of the legacy of imperialism

[or] as part of the politics of cultural production in transnational modernities and postmodernities'.[61] To future generations, our efforts may look flawed and outdated; they are as much of our own time as the works of our predecessors were of theirs. Nor should we overlook the role of earlier studies in establishing the bases on which we can build. Our own age and its texts ought not to be spared the sharp scrutiny we devote to those of earlier periods. Expansion and encroachment continue apace, in militaristic, capitalist and covert forms.

These caveats apart, I hope that the following pages offer something both to newcomers and to veteran observers of the genre. Travel writing reflects and influences the way we view the world and ourselves in relation to it. Jonathan Raban remarks that the travel book's 'essential condition ... is the experience of living among strangers, away from home'.[62] Whether and how one engages with those strangers is of much more than private or individual significance.

There are consequences far beyond literary narrative. Representations of the travel experience affect subsequent travellers. These are not simply matters of academic interest but are of pressing social and political importance. They can shape one nation's view of, and conduct towards, another. As Elizabeth Bohls points out, following the line laid down by Said, travel is 'always a source of knowledge and power'.[63] Said shows in *Orientalism* how knowledge is exercised in the service of power and is not disinterested, and Elsner and Rubiés remark that 'The desire to map is never innocent'.[64] Bohls contradicts the adage that travel broadens the mind: 'Clearly, travel does not always entail openness to unfamiliar cultures. In fact one suspects this is rarely the case. Most travelers carry with them an entire apparatus for assimilating their new experiences to comfortable systems of belief'.[65] The traveller Freya Stark asserts that explorers – that is, those who aim to grasp a little more fully the meaning of the universe and who exhibit an openness to other cultures – are likely to have their minds broadened whatever their occupation.[66] Holland and Huggan go further, contending that travel writing 'frequently provides an effective alibi for the perpetuation or reinstallment of ethnocentrically superior attitudes to "other" cultures, peoples, and places. This thesis is complicated, though, by the defamiliarizing capacities of travel writing, and by its attempts, keeping pace with change, to adjust its sights to new perceptions – both of "other" cultures, peoples, and places.'[67]

If identities and meanings are sometimes imposed on others in and through travel writing, they are as often unsettled, questioned and mediated. Travel writing has accompanied colonialism and patriarchy, but has also been utilised by postcolonial writers, by anti-capitalists and by feminists. Whatever the politics of travel texts, scholars' readings of them have led to the realisation that 'The truth claims of travel writing are increasingly being exposed as rhetorical strategy – the "other" produced by travel writing is increasingly being seen as a textual construction, an interpretation and not a reflection of reality. An important role in these constructs of reality is played by an intertextual exchange between texts'.[68] It is thus important to view travel narratives internally, intertextually and contextually.

Structure

This book is divided into three parts. The first comprises an historical survey consisting of chapters on travel writing up to the early modern period, the eighteenth century, the nineteenth century and post-1900. It sketches the development of the genre and makes some observations on the relationship between text and society. The fact that Chapter 2 covers several centuries (from the ancient to the early modern world) is not meant to signify that any of these are less important or more homogenous than the later centuries discussed in Chapters 3–5. Rather, since travel writing – as most critics understand the term – is generally considered to begin in the sixteenth or early seventeenth century, Chapter 2 outlines the precursors to and origins of the genre.[69] As Elsner and Rubiés observe, modern subjectivity in the West has been defined by and against the ancient and medieval past.[70]

The second part of the book is thematic, concentrating on four subjects that are fundamental to travel writing, whatever its period: the quest (Chapter 6), the inner journey (Chapter 7), 'race' (Chapter 8) and gender and sexuality (Chapter 9). While these are present throughout the history of travel literature, their treatment varies according to context and aesthetic convention. Between them, the two parts allow for a comparison of what we might call external factors (social and historical context) with internal ones (enduring elements that seem intrinsic to the genre).

Part III examines the writing and reading of travel narratives and attempts to predict the paths the genre might take in the future. It begins with Chapter 10, which examines how some travel writers negotiate the external and internal constraints discussed in the first two parts and considers what they themselves have said about their practice. Chapter 10 shows how they treat the form they have inherited and how they strive to communicate their individuality. Whereas other chapters up to this point concentrate on the contextual and generic forces that shape travel texts, the emphasis of this chapter is on the efforts of travel writers to establish their individuality; to clear their own path through the textual terrain in which they have found themselves. Theoretical readings of other genres, in common with theory-driven readings of travel, have tended to diminish the importance of writers' intentions and have prioritised ideological readings over what used to be called practical criticism. A consequence of this has been the downplaying of agency; of the writer's deliberate handling of techniques. Chapter 10 differs from this approach by looking at what writers themselves have had to say about their craft; it restores to them a sense of control. Chapter 11 diminishes their authority again by introducing another layer of mediation between the travel experience and the telling of it; that is, the reader. Not only do writers and publishers have to shape their stories according to formulas that appeal to readers, but the latter (as literary theory has amply demonstrated) may find in texts meanings and significance that authors do not intend. The final chapter (Chapter 12) surveys some recent developments in travel writing and tries to anticipate future directions the field may take by utilising technologies as well as theme.

Through the combination of these approaches, something of the diversity of both travel writing and the influences on it may be appreciated. Travelling and storytelling are fundamental to human existence, yet the ways in which they work together are highly complex, involving all sorts of stages between perception, experience, narration and reception. It is highly appropriate that these tales of mobility are told in a form so mixed, adaptable and resilient. For postcolonial and African American travellers, especially, this fluid genre has been used as a vehicle for the exploration and articulation of individual and group identities.[71] Travel writing is – fittingly – a dynamic genre, often employed for radical aims. It is associated with colonialism and capitalist expansion and with patriarchy, but it can also be oppositional, interrogative and subversive.[72] The structure adopted for the present volume is intended to facilitate an historical and thematic survey, to combine a diachronic and synchronic examination (i.e., both through time and at particular moments). The aim is to assess how travel writing has been affected by historical developments and by generic features, which, as we have seen from Frow's comments, are themselves open to modifications. Of relevance here also is Raymond Williams's theory of 'dominant, residual and emergent institutions and practices', which we can apply to cultural forms, too.[73] That is to say, at any one time, forms that are becoming obsolete may coincide with prevailing and new ones. I echo Elsner and Rubiés's statement that 'we should not be talking about a linear development', but I approach with more caution their belief that 'the cultural history of travel is best seen as a dialectic of dominant paradigms between two poles, which we might define as the transcendental vision of pilgrimage and the open-ended process which typically characterizes modernity'. Elsner and Rubiés explain that 'By transcendental vision we mean the sense of spiritual fulfilment with which the traveller achieves a kind of completion at the goal of his journey ... By contrast, we define as open-ended travel that process the fulfilment of which is always deferred because its achievements are relativized by the very act of travelling'.[74] Such distinctions are useful but the present volume avoids the idea of two poles, although it does recognise dominant paradigms. The genre cannot easily be fixed or contained, even within extremes. The many gaps, overlaps and misfits in the pages that follow testify to the flexibility of travel writing – mutable in itself and also, as Mary Baine Campbell observes, 'involved in the development of many new kinds of writing'.[75] They also underline that this *Introduction to Travel Writing* is, and can only be, simply a setting out.

Part I

Historical overview

Chapter 2

Medieval and early modern travel writing

stirrers abroad, and searchers of the remote parts of the world.
Richard Hakluyt[1]

You cannot discover an inhabited land.
Dehatkadons[2]

Antecedents

The origins of travel writing go back thousands of years. People have always travelled and told stories about their travels. As recorded on an Egyptian tomb, Harkuf, an emissary of the pharaohs in the third century BCE, was 'the first long-distance traveler whose name we know' and 'the first one to leave a written account, or narrative, of his [four] journeys'.[3] Modern travel literature has its roots in such older forms of writing: the factual record, as well as the mythical, the legendary and the ancient epics, including the four-thousand-year-old *Gilgamesh* from Mesopotamia, which was 'widely known in the second millennium' BCE, and through which 'we are shown a very human concern with mortality, the search for knowledge, and for an escape from the common lot of man'.[4] In it, the eponymous protagonist – part divine, part human king of Uruk – undertakes a journey through the Cedar Forest, suffers the death of his friend Enkidu and searches for ancestral wisdom and (in vain) for immortality (p.22). Gilgamesh is, Sanders observes, the 'first tragic hero of whom anything is known' (p.7). Lamenting that 'Only the gods live for ever …, but as for us men, our days are numbered, our occupations are a breath of wind' (p.71), Gilgamesh vows to go to the 'country where the cedar is cut' and to 'set up my name where the names of famous men are written' (p.72). His homecoming after his adventures, without attaining his goal of immortality, is prosaic but inscribes his name: 'He went on a long journey, was weary, worn out with labour, and returning engraved on a stone the whole story' (p.117).

Maria Pretzler hypothesises that 'The tradition of written travellers' accounts probably began with sea-farers' logs, preserving information about distances, landmarks and harbours to facilitate orientation for future voyages'. These, she suggests, are probably the origin of the *periplous*, 'an ancient genre of texts describing coastlines'.[5] Among the periploi is the Carthaginian Hanno's account of his voyage (probably in the early fifth century BCE) along the African coast, and Pytheas of Massalia's *Peri tou Okeanou* (*On the Ocean*), which recorded his voyage to northwestern Europe, most likely undertaken in the 320s BCE, including a circumnavigation of Britain (MP, p.49). Another type of text that may be seen as one of the antecedents of travel writing is the *stadiasmus* – a genre that lists places and distances along overland routes (MP, p.53).

'Travelling ... plays a pivotal role in the earliest Greek literature', notes Pretzler (MP, p.33), a fact recognised by, among others, Elsner and Rubiés, who remark that 'Since the literary creation of the *Odyssey*', with its 'portrait of a great journey home after the Trojan War ... the theme of the voyager has been central to the Graeco-Roman tradition'.[6] Travel 'had always been recognised as a way of acquiring knowledge ... By the early classical period, "travelling to see (*theôria*)" was firmly linked with acquiring wisdom (*Sophia*)' (MP, p.37), while *autopsia* denotes an author's claim to 'personal experience, or, literally, "seeing for oneself"' (MP, p.39). Elsner and Rubiés, referring specifically to the second century CE – in which 'the Roman empire enjoyed a period of immense stability' with safe roads and frequent travel – but also to classical Greece and Rome in general, observe that there is 'a rich literature of travels which combined antiquarian, literary, even touristic interests with a strong emphasis on pilgrimage to oracles, healing sanctuaries and major temples' (ER, pp.9–10).

The most famous model of travel from classical times is provided by Homer, whose *Odyssey* has influenced literary journeys for nearly 3,000 years. The 'themes of terrible danger, exotic "others," fantastic creatures, and sexual longing' that are prominent in it, and in Apollonius of Rhodes's *Argonautica* that recounts the story of Jason and the Argonauts, 'reappear frequently in later travel writing' (GS, p.26).

Travel writing itself is often traced back to Herodotus, whose *Histories*, written in the fifth century BCE, tell of the wars between the Persian Empire and the Greeks, 'using the expansion of the Persian Empire as the guiding thread and providing ethnographies of peoples the Persians conquer as their empire grows'.[7] Noreen Humble notes that 'The way Herodotus presents his narrative, in particular his insistence on autopsy (i.e. on seeing things for himself), gives the impression that he has travelled widely' (NH, p.14), an impression whose basis in fact is still argued over by scholars, but while he 'does not foreground his travels', his 'attraction to travel-writing scholars is his exploration of Otherness' (NH, p.15). In the words of Elsner and Rubiés, 'Among the other worlds mapped by Herodotus and used by him anthropologically to define Greekness by contrast with others were those of the Scythians, the Persians and the Egyptians' (ER, p.14). The *Histories* draws on Herodotus's own journeys in the Middle East, North Africa, Central Asia and the Balkans and on others' accounts of these regions. Its combination of information and the fantastic anticipates the mixture of fact and fiction, observation and speculation that has characterised travel writing ever since. Herodotus also 'took it for granted that there would be different local versions of historical events, and he accommodated them in his work' (MP, p.100).

The Athenian Xenophon's *Anabasis*, described by Pretzler as 'the longest and most extensive personal account of an actual journey that survives from antiquity' (MP, p.51), 'chronicles two years of Xenophon's life, 401–399 BCE, which he spends travelling into the hinterland of the Persian empire and back out again' (NH, p.15). It recounts the approximately 3,000 mile march of the 'Ten Thousand', an army of Greek mercenaries, begun in the spring of 401 BCE, across Anatolia into Mesopotamia and back. It is a source of information 'about the specific circumstances the soldiers faced while on the move' and about 'Anatolia, Mesopotamia and the Aegean region' (GS, p.32). Although Xenophon refers to himself only in the third person, increasing the air of objectivity (NH, p.21), which is not what we might now expect from today's personality-laden, subjective travel narratives, the *Anabasis* is 'an important text in the history of travel writing' (NH, p.25). It 'relates a journey which moves from familiar cultural territory to unfamiliar and back again, ... it reveals an exploration of both self and Other on a number of levels' (NH, p.17); it reflects on identity, and its narrator 'skilfully reveals and exploits the distance between his naïve younger self, with his expectations of homecoming and his more reflective older self, who with hindsight is able to acknowledge that he embarked on the journey without heed for the consequences' (NH, p.24). Humble also points out that even 2,500 years ago, travellers were influenced by extant accounts: 'Xenophon is no less encumbered and preconditioned by earlier literature than modern travel writers'; in his case, the *Odyssey* and Herodotus's *Histories* in particular (NH, p.23). The nineteenth-century journalist, explorer and adventurer, Henry Morton Stanley frequently invoked Xenophon in his book *In Darkest Africa* (1890), the narrative of his controversial 'relief' of Emin Pasha, the Governor of Equatoria. Stanley led Emin and his people from where it was feared they were threatened by Mahdist forces to the safety of the coast.[8] More recently (and pacifically), Justin Marozzi has travelled *In the Footsteps of Herodotus* (2008) and Ryszard Kapuściński borrows the ancient's authority, journeying with Herodotus's *Histories* in his *Travels with Herodotus* (2007).[9] By such means travellers construct images of themselves, acquiring extra depth and complexity through the added weight of the reference to previous travellers.

As with modern travel, 'From the beginning the act of travelling and the encounter with foreign lands also had a great impact on Greek self-definition' (MP, p.33). Pausanias's *Periegesis* (probably composed between 160 and around 180 BCE) has exercised a strong influence on how travellers perceived, journeyed in and represented Greece.[10] It has been described as 'a huge and well-informed guidebook to the important historic sites' in that country; a 'publication that is the true ancestor of the best modern tourist guides' (GS, p.40). From the late eighteenth century there was a 'long tradition of travellers who used Pausanias as a travel guide to Greece and its ancient remains' (MP, p.135). His text has shaped even modern '"cultural" travel guides' (MP, p.3).

Pretzler seems confident that its status as 'the most extensive text surviving from antiquity that deals with a traveller's experiences', means that it 'can therefore be considered as travel literature' (MP, p.11), even though '[t]he ancients had neither a clearly defined genre of travel writing, nor a notion of books specifically written for travellers' (MP, p.45). As a consequence, she asks, 'Is it worthwhile to use a modern category, namely "travel writing", to analyse a set of ancient texts which were not perceived as belonging to one common group in antiquity?' Her answer is that what the works she discusses have in common is that 'they tackle the problem of representing geography, landscape and travellers' observations and experiences as a text' (MP, p.45).

Although we tend to think of tourism as a comparatively new phenomenon, scholars have traced its origins to classical times. Gosch and Stearns claim that Herodotus 'might well be regarded as the classical world's first tourist', and observe that 'travel for pleasure in the Mediterranean accelerated significantly during the Roman empire. Indeed, for the Roman upper classes, tourism seems to have become a major leisure-time activity' (GS, p.40).

There are also accounts of travels in the Bible. Gosch and Stearns refer to the description of Paul's Mediterranean voyage in chapter twenty-seven of the Acts of the Apostles from the New Testament. David P. Moessner has written on the Lukan travel narrative.[11] M. H. Abrams finds in 'the early books of the Hebrew Bible', the 'major source of the image' of the 'course of the life both of the human race and of the individual as an extended journey through alien lands'. This is '*peregrinatio vitae* [life's journeying]', 'one of the enduring master tropes by which the postclassical West has endowed the course of human life with structure, purpose, meaning, and values'. He suggests that it is found notably in, among other episodes, the banishment of Adam and Eve from Eden; Cain's punishment 'to wander as a fugitive and a vagabond'; the exodus of the Hebrews from Egypt; and 'the journey of Moses up to Mount Sinai to encounter Divinity; and his later ascent of Mount Pisgah for a glimpse of the Promised Land, to which access was denied him but was later granted his people'.[12]

Pilgrimage and medieval travel

After the Bible came Christian pilgrimages, which were also connected to Greek and Roman culture. As Elsner and Rubiés observe, 'in Biblical and in Greek sources, for instance, there is a great deal of common ground between Western and Asian traditions' (ER, p.7). Indeed, justifying their pronouncement that 'Antiquity was ... the mother of the Middle Ages', Elsner and Rubiés explain that 'the archetypically Christian pilgrimage model of the Middle Ages is rooted in the ancient myths of heroes such as Apollonius, who travelled himself into sainthood, or the allegorical Odysseus, whose journeys became a metaphor for the spiritual progress of his readers' lives' (ER, p.15).

One account of Christian pilgrimage, Egeria's *Peregrinatio ad terram sanctam*, probably dating from the late fourth century CE, is, according to Mary Baine Campbell, 'the earliest extant work devoted entirely to the account of a journey beyond the borders of Europe'.[13] Campbell notes that 'The limit of geographical knowledge, wherever located, was a point commonly charged with moral significance'.[14] This is evident in pre-Christian as well as Christian literature, but the investment of landscape with moral qualities (or their lack) has become so prevalent that it remains in operation nowadays.[15] Of the period about which Campbell writes, and of pilgrimage in particular, 'the perceived nature of the Holy Land lent itself to the development of a heavily allegorical topography'.[16] The perception and representation of topography altered over time. As Elsner and Rubiés put it, 'Gradually, but systematically, the terrain of pagan Antiquity ... was transformed into a world sanctified by the exclusive God and his saints', and the Bible itself served as a guidebook to the Holy Land for Christian travellers who used it to 'redefine the actual places and landmarks they found on the terrain in relation to their dominant mythology, namely the Old and New Testament' (ER, p.16).

More enacted than written about by its participants, Christian pilgrimages to Jerusalem increased in number during the reign of Constantine (305–37 CE), the first Christian emperor of Rome (GS, p.41). The first well-documented pilgrimage is that of Helena, Constantine's mother, in 327 CE, recounted by Eusebius. The first recorded visit by a pilgrim after Helena was the 'Bordeaux pilgrim' whose record of his trip was made in 333 (GS, pp.42–3).[17] Elsner and Rubiés note that even when travel to the Holy Land was made difficult by the rise of Islam, following the fall of Jerusalem in 648 and the invasion of Spain in 711, Christian pilgrimage remained 'the fundamental paradigm of travel in the Latin West' (ER, p.21). Subsequently, travel to the Holy Land would become associated with conquest; with crusade (ER, pp.23–4). Later still, there occurred 'the sublimation of the crusading impulse into a chivalric ideal' and with it the idea of the knight errant (ER, pp.26–9).

Pilgrimage 'was one of the most important institutions of late medieval culture'.[18] The pilgrimage to Jerusalem was 'the pilgrimage of pilgrimages', for it was seen as lying at the centre of the world. It was 'the ground the Lord had walked upon' and was 'a symbol of the Heavenly City' (H, p.12). Diana Webb points out that 'by 1100, Christ Himself was shown as a pilgrim' and by the fourteenth century, Saint James was 'almost invariably depicted as a pilgrim'.[19]

According to Howard, 526 accounts of the Jerusalem pilgrimage between 1100 and 1500 survive (H, p.17), but 'the great age of pilgrimage narratives' began in the 1300s (H, p.29), the century whose end saw Chaucer's composition of *The Canterbury Tales*. Famous actual records of pilgrimage from this 'great age' include Bernhard von Breydenbach's *Peregrinatio in Terram Sanctam* (1486), regarded as the first illustrated, printed travel book, and the *Evagatorium* (*Wanderings*) of Brother Felix (Friar Felix Fabri). It should be noted that Latin was the dominant language of pilgrims' written accounts until the thirteenth century, when narratives in the vernacular began to appear, first in French and then in other languages, including English. Marco Polo's and Mandeville's narratives, as will be discussed, first appeared in French.

Throughout and after the Middle Ages, 'spiritual renderings of biblical accounts of exiles and journeys, pilgrims and prodigals, served as commonplaces in numberless commentaries, sermons, homilies, and works of literature'. Abrams writes:

> [T]he *peregrination* constituted the total plot of that familiar allegoric narrative in which the protagonist is named Everyman, or Mankind, or Christian; in which the allegory signifies the normative course of a Christian life …The chivalric romances – with their literal plots of journeying knights, quests, and perilous trials by which the protagonist proves that he merits his lady love – obviously invited adaptation into allegories of the wayfaring Christian life. A late and elaborately designed instance is Spenser's *Faerie Queene*.[20]

Abrams describes John Bunyan's *The Pilgrim's Progress* (1678), the 'story of the pilgrim who shoulders his pack and trudges sturdily through commonplace obstacles, temptations and perils, toward the celestial city for which he longs', as 'the great working-class equivalent of the adventurous quest of the aristocratic knight on horseback'.[21]

Outside the Christian tradition, 'As early as the tenth century, the Arab world identified (and sometimes taught) travel narratives as an autonomous literary genre related to the novel. ... The tradition was to last up to the seventeenth century, giving birth along the way to the vast narrative of Ibn Battuta, who from 1325 to 1345 traveled throughout Africa and Asia'.[22]

Marco Polo and Mandeville

The most famous of medieval travellers is probably Marco Polo, whose influence was and continues to be profound. His late thirteenth-century account of his travels had no obvious model (ER, p.35). Many modern readers will be familiar with part of his narrative through Samuel Taylor Coleridge's poem 'Kubla Khan', which draws on it (via Samuel Purchas's anthology), for 'When we think of Marco Polo, it is of Kublai [Khan] that we think'.[23] In the view of John Masefield, introducing an early twentieth-century edition of Polo's *Travels*, 'The wonder of Marco Polo is ... that he created Asia for the European mind'.[24] Writing in 1908, Masefield could assert that 'Even now, after the lapse of six centuries, it remains the chief authority for parts of Central Asia, and of the vast Chinese Empire'.[25] While there is still debate over the reliability of the book and its author, it is generally accepted that Marco dictated his story while in prison in Genoa in the late thirteenth century to the Italian novelist Rusticiano (also known as Rustichello) of Pisa, 'though it is difficult to distinguish what in the work belongs to him and what to the narrator'.[26]

Elsner and Rubiés believe that Polo's narrative represents the clearest late medieval manifestation of the move towards empiricism that would gather momentum in travel literature of the Renaissance (ER, pp.29–31, 35). They claim that the two authors' 'appeal was to curiosity and the desire for knowledge alone' (ER, p.35).

We are told in the prologue that 'this book will be a truthful one',[27] a declaration that immediately raises questions about its status: if so evidently truthful, why the need to assert the fact? There continues to be debate on how much of what is related Polo really did and saw; even whether he actually visited China at all.[28]

Polo's book, which recounted the adventures of himself, his father and his uncle on a mission that 'was on the whole a private enterprise which began as a business venture and ended with the peculiar job of serving the Great Khan as part of his extensive foreign contingent in China', is 'a combination of pure ethnography and historical or legendary material based on hearsay' (ER. p.35). It is noteworthy for many things. These include the extent, by Polo's account, of his immersion in the life of the places he visits. During his 'residence of so many years in the eastern parts of the world' (p.30), he 'was held in high estimation and respect by all belonging to the court [of the Grand Khan]. He learnt in a short time and adopted the manners of the Tartars, and acquired a proficiency in four different languages, which he became qualified to read and write' (p.21). But he often disparages Muslims (as well as idolators). He tells us, for example, that 'The Turkomans, who reverence Mahomet and follow his law, are a rude people, and dull of intellect' (p.32), that the 'Mahometans of Kashcar' are 'a covetous, sordid race, eating badly and drinking worse' (p.93), and that the 'Mahometan inhabitants' of 'The city [Tauris in Irak]' are 'treacherous and unprincipled' (p.48). He also writes negatively about dark-skinned people and positively about lighter-skinned ones. Thus, in Acià, ten days south of Balashan, 'the people ... have a peculiar language. They worship idols; are of a dark complexion, and of evil disposition' (p.86); of Kesmur (Kashmir), he declares that 'the women, *although dark*, are very comely' (p.88, my emphasis); and of Tenduk, he exclaims: 'The men of this country are fairer complexioned and better looking than those in the other countries of which we have been speaking, and also better instructed, and more skilful traders' (p.141). Of Zanzibaris he remarks:

> They are black, and go naked; covering only the private parts of the body with a cloth. ... They have large mouths, their noses turn up towards the forehead, their ears are long, and their eyes so large and frightful, that they have the aspect of demons. ... There are in this island the most ill-favoured women in the world; with large mouths and thick noses, and ill-favoured breasts, four times as large as those of other women. (pp.395–6)

He writes of cannibalism, including in Java and among the Angaman (Andaman) islanders, who he declares are 'idolaters, and are a most brutish and savage race, having heads, eyes and teeth resembling those of the canine species. Their dispositions are cruel, and every person, not being of their own nation, whom they can lay their hands upon, they kill and eat' (pp.347–8).

It is the horrors and the wonders that secure one's attention. Those wonders pertain to the human, the animal and the landscape. Here is what Polo's 1908 editor says is his 'distorted account of the alligator or crocodile':

> Here are seen huge serpents, ten paces in length, and ten spans in the girt of the body. At the fore part, near the head, they have two short legs, having three claws like those of a tiger, with eyes larger than a fourpenny loaf (*pane de Quattro denari*) and very glaring. Their jaws are

> wide enough to swallow a man, the teeth are large and sharp, and their whole appearance is so formidable, that neither man, nor any kind of animal, can approach them without terror. (p.246)

He states that in the kingdom of Lambri 'are found men with tails, a span in length, like those of the dog, but not covered with hair' (pp.344–5). He describes a nut 'of the size of a man's head, containing an edible substance that is sweet and pleasant to the taste, and white as milk. The cavity of this pulp is filled with a liquor clear as water, cool, and better flavoured and more delicate than wine or any other kind of drink whatever' (pp.342–3); it is, of course, the coconut. The enduring wonder is Kublai Khan, with his 'great and admirable achievements' (p.152), whose 'magnificence ... is unequalled by that of any monarch in the world' (p.187), and with his admirable and elegant palace and the 'rich and beautiful meadows' in his royal park (p.145).

Amid all these wonders, such observations as that earlier mention of the skilful traders of Tenduk (p.141) should not be passed over. Campbell notes that

> In the real world of a merchant it is the quotidian that matters. Marco Polo describes political and military structures, imports, exports, and mediums of exchange, religious customs, the protocols of marriage and burial, birds, beasts and countryside, the layout and architecture of cities. The phenomenal world is the only one we see here.[29]

Similarly, Blanton comments that Polo 'materializes everything he sees'.[30] At several points, Polo's narrative seems to offer practical advice for subsequent travellers. For example: 'A desert then commences, extending forty or fifty miles, where there is no water; and it is necessary that the traveller should make provision of this article at his outset. As the cattle find no drink until this desert is passed, the greatest expedition is necessary, that they may reach a watering place' (p.78). And 'Provisions, however, are scarce in the hilly tract passed during these two days, and the traveller must carry with him food sufficient both for himself and his cattle' (p.79). Several places do not command his attention at all. After five short sentences on the province of Karkan, he dismisses it thus: 'In this country there is not anything further that is worthy of observation' (p.95). According to Elsner and Rubiés, the 'critical innovation of the book, and what explains its influence in cartography and its ability to inspire future explorers, was the way in which the figure of the traveller became a rhetorical justification for the use of popular vernacular descriptive language in a "realist" (if rhetorically stereotyped) manner' (ER, p.36).

Before moving on, we should note the textual problems surrounding these narratives, which add to the layers of intervention between travel and its telling outlined in Chapter 1 of the present volume. As Campbell observes, Polo's tale was dictated, Mandeville's, which exists in manuscripts, was plagiarised, and the first voyage of Columbus (who considers himself the successor to Marco Polo[31]) was 'edited, abridged and partly summarized by Las Casas'.[32] In addition, their translation into English introduces further layers of mediation.

Probably the most celebrated of medieval travel texts, one that has been called the 'most important English book of travel writing of the late Middle Ages',[33] authored by the man whom Campbell claims 'we can call ... the father of modern travel writing, is Mandeville's *Travels,* which began to circulate in Europe between 1356 and 1366.[34] It was written in French, but by 1400 had appeared in several European languages, and a century later existed in many manuscript versions.[35] Campbell writes that 'With *Mandeville's* Travels, the developing genre of travel literature in the West reaches a complicated and long-sustained climax'.[36] Although now viewed as largely the product of plagiarism and invention, the text was, as Moseley reminds us, relied upon by a 'huge number of people ... for hard, practical information in the two centuries after the book first appeared'.[37] Yet it 'represented a purely fictional traveller, an invention devised to render a[n unacknowledged] compilation of pre-existing travel accounts more coherent and convincing' (ER, p.37).[38] Elsner and Rubiés write that, 'contrary to the spirit of Marco Polo's lay empiricism'[,] John Mandeville is a pilgrim, and his book is a conventional fourteenth-century pilgrimage to the Holy Land, although with the unprecedented addition of an extended journey to the East, India, Cathay, the land of Prester John, and the walls of Paradise (Paradise is itself unreachable)' (ER, p.38). The text's 'vicarious pilgrimage' is 'written for a generation who lived without hope of a successful crusade' (ER, p.38).

Moseley points out that nothing is known of the author of Mandeville's *Travels* beyond what we are told in the text, and that he 'may, of course, be creating to a greater or lesser degree a fictional *persona*'.[39] Moseley is alert to the importance of viewing the author in his time. This means recognising that 'what you see (and can write about) depends to a large extent on the conceptual and methodological structures you have in your mind'. Thus, the practice of borrowing from existing works should be seen from the medieval perspective that applauded rather than condemned it.[40] Campbell likewise warns against anachronistic readings of fourteenth-century texts such as Mandeville's, for they were 'fluid: plagiarized, misquoted, mistranslated, interpolated upon, bowdlerized, epitomized, transformed, and transformable at every stage of their complex dissemination'.[41] Yet into this 'patchwork of plagiarism' from 'encyclopedists, pilgrims, and merchant and missionary travel writers', the author, in Campbell's view, 'inserts his own person ... more forcefully than any writer but William of Rubruck had before him'.[42] A result is that Mandeville's

Travels 'discards and subverts and extends the possibilities of many of its inherited characteristics. And the spirit that shapes it is almost wholly new'.[43] Campbell hails 'Its remarkable cultural relativism ... [as] a bright spot in a picture that will almost immediately darken when the Age of Discovery begins'. She writes that 'Columbus, Frobisher, Ralegh, Ortelius, Mercator: all read him, used him, believed him. But the message of his humane rhetoric was lost on Columbus'.[44]

Columbus, who is 'new in making himself a romance hero', also 'opened up the travel account to a subjectivity and narrativity new to the form and essential to its later masterpieces. ... [I]t was in the self-love of conquering heroes that the travel memoir was born'.[45] This view of Campbell's is endorsed by Blanton, who argues that 'What matters for travel literature is the sense we get in Columbus's letters ... of an intense personal experience mediating our response to his New World. The narrator becomes a character whose responses we can feel, made more urgent by the use of the personal pronoun "I"'.[46]

Polo, Mandeville and Columbus are all Christian. I have quoted some of the anti-Muslim statements in Polo's *Travels*. By contrast, Nabil Matar observes that 'a total dismissal of Arab-Islamic travel has prevailed' that 'has persisted into modern scholarship'.[47] Matar notes that the Ottomans had 'a history of travel and cartography' (p.xiv), and that Arab 'Travelers, merchants, envoys, ambassadors, and clergymen journeyed [from North Africa and the Levant] to London and Rome, Cadiz and Malta, Madrid and Moscow' (p.xv). Indeed, 'the genre of *rihla* (travel writing) flourished in Arabic' (p.xix). Matar claims that 'No other non-Christian people ... left behind as extensive a description of the Europeans and of *bilad al-nasara* [the lands of the Christians], both in the European as well as the American continents, as did the Arabic writers' (p.xxii). He asserts that unlike their Christian European contemporaries, Arab writers of the early modern period 'described what they saw, carefully and without projecting unfounded fantasies ... because most of them were writing to governmental and ecclesiastical superiors who, if not accurately apprised, could blunder in their dealings with their European counterparts' (p.xxxi). Greater scholarly attention to such works is helping to counter some of the dominant assumptions about travel.

Early modern travel

Andrew Hadfield identifies the 'miraculous sights described in ... Sir John Mandeville's *Travels*' and Marco Polo's '*Travels* in search of the wealth of the "Great Khan", which lay behind Columbus's plans for his voyage in 1492', as the 'two paradigms of European travel writing before the discovery of the New World'.[48] Increasingly the marvels and wonders accompanied colonial and mercantile expansion. In Campbell's words, 'English travelers of the sixteenth century played a major role in ushering in the long era of England's dominance as a world power'.[49] Their travel accounts influenced and were drawn upon by writers of other genres, notably Shakespeare and John Donne, along with many others.

Travel writing of the early modern period also intervenes, if obliquely, in internal politics. Indeed, Hadfield argues that much early modern travel writing and colonial writing was written to participate in social debates and political discourse.[50] The *History of Italie* (1549), by William Thomas, who 'was executed after his prominent role in [Sir Thomas] Wyatt's rebellion',[51] 'neatly point[s] out the liminal, potentially transgressive, status of the traveller who writes back to his native country and the suspicion with which he was regarded by the authorities, as well as the ways in which he might be transformed himself by the experience'.[52] For the rest of the Tudor period, 'Travel abroad required a licence issued by the monarch. ... Large numbers of books ... gave instructions for would-be travellers, most of which emphasized the need for the traveller to serve his country through his actions. ... Travel writing as we recognize the genre today ... did not appear in any quantity until the late 1590s'.[53]

One of the most idiosyncratic of travel texts, 'hard to place ... in any previously established generic form', dates from these years.[54] *Coryat's Crudities* (1611), 'describing [the author's] observations of France, Savoy, Italy, Switzerland, Germany, and the Netherlands', has been called 'the first self-consciously styled work of English travel writing' and led to the publication of similar works during James I's reign by, for example, Fynes Moryson, George Sandys and William Lithgow.[55] Coryat emphasised the importance of Venice in Europe as 'a symbolic core of democratic values and traditions'.[56]

We should not be deceived by its eccentricity, for while Coryat represents himself as 'an obsessive buffoon', that is 'a mask'; *Coryat's Crudities* is 'a work of self-fashioning, and ... its mode of presenting its author needs to be taken seriously'.[57] Hadfield views Coryat's self-construction as '"a private man" ... too eccentric to fit into any recognizable categories of state control, [and] also a political act of resistance to an over-mighty and intrusive state'.[58] Thus, we must be alert to the political connotations of the most idiosyncratic of voices.

Besides notable individual works, the early modern period gave rise to great collections of travel. The first collection of voyages in English was Richard Eden's *Decades of the Newe Worlde* (1555), revised and expanded by Richard Willes as the *History of Travayle* (1577). Both included 'a few English voyages ..., reflecting the relatively late English contribution to the discovery and description of distant lands in the sixteenth century'.[59] But the most famous endeavour in early modern travel writing is the collection of voyages and discoveries compiled and edited by Richard Hakluyt (1552–1616), who drew on the English voyage material in both these collections in compiling the *Principall Navigations* (AP, p.36). Hakluyt's work was designed to demonstrate the achievements of Protestant England. It manifests the connections between travel, nation, commerce and colonial expansion that have been evident in so much travel writing, and that would appear strongly again in the mid to late nineteenth century. The first edition of *Principall Navigations* appeared in 1589 and comprised 825 pages; the second, published in 1600, filled three folio volumes totalling around 2,000 pages.[60] From Hakluyt's 'Epistle Dedicatorie' to Sir Francis Walsingham, we learn that at Oxford – where he was educated at Christ Church after attending Westminster School, taking his BA in 1574 and his MA in 1577 – he 'read over whatsoever printed or written discoveries and voyages I found extant either in the Greeke, Latine, Italian, Spanish, Portugall, French, or English languages'.[61] Hakluyt 'both heard in speech, and read in books other nations miraculously extolled for their discoveries and notable enterprises by sea, but the English of all others for their sluggish security, and continuall neglect of the like attempts ... either ignominiously reported, or exceedingly condemned'.[62] Hakluyt, however, commends the English nation:

> It can not be denied, but as in all former ages, they have bene men full of activity, stirrers abroad, and searchers of the remote parts of the world, so in this most famous and peerless governement of her most excellent Majesty, her subjects through the speciall assistance, and blessing of God, in searching the most opposite corners and quarters of the world, and to speake plainly, in compassing the vaste globe of the earth more than once, have excelled all the nations and people of the earth.[63]

His elaborately constructed Elizabethan sentences bestride the page as his subjects do the globe. While Mackenthun calls Hakluyt 'the rational reverend and propagator of English imperialism',[64] Payne reminds us that 'Any consideration of the contemporary reception of Hakluyt's books should of course bear in mind the high illiteracy of the era – perhaps seventy per cent of the male, ninety per cent of the female population were illiterate – and that the number of copies printed is unlikely to have been more than a few hundred' (AP, p.44). As Payne points out, 'The long-term impact of the *Principal Navigations* is to be found in the transmission of texts' (AP, p.46). In the years from 1580 to 1616, 'Hakluyt influenced or was directly responsible for the printing of no less than twenty-six travel books' out of roughly 160 travel books printed in England during this period (AP, p.38).

It is not simply the content that conveyed the meaning. Mackenthun has suggested that the main ideological function of Hakluyt's anthology is performed by the formal organisation of the texts.[65] Mary Fuller has noted the material, as well as textual effects, of his enterprise: '[T]here was also alongside the process of material exploitation and profit, the loop of voyage, report, repeated voyages, repeated investment, a process of *textual* generation and accumulation with which Hakluyt is identified. … Hakluyt stimulated writing by soliciting narratives, and in so doing helped to create an ongoing demand for such narratives'.[66] His anthology continues to fascinate, and, as I write, a 'new scholarly edition for the 21st [c]entury' is in preparation.[67]

According to Peter Mancall, the 'most significant travel account published in the entire sixteenth century' was the four-language edition of Thomas Harriot's *Briefe and True Reporte of the New Found Land of Virginia*.[68] Harriot's report, writes Mancall, had a dual purpose: that, shared by its author and Hakluyt, of encouraging English colonisation; and, although 'a piece of nationalistic propaganda, it is also without question a genuine work of ethnography'. It is 'famous in American history for telling much about the nascent English settlement at Ronaoke, the fabled "lost colony" of the English … [and] has become an epitaph for the Carolina Algonquians, a people obliterated by the forces of European colonization'.[69] This combination points to what some might see as a paradox and others as the frequent consequence of expansion: that travel accounts describe people and ways of life that are undergoing enforced change and often extinction. Harriot's report recounts the Algonquians as being so mystified by scientific instruments, books and writing that they 'thought they were rather the works of gods than of men, or at the leastwise they had been given and taught us of the gods'.[70] The report also includes the illness that follows the white men's movements and that cause the Algonquians to 'die very fast, and many in short space, in some Towns about twenty, in some forty, and in one six score, which in truth was very many in respect of their numbers'. The disease is new to the people. What they do not understand they attribute to magic, so that, in trying to account for the deaths from sickness, 'they were persuaded that it was the work of our God through our means, and that we by him might kill and slay whom we would without weapons, and not come near them'.[71] Harriot further reports that because none of the whites died, and there were no women with the whites, 'Some therefore were of opinion that we were not borne of women, and therefore not mortal, but that we were men of an old generation many years past, then risen again to immortality'. Some of the Algonquians, relates Harriot, further believed that people were dying because whites were 'shooting invisible bullets into them'.[72]

Harriot confesses that towards the end of the year some of the whites 'showed themselves too fierce in slaying some of the people in some Towns, upon causes that on our part might easily have been borne withal' but he suggests that the deaths were deserved and that the Algonquians will have nothing to fear if they deal carefully with the Englishmen.[73] He assures his readers:

> If that those which shall thither travel to inhabit and plant be but reasonably provided for the first year, ... and being there, do use but that diligence and care, that is requisite, and as they may with ease. There is no doubt, but for the time following, they may have victuals that are excellent good and plenty enough, some more English sorts of cattle also hereafter, as some have been before, and are there yet remaining, may, and shall be God willing thither transported. So likewise, our kind of fruit, roots, and herbs, may be there planted and sowed, as some have been already, and prove well. And in short time also they may raise so much of those sorts of commodities which I have spoken of, as shall both enrich themselves, as also others that shall deal with them.[74]

Ralegh's Guiana

One of the most famous and enduring narratives of travel from the early modern period is the account of an expedition which, in its main phase, lasted less than six weeks, between May-June 1595: that is, Sir Walter Ralegh's *The Discoverie of the Large, Rich, and Beautifull Empire of Guiana*, relating his quest for El Dorado.[75] *The Discoverie* was written within a few weeks of Ralegh's return to England, published early in 1596, and reprinted twice that year.[76]

As Gesa Mackenthun notes of *The Discoverie*, 'It has since been regarded as a classic of Elizabethan travel writing and, less frequently, as a classic of empire'.[77] At the same time, according to Campbell, 'Ralegh's book is characteristic of travel literature as we know it today: fully narrative, fully inhabited by its narrator, self-conscious about the problem of presenting difference in terms that neither inadvertently domesticate nor entirely alienate'.[78]

In 1595, the year of the Guiana expedition, Ralegh turned forty. In the early years of the decade, he became eclipsed at the royal court by the Earl of Essex and in the summer of 1592 was sent with Elizabeth Throckmorton to the Tower of London and then to his estates in Dorset. Throckmorton was Lady-in-waiting to the Queen and had secretly married Ralegh, with whom she had a son. Nicholl also notes that Ralegh was under investigation for holding heretical views and was experiencing financial problems: 'His ill-fated attempts to colonize Virginia in the 1580s had cost him over £40,000; his attempts to profit from the Irish lands he had been given were unsuccessful'.[79] The expedition was an attempt to win back some favour from the Queen. Ralegh's narrative of his quest, his travails and the wonders he saw and heard of along the way, distracted from the fruitlessness of his search for the mythical land of gold.

The features of the *Discoverie* that lead some critics to identify it as a transitional text, one that bridges the medieval and modern eras, include the use it makes of its literary antecedents, the relationship it establishes between its symbolic and external referents (one might say between the mythical and realism), and the artful self-construction of its protagonist/narrator. Several critics trace the influence on it of earlier works. Nicholl notes that Spenser's *Faerie Queene* was dedicated to Ralegh in 1590,[80] and observes similarities in each text's view of American Indians. Besides the *Faerie Queene*, Nicholl notes, the precursors of Ralegh's *Discoverie* include Montaigne's essay 'Des Cannibales', the accounts of Virginia by Arthur Barlowe and Thomas Harriot, and Thomas More's *Utopia* (1516),[81] 'a work which overshadows much subsequent literature dealing with overseas travel, colonial expansion, and contact with non-European peoples' and one that 'can be seen as a foundational text of early modern English travel and colonial writing'.[82] Mackenthun also finds echoes of the *Faerie Queene* in the *Discoverie*, along with traces of Dante's *Inferno* and Columbus.[83] Two main points from this concern us here. First, as Nicholl recognises, the conception formed by Ralegh from his reading 'suffuses the actuality of his encounters' with the American Indians and 'his experience of the South American wilderness'.[84] Second, the earlier literature offers models on which Ralegh can draw for his self-construction in his text.

Mackenthun and Nichol are among those who have commented on the echoes of Spenser. Mackenthun explains: '[T]he *Discoverie* is in part modeled after an archetypal narrative of knight errancy that finds its most aestheticized contemporary expression in Spenser's epic poem'. She continues: 'The relationship between the imaginative journey of Spenser's Red Crosse Knight and the actual journey of Sir Walter Ralegh, which is inscribed in Ralegh's choice of similes and names, to a large part determines Ralegh's view and his presentation of colonial relationships as well'.[85] Similarly, Nicholl sees in Ralegh's naming of the Red Cross River an allusion to Spenser's Red Cross Knight, 'himself a version of St. George, particularly as a defender of the Anglican church'.[86] So far as readings of travel texts are concerned, the significant thing about Ralegh's identification of himself with Spenser's hero is that, in Nicholl's words, 'we find [a] blurring between the symbolic and the physical'.[87] This is one of the features that has led scholars to regard the *Discoverie* as a transitional text that contains elements of medieval and early modern narratives while ushering in the modern.

The most famous passage from the *Discoverie*, and one that will later be referenced by V. S. Naipaul and Graham Greene, is the one figuring Guiana as unspoilt; unplundered. It implicitly draws a link between Elizabeth, the Virgin Queen, and the South American country, just as Ralegh had renamed Wingandacoia 'Virginia'. Mackenthun describes this act of 'bestowing a new name on a future colony to express his and his country's indebtedness to the benevolence of the virgin queen Elizabeth' as marking 'an important juncture of the discourse of colonialism with another powerful discourse of the English Renaissance, that of female rulership'.[88]

> To conclude, *Guiana* is a Countrey that hath yet her Maydenhead, never sackt, turned, nor wrought, the face of the earth hath not beene torne, nor the vertue and salt of the soyle spent by manurance, the graves have not beene opened for gold, the mines not broken with sledges, nor their Images puld down out of their temples. It hath never been entred by any armie of strength, and never conquered or possessed by any Christian Prince. It is besides so defensible, that if two fortes be builded in one of the Provinces which I have seen, the flood setteth in so neere the banke, where the channell also lyeth, that no shippe can passe up, but within a Pikes length of the Artillerie, first of the one, and afterwards of the other: Which two Fortes wilbe a sufficient Guard both to the *Empire* of *Inga*, and to an hundred other severall kingdoms, lying within the said River, even to the citie of *Quito in Peru*.[89]

The other, almost equally famous passage from the *Discoverie* is Ralegh's description of the Ewaipanoma. He writes that although the stories of them 'may be thought a meere fable, yet for mine owne parte I am resolved it is true, because every child in the provinces of *Arromaia* and *Canuri* affirme the same':

> [T]hey are reported to have their eyes in their shoulders, and their mouths in the middle of their breasts, & that a long train of haire groweth backward between their shoulders. . . . Such a nation was written of by *Mandevile*, whose reportes were held for fables many years, and yet since the East *Indies* were discovered, wee finde his relations true of such things as heeretofore were held incredible: whether it be true or no the matter is not great, neither can there be any profit in the imagination, for mine own part I saw them not, but I am resolved that so many people did not all combine, or forethink to make the report.[90]

Ralegh's account simultaneously avows the truth of what he has heard and invites doubt (at least to the modern reader). He has not seen the Ewaipanoma himself but takes the word of children for their existence. His mention of

Mandeville – and of wonders that were thought false but, he says, turned out true – helps us see why critics view him as still linked to the medieval world but ushering in the modern.[91] One of the characteristics of Ralegh's narrative that encourage readings of it as modern is its author's conscious representation of himself. Mackenthun succinctly expresses a view that is held by several critics and that Ralegh himself proposed: 'The main force that drove him to Guiana, Ralegh claims in an unmatched act of courtly self-fashioning, was his passionate desire to regain the favour and sympathy of Elizabeth by presenting to her a new and rich colony in South America'.[92] Mackenthun even refers to Ralegh's 'notorious practice of hyperbolic self-dramatization'.[93] And Blanton suggests that Ralegh's 'withhold[ing] of the failure of his quest until the end while recounting in detail the history of the search for El Dorado at the beginning' creates tension and 'at the same time elevates his quest to almost mythic status', fashioning himself 'as the hero of his tale, not only as its organizing principle but also as its spiritual center'.[94]

More modern narratives witness a shift of focus. Charles Nicholl remarks of the Indians of the region around Venezuela's Angel Falls (named after Jimmy Angel) that they are 'understandably sceptical about these daring "discoveries" of places they had known about all along'.[95] The effects of sixteenth-century adventures are still felt. Observing the dirty reality of the search for gold now, Nicholl muses: 'I suppose just by coming here Ralegh is partly responsible for this devastation. I suppose all of us who come to these places take rather more than we give'.[96]

As we move towards the close of this chapter, there are some caveats to note. First, there are plenty of important travels that have not resulted in travel writing (according to our definition of it as a first-person narrative by the traveller). Mary Fuller reminds us, for example, that Drake's 1577–80 circumnavigation of the world 'produced no important printed account by a participant'.[97] Second, the Others of the text are represented, usually for self-serving motives, by the author; when their voices are supposedly present they are ventriloquised. Modern literary theory may allow us to discern them in the shadows (or to comfort us with the possibility that we can). For instance, Fuller listens for voices around the margins of texts (p.46), including a silent Inuit woman captive (pp.53–5). Third, the genre that we have been discussing and to which this volume forms an introduction, was not understood in the same way in the years covered by this chapter as it is now; the expectations, practices and reception of genre changes over time. In the early modern period, 'the use of print as a medium for the dissemination of information was uncertain and fluid, and certain generic distinctions which we take for granted today – including that of travel writing – were by no means clear or distinct'.[98] Finally, the very idea and discourses of discovery are ideological. Just as history is written by the victors, so any discussion of exploration tends to be written from the point of view of the explorer. The language of exploration history perpetuates the idea of active, inquiring Europeans and static, passive indigenes. A writer who has attempted to reverse this view, Ronald Wright, records being 'told by Dehatkadons, a traditional chief of the Onondaga Iroquois, "You cannot discover an inhabited land. Otherwise I could cross the Atlantic and 'discover' England"'.[99]

Chapter 3

Travel writing in the eighteenth century

I found I could not avoid being continually the first person – 'the little hero of each tale'

Mary Wollstonecraft[1]

[I]n what other light can they at first look upon us but as invaders of their Country

James Cook[2]

Picaresque to picturesque

The narrators of many of today's travel books owe something of their character to the humorous protagonists and comic adventures of the eighteenth-century novel, as well as to the introspection of the literature of the later decades of that century. The eighteenth century saw the rise of the modern novel as Ian Watt labels it in his influential study.[3] Daniel Defoe's *Moll Flanders* (1722), Henry Fielding's *Joseph Andrews* (1742) and *Tom Jones* (1749) and Laurence Sterne's *Tristram Shandy* (1759–67) and *A Sentimental Journey* (1768) are among the fictions whose plots are structured around the travels of their heroes and that draw on the conventions of the picaresque. Their mock-heroic narrators experience misfortunes that are echoed by the mishaps of twentieth-century travel narrators.

The link between travel writing and these fictions is close. The major novelists also wrote travel books, and 'the eighteenth century ... witnessed a new era in which non-fiction travel literature achieved an unparalleled popularity'.[4] Defoe's other works include *A Tour through the Whole Island of Great Britain* (1724–6); Fielding's include *The Journal of a Voyage to Lisbon* (1755). Many of the fictions are modelled on varieties of the travel book. At least two of them, Defoe's *Robinson Crusoe* (1719) and Swift's *Gulliver's Travels* (1726, 1735), have outlived their times and grown into powerful cultural myths. The interrelationship between the novel and travel writing helped forge the individual narrative voice that remains familiar to us now.

One critic remarks of Defoe's *Tour thro' the Whole Island of Great Britain*,

> the itinerary [he] reports having followed serves as a central fiction by which he draws together both personal observations gleaned from various trips through Great Britain as well as facts often taken without acknowledgment from other books. Consequently, Defoe's descriptions *seem* essentially truthful, but the narrative that connects them is largely fictional. Yet instead of casting doubt on the instructional value of the whole work, the fictionality of the narrative serves to make the travel book more pleasing. The narrative unites and orders his descriptions; through it Defoe presents, in a pleasing manner, descriptions that should be instructionally profitable to his readers.[5]

The overlapping of fact and fiction at this time is particularly enabled by the shared traits of the *picaro*. Although the protagonists of the eighteenth-century travel book tend to be of a higher social class than their novelistic counterparts, they, too, are often rascals. In narrative tone and style, travel books of the period also exhibit characteristics of the picaresque. For example, the narrator of *Another Traveller! Or Cursory Remarks and Critical Observations Made upon a Journey through Part of the Netherlands in the Latter End of the Year 1766*, makes the kind of humorous address to the audience that is typical of that genre. Like Sterne and others, he draws explicit parallels between travel and narration; between the journey and writing. Thus, of 'Louvain, or Lovens', he exclaims: 'its agreeable situation, the salubrity of the air, the great number of ecclesiastic and civil antiquities; its learned societies and plentiful markets; its delightful environs and the courtesy of the inhabitants, cannot but invite the curious passenger to stop a little and look about him'.[6] However, he goes on:

> But surely it will not be expected that I should speak at large upon all these heads; each of which would be sufficient to fill half a dozen chapters? – In that case I shall never get to my journey's end. – I rather chuse, in pursuance of my old plan, to touch only upon a few particulars, ... submitting the topographical and historical parts to be treated at large by future travellers of more abilities and industry than myself.
>
> 'Tis certainly a most unfair way of proceeding; so to exhaust the subject, as to leave no harvest for others.[7]

This passage comes from chapter 34, whose heading, 'In proof that the Traveller made some short stay at Louvain', alludes to the doubts over authenticity that other accounts had produced. The narrator's need to state his evidence has the effect of reminding readers that other authors had made claims to travels they had not really undertaken.

There are also similarities between the adventures of the protagonists of eighteenth-century novels, travel writing and the Romantic poets (although in some cases, as with Byron and Shelley, death tragically results). Carl Thompson refers to 'the romantic tendency to construct travel as an enterprise that ought ideally (or properly) to involve travails and misadventures'.[8] He identifies the Romantic era as the period in which a 'fascination with such misadventures becomes especially prominent in British culture'.[9] Crucial here is what Thompson labels the 'tendency in much Romantic poetry to suggest that the poet himself is, or has been, some sort of suffering traveller'.[10] The means by which this is communicated is Romantic travellers' self-fashioning, or what Thompson prefers to call self-dramatisation, one of the most distinctive of which roles is as misadventurer.[11] Wordsworth and Byron are 'especially influential in terms of establishing new personae, and new patterns of travel, for subsequent generations of British travellers'.[12] It is not simply a matter of personalities. Thompson claims that 'the influence of romance, sentimentalism, and Gothic all have some part to play in the Romantic interest in travel as misadventure', and also the sublime, primitivism and pedestrianism, the last of which 'became popular, amongst a particular subset of British travellers, in the 1780s and 1790s'.[13]

Images and motifs from earlier voyages and travels were incorporated by Romantic poets. Donald Howard refers to the fact that the Romantic poet Samuel Taylor Coleridge (1772–1834) claims to have been reading Purchas's anthology of travels while composing 'Kubla Khan'. Coleridge writes that he had Purchas's book open at a passage that reads 'In Xamdu did Cublai Can build a stately Palace, encompassing sixteene miles of plaine ground with a wall, wherein are fertile Meddowes, pleasant springs, delightfull Streames, and all sorts of beasts of chase and game, and in the middest thereof a sumptuous house of pleasure, which may be removed from place to place'.[14] Howard also reminds us that Mandeville's *Travels* was a great favourite of Coleridge's. The case of Romantic poets, and particularly Coleridge, shows how travel accounts may be utilised in other forms of literature and influence their representations – and thus, in turn, readers' images – of other places.

Just as the novel arose in response to and reflected particular social and economic conditions, so travel writing also reacted to those. Nigel Leask explains that, 'The eighteenth-century popularity of books of voyages and travels reflected the rise of European commercial and colonial expansion'.[15] Roy Bridges outlines something of the situation: 'By 1720, among the European powers struggling for primacy in the wider world, Spain and Portugal had been eclipsed by France, Britain, and the Netherlands. These three societies now competed to control what was assumed in the current "mercantilist" theory to be a limited supply of wealth. All three were successful because they had linked state and capitalist mercantile interests'.[16] Britain became more dominant, gaining territories in 1744–8 and 1763 after the Seven Years War.

Besides leisure travel, the outward movements associated with trade, science and colonialism consolidated the production of and audience for various subgenres of travel writing, such as narratives of shipwreck, captivity and exploration.[17] The Romantic period especially saw 'a dramatic upsurge' in 'the genre known to contemporary readers as Voyages and Travels, a huge and highly heterogeneous branch of the eighteenth-century literary scene'.[18]

Anthologies of travels helped meet the appetite for accounts of these activities: 'From 1660 to 1800 over a hundred such collections were made, many in several editions, many translated into more than one language, and some that included twenty, thirty, even one hundred volumes'.[19] One of the best-known is Thomas Astley's modestly titled *A New General Collection of Voyages and Travels: Consisting of the Most Esteemed Relations Which Have Been Hitherto Published in Any Language, Comprehending Everything Remarkable in Its Kind in Europe, Asia, Africa, and America* (1745–7).

Although the common critical view is that the eighteenth and nineteenth centuries saw scientific and 'pleasurable' narratives (in Batten's term), each going its own way, the scientific narratives are neither objective nor innocent. Dennis Porter has pointed out:

> The age of the Enlightenment ... saw itself as the triumphant culmination of some two thousand years of European cultural development.... [O]ne consequence of that progress was the extension and consolidation of European power over the course of the century to the remotest regions of the globe....
>
> The voyages of world travellers ... were therefore integrally connected to the project of the Enlightenment in all kinds of ways.[20]

The 'age of discovery' was part of this movement; it was not a disinterested collection of information.

The voyages of discovery have been the subject of postcolonial re-readings, including ones that assume the position of those on the shore rather than on the ship and of ordinary sailors.[21] Nigel Leask, however, implies that some of these have overstated their case. Leask explains that he is 'wary of underestimating the degree to which eighteenth- and early nineteenth-century travellers were bound by empirical protocols which demanded rigorous practices of description and notation, however distorted these reports now seem to us'.[22] Leask takes as his starting point, 'the *vulnerability* rather than self-sufficiency of European travellers, in relation to the lands and peoples in which they travelled, and the instability rather than the authority of their published narratives, in the eyes of metropolitan readerships'.[23] For Leask, 'there is an urgent political need to contest the tendency (ironically enough, often manifested by post-colonial critics themselves) to exaggerate the historical and geographical reach of European hegemony, and its power over different cultures'.[24]

Leask does not deny the horrors of the slave trade or of aspects of European imperialism, but points out that in the 1770s and 1780s, British forces suffered defeats in India, Abyssinia remained free from colonial rule until the twentieth century, and Egypt and Mexico freed themselves from European rule in the early nineteenth century. He commends Mary Louise Pratt for 'acknowledg[ing] the historical agency of those peoples who were in constant (and often effective) struggle against the imposition of colonial subalternity', but believes that she 'does not go far enough in breaking up and discriminating the grand historical narrative of European global dominance'.[25] In Leask's view, Pratt's reading is inflected with terms more appropriate to an analysis of narratives imbued with the 'hawkish imperatives of Victorian high imperialism'. Regarding eighteenth-century travellers, Leask remarks that 'Even in an age of sensibility, the rhetoric of vulnerability in travel writing was not merely feigned'.[26] Leask's arguments constitute a valuable corrective to studies that overemphasise domination, but the travellers' influence was felt in material ways and helped pave the way for those that followed them, even if the attitudes and methods of those later travellers differed. Theirs were incursions.

The Picturesque

While the picaresque novel and the travel writing that shares its features direct attention to the character of protagonists and their adventures, William Gilpin focuses on particular views of the landscape, and in highly contrived ways. Gilpin appears to offer the picturesque as a kind of antidote to practical travel. In his essay 'On Picturesque Travel' (1792), he refers to the object of picturesque travel as being 'beauty of every kind, which either art, or nature may produce.... This great object we pursue through the scenery of nature; and examine it by the rules of painting. We seek it among all the ingredients of landscape'.[27] In his *Observations on the River Wye ...* (1782) he announces:

> The following little work proposes a new object of pursuit; that of examining the face of a country *by the rules of picturesque beauty:*

> opening the sources of those pleasures which are derived from the comparison.
>
> Observations of this kind, through the vehicle of description, have the better chance of being founded in truth, as they are not the offspring of theory, but are taken immediately from the scenes of nature as they arise.[28]

Of course, such observations are manifestly the 'offspring of theory', deriving, as they do, from the idea of the picturesque and its view of beauty and truth in nature. It is a highly prescriptive theory at that. Thus, crossing 'Hounslow-heath, from Kingston in Surry, we struck into the Reading road', and

> turned a little aside to see the approach to Caversham-house, which winds about a mile along a valley, through the park. This was the work of [Lancelot 'Capability'] Brown, whose great merit lay in pursuing the path which nature had marked out. Nothing can be easier than the sweep, better united than the ground, or more ornamental than several of the clumps; but many of the single trees, which are beeches, are heavy, and offend the eye. Almost any ordinary tree may contribute to form a group.... But few trees have those characters of beauty which will enable them to appear with advantage as individuals. (pp.2–3)

In similar vein, Gilpin writes of leaving Lord Cadogan's and taking the Wallingford Road to Oxford, which overlooks one of the valleys of the Thames:

> [T]hese scenes afford nothing very interesting. The Thames appears; but only in short reaches. It rarely exceeds the dimensions of a pool; and does not once, as I remember, exhibit those ample sweeps, in which the beauty of a river so much consists. The woods too are frequent; but they are formal copies: and white spots, bursting everywhere from a chalky soil, disturb the eye. (p.3)

In Gloucester, on the ridge of the Cotswolds, Gilpin looks down on the Severn Vale, and doubts he has ever been 'more struck with the singularity and grandeur of any landscape' (p.7). He observes that: 'When nature works in the bold and singular stile of composition in which she works here; when she raises a country through a progress of a hundred miles, and then breaks it down at once by an abrupt precipice into an expansive vale, we are immediately struck with the novelty and grandeur of the scene' (p.8). This is not seeing nature for what it is, but for how it measures up to a culturally shaped aesthetic.

Of the situation of Tintern Abbey, he judges, 'The woods and glades intermixed; the winding of the river; the variety of the ground; the splendid ruin, contrasted with the objects of nature; and the elegant line formed by the summits of the hills which include the whole, make all together a very enchanting piece of scenery' (pp.48–9). Gilpin's description of the Abbey illustrates how prescriptive the picturesque's view of nature (and of objects in it) was. Thus, from a distance:

> Though the parts are beautiful, the whole is ill-shaped. No ruins of the tower are left, which might give form and contrast to the buttresses and walls. Instead of this, a number of gabel-ends hurt the eye with their regularity, and disgust it by the vulgarity of their shape....
>
> But if Tintern-abbey be less striking as a *distant* object, it exhibits, on a *nearer* view, (when the whole together cannot be seen,) a very enchanting piece of ruin. The eye settles upon some of its nobler parts. Nature has now made it her own. Time has worn off all traces of the chisel: it has blunted the sharp edges of the rule and compass, and broken the regularity of opposing parts. (pp.49–50)

Gilpin's version of the picturesque allows us to see more clearly what is implicit in other, if not all, travel writing: that travellers' accounts of the landscape do not provide neutral versions of it; they do not simply describe it; they *construct* it, too. They regard it not as it is but as it strikes and affects us. The same is true of responses to those who inhabit the landscape.

The grand tour

We saw in Chapter 2 that tourism has its origins in classical times but, as Ian Littlewood is one of many to have observed, 'modern tourism may reasonably be said to date from the spread of the Grand Tour in the eighteenth century'.[29] With it arose the modern guidebook and its prescriptions for the acquisition of cultural taste. One of the influential works was Thomas Nugent's *The Grand Tour* (1749), of which Littlewood writes: 'Today's guidebook, with its list of monuments and its advice on local purchases, is a direct descendant of [it]'.[30]

The 1700s saw the consolidation of the Grand Tour, a phenomenon usually identified as having begun in the seventeenth century. The first recorded use of the term is widely cited as being in Richard Lassels' *The Voyage of Italy* (1670), the 'charter or foundational text for the [Grand] Tour',[31] and 'the first really popular English guidebook'.[32] Redford notes that it 'conditioned the reactions of thousands of Tourists' and emphasised the intellectual, social, ethical and political advantages accruing to the traveller (R, p.10).

The Tour had no fixed route or duration but on average 'lasted longer than a year',[33] and was generally expected 'to include France, Switzerland and Italy, probably taking in Germany and the Netherlands on the way home'.[34] Whereas

'Italy was essential' to it, ways of reaching that country varied.[35] For most, the first destination was Paris, seen by many 'as the most important sight not only in France, but in Europe'.[36] The Low Countries, which served as a thoroughfare, were themselves a goal for large numbers of people. According to Black, they were, after Paris and Italy, 'the third most important group of places visited by British tourists', and the subject of an 'extensive literature'.[37] Itineraries remained flexible even when the Tour became 'increasingly *pre*scriptive' during the second half of the seventeenth century.[38] But for all who made the Tour, Rome was '"the great object" of the exercise' (R, p.1). It was 'where the traveler completed his transformation into gentleman-classicist, possessor of the past' (R, p.9). As Black observes, 'The strong influence of a Classical education and of a public ideology that drew strongly on Classical images and themes can be seen in the accounts of many tourists'.[39]

The significance of Venice was more double-edged. It

> helped to form the gentleman as contemporary cultural leader; it taught modern art, politics, economics, and sexuality. Venice also gave a local habitation and a name to the ambivalence that surrounded the Tour in eighteenth-century culture, which viewed it as a phenomenon both deeply necessary and deeply dangerous, a prop of the hierarchical status quo and a subversive force within it. (R, p.9)

Redford also claims that 'the mythology and ideology of Venice are intimately connected to the mythology and ideology of the Tour, an institution that decisively shaped eighteenth-century culture and politics. It did so by helping to form, strengthen, and sustain the patriciate of Great Britain' (R, p.7). Redford follows Gerald Newman and E. P. Thompson in suggesting that the power of the patriciate depended not so much on economic or material factors as on '[h]egemony based upon differentiation through style' (R, p.8). This point is arguable: style accompanied and complemented the financial status that made its exhibition possible. Nevertheless, Redford is right to underline this as a means by which the ruling class asserts its superiority over those it sees beneath it. 'To make the Grand Tour was to acquire a special sort of cultural power. Such power depended upon display. Indeed one might go so far as to say that travel abroad existed for the sake of ostentation at home' (R, p.81).

The Tour's 'protracted travel for pleasure' was a part of the 'ideal education of the social élite, as well as an important source of descriptive and imaginative literature'. Despite its associations with the aristocracy, the 'majority of travel accounts were not by aristocrats'.[40] On the other hand, there was a fear that the Grand Tourist would 'go native' in Europe; that 'Foreign cultural preferences could be held to be more widely indicative, to reveal political and ideological tendencies'.[41]

The Grand Tour was not just about art, architecture, languages and politics. It was about sex, too. In all these aspects it was a rite of passage for aristocratic and upper-class males (R, p.15). Referring to the escapades of Samuel Johnson's biographer, Littlewood asserts that 'If we want to understand the Grand Tour and its relation to modern tourism, it is quite as important to take account of Boswell's visits to Dresden streetwalkers and Venetian courtesans as of his visits to the Dresden picture gallery and the Doge's Palace'.[42] The Grand Tourist 'expected to have amours' but had fun poked at him too: 'By the 1730s, the syphilitic alumnus of the Grand Tour had become a standard target of satire' (R, p.21). Those amours were both heterosexual and same sex. Italy in particular became 'firmly associated in the English imagination with rampant homosexuality' (R, p.21). Links between effeminacy, homosexuality and the sultry climes of the south were reinforced. In sex as well as potentially in politics and social conduct, there was, in Redford's words, 'the transgressive as well as the transformative aspect of the Grand Tour'. Redford continues: 'Britain's young patricians, propelled toward adulthood through systematic border-crossing, transgressed boundaries that were meant to remain inviolate'; it was Venice 'that most fully embodied the paradox and focused the anxieties'(R, p.25).

At the end of the century and in the early nineteenth century, the Grand Tour was interrupted by the French Revolution and the Napoleonic Wars. It was 'undermined for good by the invention of steam travel and the development of package tourism for a middle-class clientele. In losing its exclusivity, it lost its *raison d'être*' (R, p.15).

The first person

The prescriptions of the Tour provoked satire and parody. For example, Tobias Smollett's *Travels through France and Italy* (1766) subverted the conventions of narratives of the Tour (R, p.43). There was, in turn, a humorous response to the mocking. Laurence Sterne's *A Sentimental Journey* (1768) may be read as a riposte to Smollett's *Travels* but both 'define themselves in opposition to the Tour and narratives spawned by it' (R, p.46). Volume VII of *Tristram Shandy* was described by Sterne himself as a satire against travelling (R, p.46). Littlewood writes that 'Sterne shifts the whole emphasis from the exterior to the interior journey. He is less interested in places than people and less interested in both than in their impact on the consciousness of the traveller'. Littlewood views this as 'part of a wider trend', with Sterne's *A Sentimental Journey* 'foreshadowing a new theory of travel. For the Romantic, travel was not simply about seeing new sights, acquiring new information, making new contacts; it could also be about becoming a new person'.[43] This transformational aspect of travel would continue into the twenty-first century.

Yorick, the protagonist of Sterne's *A Sentimental Journey*, writes of his awareness that 'both my travels and observations will be altogether of a different cast from any of my fore-runners'.[44] His words illustrate the move by travellers to distinguish themselves from other travellers and their accounts. No one does this more than Lady Mary Wortley Montagu, who frequently disparages previous travel accounts and their authors for their inadequacy, inaccuracy and invention. In just one of very many examples, she expresses to one correspondent her annoyance with another who she thinks suspects her of withholding tales of marvellous sights: 'She is angry that I won't lie like other travellers. I verily believe she expects I should tell her of the anthropophagi, and men whose heads grow below their shoulders'.[45]

The narrative emphasis on individualism coincides with the introspection, or association between the external and internal, that accompanies Romanticism. Redford notes that William Beckford's and Byron's versions of the Grand Tour included a subordination of 'the external world to the troubled consciousness of a traveler whose primary quest is directed inward' (R, p.105). Beckford's suppressed narrative, *Dreams, Waking Thoughts and Incidents* (1783) transforms the Tour in significant ways, including the insistence on the primacy of the subjective viewer; 'cultivat[ing] with the reader a relationship of confessional intimacy'; and 'displac[ing] education in favor of imagination' (R, p.107). Canto IV of Byron's *Childe Harold's Pilgrimage* is 'about the memory of landscape and the landscape of memory'; in the Canto 'topography is always turning into autobiography'(R, pp.115, 116). It is the 'last important Grand Tour narrative'(R, p. 117). With this, 'Intensity of sensation has become the most important goal of travel, and the principal criterion of success' (R, p.120).

The literature discussed so far in this chapter – the picaresque, the Grand Tour narratives and Romantic writing – is usually seen as dominated by men. Yet the eighteenth century saw a significant increase in female authorship. According to Carl Thompson, 'Only one travel account by a woman seems to have been published before 1763 ... Between 1763 and 1800, however, some twenty female-authored travelogues appeared'.[46] A similar picture emerges from Elizabeth Hagglund's survey of reviews of travel books and pamphlets in the periodical the *Monthly Review* between 1749 and 1758. Explaining that 'Book reviewing in the way we now understand the term began with the *Monthly Review* in 1749', Hagglund notes that in the years covered by her survey 'None of the [travel] books on the list was written by women, although reviews of other books by women – usually fiction and poetry – appeared. It was later in the century that accounts of women's travel began to be published and reviewed'.[47]

A noteworthy example of one of the new women travel writers is Mary Wollstonecraft whose *Letters Written During a Short Residence in Sweden, Norway and Denmark* was published in 1796, the year before her death. Wollstonecraft was the author of the radical *A Vindication of the Rights of Men* (1790) and of the proto-feminist *A Vindication of the Rights of Woman* (1792). Her travel book – comprising letters to unnamed recipients, but known to be to her lover, Gilbert Imlay – was 'an immediate success', being '[w]idely read in England and America' and translated into German, Dutch and Portuguese, and 'reviewed in glowing terms'.[48] Wollstonecraft made her trip when she was thirty-six, accompanied by her infant daughter and a French nursemaid. She returned to England with her child on 4 October, 1795 and within weeks attempted suicide for a second time by drowning, following Imlay's desertion of her. (She had also tried to kill herself shortly before her journey.) Wollstonecraft shows that how one looks at and judges a country is affected by one's thoughts and moods; by one's private situation. This is signalled from the start, in her Advertisement, where she announces:

> I found I could not avoid being continually the first person – "the little hero of each tale." I tried to correct this fault, if it be one, for they were designed for publication; but in proportion as I arranged my thoughts, my letter, I found, became stiff and affected: I, therefore, determined to let my remarks and reflections flow unrestrained, as I perceived that I could not give a just description of what I saw, but by relating the effect different objects had produced on my mind and feelings, whilst the impression was still fresh.[49]

Wollstonecraft's politics ensure that her emotions are not confined to the merely personal. Rather, her interjections of her mood often see her despairing at her lot or at that of women in general. For example, recording her 'sort of weak melancholy that hung about my heart at parting with my daughter for the first time', she writes: 'You know that as a female I am particularly attached to her – I feel more than a mother's fondness and anxiety, when I reflect on the dependent and oppressed state of her sex. I dread lest she should be forced to sacrifice her heart to her principles, or principles to her heart' (p.66). Moving to the larger view, she states: 'most of the struggles of an eventful life have been occasioned by the oppressed state of my sex' (p.214). She is open about how her personal mood may affect her observations: 'I am perhaps a little prejudiced, as I write from the impression of the moment; for I have been tormented to-day by the presence of unruly children' (pp.202–3). Unsurprisingly, given her circumstances, a sombre, even depressive mood shadows the book, arising into expression intermittently. For example, she muses: 'How frequently has melancholy and even mysanthropy [sic] taken possession of me, when the world has disgusted me, and friends have proven unkind' (p.15).

In 1792 Wollstonecraft had travelled to France where she met, among others, the radical Tom Paine. Two years later she published *An Historical and Moral View of the Origin and Progress of the French Revolution*. Having eagerly embraced the French Revolution,[50] she writes of Norway that the revolution will lead to politics becoming a matter of discussion and will enlarge the understanding (p.79). Her politics evince a concern with class and gender. In *Letters* she has a dig at men: 'the [Swedish] men stand up for the dignity of man, by oppressing the women' (p.27). Yet she also looks at servitude in class terms: 'The treatment of servants in most countries, I grant, is very unjust; and in England, that boasted land of freedom, it is often extremely tyrannical.... We must love our servants, or we shall never be sufficiently attentive to their happiness' (p.28). As for property, 'Every where wealth commands too much respect' (p.136). She warns that 'an adoration of property is the root of all evil' (p.211) and declares: 'You may think me too severe on commerce; but from the manner it is at present carried on, little can be advanced in favour of a pursuit that wears out the most sacred principles of humanity and rectitude' (p.157).

Wollstonecraft comments several times on the intellectual and moral benefits of travel, and on writing about it. She suggests that, like travel, keeping a journal can introduce more useful enquiries 'that would not have been thought of, had the traveller only determined to see all he could see, without ever asking himself for what purpose' (p.32). With visits to the metropolis in mind, she states that: 'Mixing with mankind, we are obliged to examine our prejudices, and often imperceptibly lose, as we analyze them' (p.33); the same is true of journeying among populated areas in general.[51] She presumes that:

> The most essential service ... that authors could render to society, would be to promote inquiry and discussion ...
>
> This spirit of inquiry is the characteristic of the present century, from which the succeeding will, I am persuaded, receive a great accumulation of knowledge; and doubtless its diffusion will in a great measure destroy the factitious national characters which have been supposed permanent, though only rendered so by the permanency of ignorance. (p.59)

Her hopes for the erasure of 'factitious national characters' would not be realised in the centuries that followed.

As the eighteenth century drew to a close, so, too, in the eyes of some, did a type of literary travel. Adams claims that the 'great age' for literature in which an invented traveller served as 'the vehicle for a body of knowledge about foreign countries' ended with

> the advent of the steamboat and the steam locomotive, when real travelers became so numerous that false ones were both less necessary and more easily exposed. But the fireside travelers of the eighteenth century continued to exert their influence.... historical and adventure novels ... learned from the school of Defoe that by applying the tools of the scholar they can add color, concreteness, and verisimilitude to the lands where their heroes go.[52]

In other words, the growth in popular tourism meant that invention no longer held the same authority – it could be tested by its readership, who could travel themselves – but that the techniques of fiction were borrowed for effect. Charles Batten observes that by the end of the eighteenth century, 'significant amounts of autobiographical material had become integral parts of many travel accounts, making them seem increasingly like memoirs', an influence on which he names as Sterne's *Sentimental Journey*.[53] The approach of the nineteenth century ushered in social and literary changes: with more people travelling and a more subjective approach to writing about travel.

In the nineteenth century, the autobiographical material was often blended with colonial, imperial and missionary aims before becoming more obtrusive again in the twentieth century in the era of post-war introspection and decolonisation. The last text from the eighteenth century that we shall look at, James Cook's *Journals*, combines the personal and scientific in ways that may seem incongruous to modern readers. Although a huge popular and commercial success at the time, Cook's journals were not at first published as he wrote them. In the words of Australian historian Richard White:

> Cook's plain man's writing was not considered fit for publication; such was the vogue for travel writing that his and Joseph Banks' journals were handed over to the minor literary celebrity, Dr John Hawkesworth, to produce, with a huge advance of £6,000, the most popular travel book of the century. Hawkesworth set out to "afford more entertainment" ... and sought in turn to correct Cook's subversive sentiments: "if we admit that they are upon the whole happier than we, we must admit ... that we are the losers by the perfection of our nature".[54]

In Cook's journal, we can clearly see the mixture of personal, scientific, commercial and exploration discourses that we shall also find in the nineteenth-century productions of figures like Henry M. Stanley, but that later become separated out with the professionalisation of science. Roy Bridges identifies the three voyages of James Cook as setting 'the pattern of government demanding scientific investigation as part of a search for precise and accurate information whether or not this pointed to economic opportunities'.[55] It is important to note that science was not disinterested. Cook writes about the prospects of increasing natives' wants (e.g., p.560), and constant refrains are his taking possession of land 'in the name of His Majesty' (e.g., p.92) and bestowing European names on natural features.

One of the many interesting aspects of Cook's narrative is his direct references to the likely reception of his accomplishments and writings. He complains of the 'Vicissitudes attending this kind of service and [that] must always attend an unknown Navigation: Was it not for the pleasure which naturly results to a Man from being the first discoverer, even was it nothing more than sands and Shoals, this service would be insupportable especially in far distant parts, like this, short of Provisions and almost every other necessary'. The pressure that he feels is evident when he continues: 'The world will hardly admit of an excuse for a man leaving a Coast unexplored he has once discover'd, if dangers are his excuse he is than charged with *Timorousness* and want of Perseverance and at once pronounced the unfittest man in the world to be employ'd as a discoverer; if on the other hand he boldly incounters all the dangers and obstacles he meets and is unfortunate enough not to succeed he is than charged with *Temerity* and want of conduct' (p.168). Cook exempts himself from both charges.

Cook's representation of the Noble Savage reveals some of the tensions in his thought. He states that 'From what I have said of the Natives of New-Holland [Australia] they may appear to some to be the most wretched people upon Earth, but in reality they are far more happier than we Europeans, being wholly unacquainted not only with the superfluous but the necessary Conveniences so much sought after in Europe, they are happy in not knowing the use of them'. What Cook then writes goes beyond a standard expression of happy primitives unburdened by desires for material goods, for he proceeds to comment that 'They live in a tranquillity which is not disturb'd by the Inequality of Condition: The Earth and sea of their own accord furnishes them with all things necessary for life, they covet not Magnificent Houses, Household-stuff &c ...' (p.174). The observation clearly invites reflection on the situation in the country Cook has left behind: his own. There is no other way to read his remark on inequality than as an implicit criticism of its existence and effects in Britain.

Later, Cook is more explicit in his criticism of his home society and its methods. Musing on the changes (for the worse) in the sexual behaviour of indigenous peoples at St Charlotte Sound, he exclaims:

> such are the consequences of a commerce with Europeans and what is still more to our Shame civilized Christians, we debauch their Morals already too prone to vice and we interduce among them wants and perhaps diseases which they never before knew and which serves only

> to disturb that happy tranquillity they and their fore Fathers had injoy'd. If any one denies the truth of this assertion let him tell me what the Natives of the whole extent of America have gained by the commerce they have had with Europeans. (p.277)

Among its descriptions of physical punishments meted out to crew and indigenous peoples alike, there is also in Cook's journals an acknowledgement of how his actions may be viewed by the people whose lands they visit. He writes:

> we enter their Ports without their daring to make opposition, we attempt to land in a peaceable manner, if this succeeds its well, if not we land nevertheless and mention the footing we thus got by the Superiority of our fire arms, in what other light can they than at first look upon us but as invaders of their Country; time and some acquaintance with us can only convince them of their mistake. (p.386)

Cook's manoeuvring in this passage is very interesting. He attempts to see his arrival from the point of view of the islanders but he has quickly to suspend that exercise, dismissing the logical inference as a 'mistake'. There is in his writing a melange of discourses: official and individual; scientific and romantic; formal and personal; racial superiority but strong criticism of the country he serves. There is acknowledgement, but then suppression, of objections to his mission. All this is contained within prose that reveals his basic education and humble origins, circumstances that contributed to his journal being handed over to Hawkesworth. In the century that followed, few figures other than Henry Morton Stanley, who shared his ambivalence about indigenous peoples, would match this complexity and range.

Chapter 4

Travel writing in the nineteenth century

I read one or two shallow books of travel in the intervals of my work, till that employment made me ashamed of myself, and I asked where it was then that *I* lived.

Henry David Thoreau, *Walden*[1]

We wanted something thoroughly and uncompromisingly foreign.

Mark Twain[2]

Studies of nineteenth-century poetry and the novel tend to focus either on Romanticism or on the Victorian period. The same is true of travel writing criticism. Yet while the changes that occurred in society and culture over the course of the 1800s make coherent commentaries on the literature of the entire 100 years difficult to construct, there are benefits in considering the century as a whole. Across the shifts in literary form, style and conventions over the decades, there are clear continuities as well as breaks. The factors to consider in assessing these include the revolution in transport and communications, emigration to the colonies, imperial activity, scientific thought and practice and intellectual currents.

Much travel writing of the 1800s owes its existence to new forms of transport: the steamship, the railway, the bicycle and, at the century's end, the motor car. The first regular cross-Channel steamer service began in 1820 and in the decades that followed, rail networks spread across Europe. 'Within thirty years Continental travel had become dramatically quicker, cheaper and more widely available'.[3] Meanwhile, huge increases in literacy rates and book production facilitated the circulation of travel narratives.[4] These developments affected how people travelled and how the accounts of their journeys were written, distributed and read.

As we saw in Chapter 3, the Grand Tour underwent a transformation at the turn of the eighteenth century. Both it and Romantic-period travel survived into the nineteenth century, the Romantic movement lasting, according to most definitions, until the 1830s. By the end of the 1790s, the 'Tour in its classic form was more or less over, killed by the French Revolution and the continuing hostilities between France and England',[5] but it prevailed in modified form. The Napoleonic Wars may have 'effectively clos[ed] the Continent to British travellers for twenty years', but, 'after 1815 Britons ... head[ed] abroad in greater numbers than ever before'.[6] The Grand Tour 'enjoyed a brief revival in the nineteenth century ... but tourism was entering a new phase. Railways brought with them the age of the package tour and the guidebook. ... [T]he dominant characteristics of tourism had changed'.[7] The progression of nineteenth-century tourism is characterised by the increasing access of the middle classes to travel as a result of improved transport and greater affordability. In this respect, the shift in the demographics of tourism reflects the social movements in the relationship between classes. The gradual decline of the aristocracy and the rise of the middle classes helped effect the democratisation of travel, but, as with responses to democracy in general, reactions were often cautious or hostile. Those who regarded themselves as travellers rather than tourists insisted on the distinction with heightened intensity. Buzard's suggestion that the Grand Tourist's nineteenth-century counterpart would 'lay claim to an aristocracy of inner feeling' in place of the earlier 'repetitive ritual of classicism and class solidarity' is a reference to one of the ways in which the latter-day Grand Tourists in the new age of mass travel aimed to differentiate themselves from others who made similar journeys.[8] The example cited by Buzard is Lord Byron, who, as Ian Littlewood has stated, 'turned travel into an act of defiance'.[9] In Littlewood's words, Byron set out on his first journey abroad 'with the clear intention of using the trip to sample homosexual pleasures that were illegal at home'.[10] Littlewood places Byron at the head of the 'long and important tradition of rebel tourism ... motivated by sexual dissatisfaction', though one should not overlook Byron's political and intellectual interests as motives also.[11]

The importance of Romanticism to the representation of modern travel cannot be overstated. Littlewood's emphasis is on the sexual element of the Grand Tour, which Byron exemplified. As Littlewood puts it, Byron brought 'romantic glamour' to 'the figure of the wanderer', and 'the Byronic traveller carries within him a fantasy of escape from all that defines their ordinariness. It is a dream whose chief ingredient is sexual freedom'.[12] More generally, the Romantics furnish an example of individuals finding themselves reflected in the landscape and turning to nature for social and political criticism. The correspondence between mood, thought and nature signifies a deep relationship between the figure and the environment that distinguishes the subject from the tourist who passes unseeingly, and unfeelingly, through it. This feature of Romanticism would inform the transcendentalist movement in the United States, and both movements, in turn, have influenced twentieth- and twenty-first environmentalism and ecocriticism. 'Romanticism played an important part in shaping the development of tourism', notes Buzard.[13] It also played a very large part in shaping the development of travel writing. The appeal of the suffering traveller and the drawing of material from travel and exploration texts was discussed in Chapter 3.

Romanticism's focus on individual reflection can be linked with Buzard's observation that 'Many nineteenth-century visitors to the Continent felt the onus of proving they had significantly diverged from the track of familiar itineraries and stock responses laid down in texts'.[14] The trend began earlier as we saw in Sterne's *A Sentimental Journey*. Buzard acknowledges that 'A travel writer's perception that the place he or she visits has already been "covered" by others is not new to the nineteenth century' but points out that 'during that post-Napoleonic period in which Continental travel seemed remade, the sense of having been preceded reached crisis proportions: accounts of European tours became susceptible to that dilemma of *belatedness* which readers after Walter Jackson Bate and Harold Bloom have come to regard as a pre-eminent concern of Romantic literature'.[15]

Britain and the wider world

Providing a summary of the historical contexts of travel in the period 1720–1914, Roy Bridges writes: 'As the relationship between Britain and the wider world changed …, there were many pressures tending to make travel writing not only more precise and scientific but also more obviously utilitarian, more explicitly concerned with issues of trade, diplomacy and prestige'.[16] Bridges identifies three broad phases to this near two hundred-year period: from the mid-eighteenth century 'the beginning of the end of the old mercantilist empire of plantations, slavery and Atlantic trade is apparent' and a turn to the East and to Africa may be discerned; from around 1830 to 1880 occurred the period of 'Victorian non-annexationist global expansion characterised by considerable confidence about Britain and its place in the world'; and 1880–1914 were years of 'severe international competition and territorial annexations accompanied by considerable anxiety'.[17]

Near the beginning of the nineteenth century, 'Britain emerged as a truly global power' after the naval victory at Trafalgar. Large areas of Canada, Australasia and the West Indies were under direct rule, and much of India at that time was controlled by East India Company officials. There were new opportunities for British traders and financiers to operate in the former Spanish and Portuguese territories of the New World. West Africa was coming to be seen as a promising market. Bridges makes the crucial point that 'Britain's ever closer engagement with the wider world meant that larger and larger numbers of travellers and explorers made journeys to report upon it'.[18] The importance of this observation cannot be exaggerated. The nineteenth century bears many similarities to the late sixteenth and seventeenth centuries in its production of exploration narratives and anthologies of travel. But increased literacy rates and innovations in printing led to more affordable editions. Many narratives were written for general readers: although containing scientific information, they were accessible both financially and intellectually. Charles Darwin's *Journal of Researches into the Geology and Natural History of the Various Countries Visited by H. M. S. Beagle under the Command of Captain Fitzroy, R. N. from 1832 to 1836* (1839), better known now as *The Voyage of the Beagle*, is one of several works to fuse travel narrative and scientific observation. The nineteenth century also saw many 'armchair scientists' drawing on travellers' reports to assist in the development of their theories. Travellers would often receive instructions from scientists on what to look for and how to report back to them. Towards the end of the century, as disciplines such as anthropology came to be more professionalised, the different functions of the travelogue (to inform and to entertain) moved apart and there was a movement towards greater specialism.

What seems to modern eyes remarkable in texts written before that divergence is the combination of ethnographic, geographical and other scientific information with personal travel narrative, written with sufficient clarity for the understanding of a general audience. This blend also allows for the expression of distinctive voices. One of the most striking of these belonged to Henry Morton Stanley, the Welsh-American reporter-cum-explorer, whose narratives of travel in Africa are an extraordinary mixture of information, romance, racial theorising and stereotypes, individual and cultural portraits and self-aggrandisement. Stanley was culturally and psychologically a very complex figure, a fact that contributes to the uneven tone of his books. Those draw on readings of the classics, romance, adventure stories and the new journalism to create a composite that elevates the constantly self-justifying explorer above those around him: his white companions, his African and Arab-African porters, and local Africans, friendly or (in his view) hostile. Comparison of Stanley's notebooks, journals, newspaper reports and published books shows that he reworks his descriptions from one form to another, even changing or inventing incidents for dramatic effect. The most arresting example of this is his account in *Through the Dark Continent* (1878) of handing over to Africans, whom he presents as superstitious natives demanding that he burn his valuable notes, a well-thumbed volume of Shakespeare instead. The episode powerfully emblematises the attack on civilisation and culture by savagery. Yet, in another account of the same incident, he states that what he actually handed over was a worthless piece of paper covered with careless scribbles.[19] Stanley is inconsistent, except in his self-regard. He is murderous towards some Africans (literally so) and acted for King Leopold of Belgium, facilitating his genocidal plundering of the Congo, but on occasion he offers respectful, individually detailed portraits of others. Likewise, any reading of the polyglot Richard Francis Burton will show that it can be difficult to generalise about an explorer's racial attitudes or character. Burton was an admirer of and knowledgeable about Islamic culture, making the hajj in disguise, as recounted in his *Personal Narrative of a Pilgrimage to El-Medinah and Meccah* (1855–6), but was viciously negative about Africans. What the examples of Stanley, Burton and other explorers show (especially Stanley) is that there is a high degree of self-construction taking place. The writing is tailored for the audience, and literary genres, styles and conventions are adapted for the purpose. Of course, sometimes the authors get it wrong. One of Stanley's misjudgements was so spectacularly silly that it quickly entered, and survives in, popular culture: his self-reported greeting, 'Dr. Livingstone, I presume', by which he meant to avoid an unseemly display of emotion that he thought would appear un-British.[20] The writings also reflect their context: Stanley, although loathed by the British establishment, is the figurehead of the new imperialism, and the attitudes that accompanied – even helped enable it – are obvious in his texts. 'Oh for the hour when a band of philanthropic capitalists shall vow to rescue these beautiful lands, and supply the means to enable the Gospel messengers to come and quench the murderous hate with which man beholds man in the beautiful lands around Lake Victoria!', he apostrophises.[21]

Stanley's appeal to missionaries is far from unusual. The nineteenth century was also the age of the missionary narrative. Often taking the form of letters home to family or missionary societies, or of diary entries, these may be seen as another subgenre of travel writing. In Britain, missionary activity was linked with abolitionism. The Church Missionary Society was founded in 1799 and the London Missionary Society in 1795. Missionaries from more modest walks of life began to travel and to write. Devoting themselves to the spread of Christianity, missionaries spread other values they associated with it. David Livingstone was perhaps the best-known advocate of what became known as the three Cs: Christianity, commerce and civilisation. Missionaries (and the societies for which they worked) needed to encourage more donations and so tended to report successful progress while emphasising that more work remained to be done. R. Wardlaw Thompson, author of the popular book

My Trip in the 'John Williams', combined in his preface the vicarious function performed for the reader with an appeal for further assistance:

> I wish all who will read this book could have shared in the many and varied interests of the trip it describes, and could see with their own eyes the wonderful change which the Gospel is making among the South Seas Islanders. As this is not possible, I hope the story of my travels will prove interesting, and will encourage them to continue their efforts to help the [London Missionary] Society.[22]

Tourists and travellers

In the wake of exploration and missionary activity came tourism, sometimes in places such as the Congo, which because of their associations would surprise us now.[23] The years from 1830 to 1870 have been described as 'the high watermark of English tourism, of what one might term imperialism through tourism'.[24]

Modern tourism, which arose from industrialisation and urbanisation, was 'represented as a broadly accessible form of leisure travel no longer based in the overt class and gender prerogatives of the Grand Tour'.[25] Also different in its nineteenth-century manifestation was its institutionalisation. Tourists were now travelling in larger groups and having their plans made for them. 'If the years 1820–1850 saw the expansion and consolidation of the new means of transport, they also saw the establishment of numerous institutions either indirectly enabling tourism or designed expressly to facilitate it'.[26] One of those new institutions was Thomas Cook and Company, whose first excursion was made in 1841. Fifty years later, celebrating a half-century of Cook's Tours, W. Fraser Rae observed: 'Now an excursion trip is a matter of course'. He continues:

> When Lord Anson and Captain Cook sailed round the world, they were regarded as heroes of an adventure as daring and wonderful as any which can be found in the histories and poems of Greece and Rome. Now the tour of the globe is a matter of everyday occurrence. Steam on land and sea has brought the farthest parts of the earth into proximity.[27]

Along with this democratisation comes a fear of the loss of special privilege and exclusive experience. As still happens today, there is a perception that mass travel is a dilution of something precious; that neophytes are incapable of proper appreciation and spoil the rewards for the *cognoscenti*. It leads to intensified attempts to distinguish travellers from tourists, both in travel practices and travel narratives. As Buzard writes:

> The democratising and institutionalising of tourism that developed in the nineteenth century transformed the experience of tourism by making it a mass experience. This ensured that tourists who sought to be distinctive were reacting against other tourists as much as in response to what they were visiting. It also created a challenge for modern travel literature, most of which deliberately searches for the atypical and presents the maverick.[28]

Another consequence is the redefinition of heroism. The nineteenth century is the age of modern heroes. The growth of empire led to a new pantheon of explorer-heroes – many of them explorers of Africa – and to the resurrection of earlier heroes, especially from the Elizabethan age, whose maritime adventures and mercantile expansion laid the foundations for their nineteenth-century versions.[29] In 1846, the Hakluyt Society was founded to print early narratives of voyages and exploration. Six years later, J. A. Froude described Hakluyt's *Principall Navigations* as 'the prose epic of the modern English nation'.[30]

This was also the era of mass emigration to the colonies, a kind of travel that produced settlers' letters and diaries, as well as booster literature, aimed at promoting the new settlements to attract new colonists. This, in turn, spawned travel books and articles from visitors who returned from or remained resident in these destinations. The voyages to North America and, especially, to Australia, were lengthy and hard. The writings made during them are the object of fascinating, theory-led inquiry from scholars interested in ships as liminal places: the site of transformation for those leaving home for a new country.[31] The reverse journey, from the colonies to Britain, gave rise to its own body of travel literature.

James Buzard notes that the word 'tourist', which, according to the *Oxford English Dictionary*, first made its appearance in the late eighteenth century as synonymous with 'traveller', began to be used pejoratively by the mid-nineteenth century.[32] In that century:

> Travel's educative, acculturating function took on a newly competitive aspect, as travellers sought to distinguish themselves from the "mere tourists" they saw or imagined around them. Correspondingly, the authentic "culture" of *places* – the *genius loci* – was represented as lurking in secret precincts "off the beaten track" where it could be discovered only by the sensitive "traveller", not the vulgar tourist.[33]

Scrutiny of the disparagement of tourists can tell us much about dominant social attitudes and perceived challenges to these. Buzard's summary on this point is helpful: 'scores of passages in nineteenth-century travel-writing comment disdainfully on tourists' conspicuous failures of taste. … the tourist is an unwelcome reminder, to self-styled "travellers", of the modern realities that dog their fleeing footsteps. … Abroad, the tourist is the relentless representative of home'.[34] In the outlook referred to by Buzard here, the so-called traveller seeks authenticity through a difference from home. The genuine is sought in a flight from modernity; from machines, money and, often, from urbanisation, too. The idea is that the traveller will respect difference whereas the tourist will bring about a transformation that will diminish it.[35] It is of course a delusional flight since the means for its accomplishment are derived from the very lifestyle from which a retreat is desired. We can contrast this impulse with the travel writing that accompanied imperial and colonial expansion. Those texts encouraged export of the lifestyle and values of the home society.

Chloe Chard distinguishes the approach of the tourist, 'who … attempts to keep the more dangerous and destabilizing aspects of the encounter with the foreign at bay', from the Romantic view of travel, in which 'travel is a form of personal adventure, holding out the promise of a discovery or realization of the self through the exploration of the other'. In this light, 'travel entails crossing symbolic as well as geographical boundaries, and these transgressions of limits invite various forms of danger and destabilization'. Chard stresses, however, that both approaches 'still play a crucial part in determining the ways in which encounters with the foreign can be described or imagined today'.[36]

Giles Barber's summary of the history of modern guidebooks shows the importance of nineteenth-century developments. Barber identifies four periods:

> 1660–1690, the age of Italy and of the translation of foreign guides; 1690–1790, the period of development of the gentleman's guide; 1815–1840 the time of the development of the systematic, all-over guide produced by specialist publishers for a numerically growing market; and finally from 1840 onwards the evolution of both upper class, "comfort and culture" guides such as Murray and Baedeker, and the simultaneous exploitation of a more popular, mass market. Publishers naturally reacted to the growth of, and the changes in, the travel and tourism markets.[37]

According to Barber:

> The changed world circumstances saw four different developments: first, the systematic translation of the leading foreign guides …, secondly the commissioning of new works …; thirdly the evolution of … specialist firms such as Sherwood, Nelly and Jones, Samuel Leigh, and eventually

> Murray; and lastly the rise of active foreign firms, often using destitute expatriates as authors, who provide detailed on-the-spot guides.[38]

John Murray III's *Handbook for Travellers on the Continent* (1836) covered Holland, Belgium, Prussia, northern Germany and along the Rhine to Switzerland. Volumes followed on Southern Germany (1837); Switzerland (1838); Denmark, Norway, Sweden and Russia (1839); the Ionian Islands, Greece and Turkey (1840); and Italy (1842).[39] Buzard notes that Murray and Baedeker 'struck readers from the start as a wholly new phenomenon in the literature of travel. [They] brought an inspired diligence and thoroughness to the guidebook; they standardized it, from outer covers to inner organization; they relentlessly updated it, making it not the record of someone's tours but a description of what current tourists could anticipate'.[40]

It was not only the contents of travel books that were affected. Their appearance could be, too. Buzard observes of Murray's and Baedeker's that as their volume of information grew, 'Murray's texts were printed in double columns of extremely fine print; the Baedeker firm introduced the extra-thin paper used for Bibles (*Dünndruckpapier*) for all its handbooks after 1872. Their compactness and lightness made them all the more appealing to travellers riding the railways'.[41] Beyond appearance, these new publications helped introduce a generic shift in travel writing. As Buzard explains:

> Partly as a result of the efforts of Murray and Baedeker, we today perceive a fairly fixed distinction in the field of travel literature between the objective, informative "guidebook" on the one hand and the impressionistic "travel book" (or the more tentative "travel sketch") on the other. In the days before the modern handbook, however, this separation of functions was barely established.[42]

Yet, 'Founded by great "independent travellers", the Murray and Baedeker guides sought to retain the flavour of independent travel while increasingly relying on corporate endeavours'.[43] This apparent contradiction is a phenomenon observable a century later in the evolution of the *Lonely Planet* guide from counter-cultural alternative to canonisation by backpackers, a process given humorous treatment in the travel novels *The Beach* by Alex Garland (1996) and *Are You Experienced?* by William Sutcliffe (1997). One of the paradoxes was that 'although they guided tourists with a truly unprecedented diligence and efficiency, the creators and managers of the new handbooks regarded their labours as enabling their readers to be more *independent* in their travels'.[44] They also commodified the tourist experience: 'Murray and Baedeker translated cultural meaning into the language and logic of commerce. Buying and using the guidebook was like imaginarily buying the things themselves'.[45]

'It has been done before'

New modes of travel brought about new ways of seeing and writing. These produced a self-consciousness about tradition and the modern. That is seen in many of the century's exploration texts, especially Stanley's, but they have received much attention and I want to focus on less predictable examples. We normally associate meta-commentary and parody with the postmodern, although Chapter 3 mentioned the example of Samuel Paterson (writing as Coriat Junior) and of Sterne's *A Sentimental Journey*. Probably the most notable of nineteenth-century examples is Mark Twain's *The Innocents Abroad, or The New Pilgrim's Progress* (1869). The subtitle of this work suggests something of the shift that has occurred. After some pages on Rome, Twain's narrator writes of that city: 'I have drifted along hopelessly for a hundred pages of manuscript without knowing where to commence. I will not commence at all. Our passports have been examined. We will go to Naples' (p.206). At the end of the following chapter, under the subheading 'ASCENT OF VESUVIUS – CONTINUED', which has already appeared three times in succession and will appear four times more after it, the narrator writes: 'This subject will be excellent matter for a chapter, and tomorrow or next day I will write it' (p.210). It is one of many instances of Twain's satirising of touristic practices – both the 'doing' and the writing of tourism. Another example alludes to the ownership of descriptions; to the profiting from them:

> Towards nightfall the next evening, we steamed into the great artificial harbor of this noble city of Marseilles, and saw the dying sunlight gild its clustering spires and ramparts, and flood its leagues of environing verdure with a mellow radiance that touched with an added charm the white villas that flecked the landscape far and near. [Copyright secured according to law.] (p.62)

It is perhaps a related concern that has the protagonist remark bluntly, in Rome, 'I prefer not to describe St. Peter's. It has been done before' (p.181). His disinclination to repeat others' descriptions draws attention to tropes of originality and ribs them.

Twain employs his famous humour to puncture the romantic illusions of travel. Recounting his experiences in Paris, the narrator writes:

> Ah, the grisettes! I had almost forgotten. They are another romantic fraud. They were (if you let the books of travel tell it) always so beautiful – so neat and trim, so graceful – so naive and trusting – so gentle, so winning – so faithful to their shop duties, so irresistible to buyers in their prattling importunity – so devoted to their

> poverty-stricken students of the Latin Quarter – so lighthearted and happy on their Sunday picnics in the suburbs – and oh, so charmingly, so delightfully immoral!
>
> Stuff! (p.99)

Twain and his narrator know, too, that travellers' responses to places are shaped by material circumstances such as the ways in which one enters or otherwise experiences a city. Exclaiming 'How the fatigues and annoyances of travel fill one with bitter prejudices sometimes!' the tourist reports that 'I got lost in Florence at nine o'clock one night, and stayed lost in that labyrinth of narrow streets and long rows of vast buildings that look all alike until toward three o'clock in the morning', with the effect that 'My experiences of Florence were chiefly unpleasant. I will change the subject'. So, although 'I might enter Florence under happier auspices a month hence and find it all beautiful, all attractive', he does 'not care to think of it now at all' (pp.162–3).

Twain's protagonist and his companions also make fun of guides, refusing to be impressed. They call all of them Ferguson, in part because, 'We cannot master their dreadful foreign names' (p.254). Here Twain scorns not foreigners but the attitudes of tourists towards them. He also makes fun of guidebooks and of those that use them. In Athens, for example, he writes: 'I remember but little about the Parthenon, and I have put in one or two facts and figures for the use of other people with short memories. Got them from the guidebook' (p.231). Twain deliberately cheapens the authority of such volumes. He does the same with other works of travel (besides parodying them in the very form and tone of his book). Thus: 'When I think how I have been swindled by books of Oriental travel, I want a tourist for breakfast'. In this instance, the narrator is contrasting his experience of a Turkish bath with the 'wonders' of it that he has anticipated for years and years (p.250). The luxurious picture he has got from 'incendiary books of travel' is a 'poor, miserable imposture' (p.251). In the 1860s, Twain's tourist to the Mediterranean could exclaim: 'We wanted something thoroughly and uncompromisingly foreign – foreign from top to bottom – foreign from center to circumference – foreign inside and outside and all around – nothing anywhere about it to dilute its foreign-ness – nothing to remind us of any other people or any other land under the sun' (p.51). His party finds what they are seeking in Tangier but it is not enough to detain the narrator, who pronounces himself 'glad to have seen' it but 'ready to bid it good-bye, I believe' (p.61).

For all the international activity occasioned by exploration, scientific inquiry, tourism, emigration, trade and colonialism, it would be wrong to suggest that nineteenth-century travel writing was always looking to the outside world. The U.S. writer Henry David Thoreau announces near the beginning of his now famous work *Walden* (1854):

> I would fain say something, not so much concerning the Chinese and Sandwich Islanders as you who read these pages, who are said to live in New England; something about your condition, especially your outward condition or circumstances in this world, in this town, what it is, whether it is necessary that it be as bad as it is, whether it cannot be improved as well as not. (p.7)

Walden is not, strictly speaking, a travel text, but it has a great deal to say about travel and the writing and reading of it. Thoreau deliberately turns his attention from the exotic to the local, and he finds in his vicinity the inhabitants doing penance in ways more remarkable than he has heard of Brahmins doing in India, 'sitting exposed to four fires and looking in the face of the sun; or hanging suspended, with their heads downward, over flames', or than the twelve labours of Hercules (p.8). As well as eschewing the luxury of foreign travel, Thoreau embraces simplicity of vision: 'Most of the luxuries, and many of the so-called comforts of life, are not only not indispensable, but positive hindrances to the elevation of mankind' (p.14). He criticises the condition of factory workers producing clothing, remarking: 'as far as I have heard or observed, the principal object is, not that mankind may be well and honestly clad, but, unquestionably, that the corporations may be enriched' (pp.22–3).

In *Walden* Thoreau prefers simplicity over sophistication; slowness to speed; directness over detachment. To him, modernity displaces meaning: 'Our inventions are wont to be pretty toys, which distract our attention from serious things. … We are in great haste to construct a magnetic telegraph from Maine to Texas; but Maine and Texas, it may be, have nothing important to communicate' (p.40). (Precisely the same objection to speed of communication over content is made of Internet and social media activity today.) There is a line to be traced here from Thoreau and his fellow transcendentalist, Ralph Waldo Emerson, to D. H. Lawrence, with their shared anxiety that modern industrialism has alienated us from our souls and from the life that really matters. According to this view, a pre-industrial, unmediated experience of nature will enable a rediscovery of it and of ourselves. Such an attitude is linked with late nineteenth- and early twentieth-century manifestations of primitivism, and presages the reaction against modernity that we see in twentieth- and twenty-first century nostalgia for slower travel and a more direct experience of nature. Thoreau writes: 'I have learned that the swiftest traveller is he that goes afoot' (p.40). His explanation shows that he means this literally as well as figuratively: that the time spent labouring to earn the fare to travel by rail will be greater than that spent walking to one's destination. Yet he also means that walking will produce a closer appreciation of the country and its people. He is concerned, too, that we are subordinating our true interests and activities to the railway: 'We do not ride on the railroad; it rides upon us. Did you ever think what those sleepers are that underlie the railroad? Each one is a man, an Irishman, or a Yankee man' (p.67).

One must certainly not exaggerate the representativeness of figures like Thoreau, but it would be just as wrong to see travel writing of the nineteenth century as concerned exclusively or perhaps even predominantly with overseas expansion. Furthermore, the attention to the local that *Walden* promotes anticipates both the micro-travel of texts such as William Least Heat-Moon's *PrairyErth* (1991) and the 'green' movement that has developed in recent years, although the refrain of self-sufficiency speaks also to U.S. ideologies of the self-made man: 'For more than five years I maintained myself ... solely by the labor of my hands, and I found that, by working about six weeks in a year, I could meet all the expenses of living' (p.51). The injunction to take close notice of one's immediate surroundings, and the conviction that doing so will result in a better understanding of oneself also prefigures the idea of inner travel that we shall turn to in Chapter 7.

In opposition to the kind of travel writing that accompanies or promotes the spread of goods and expansion of capital, texts such as Thoreau's promote the virtues of an uncluttered existence.[46] Thoreau explains that: 'I went to the woods because I wished to live deliberately, to front only the essential facts of life, and see if I could not learn what it had to teach, and not, when I came to die, discover that I had not lived' (p.66). For Thoreau, 'Our life is frittered away by detail'. His antidote is: 'Simplicity, simplicity, simplicity! ... Simplify, simplify' (p.66). There is, of course, an irony in that Thoreau's statements on how we should attend to the local are accompanied by references to Eastern philosophers and religions.

Thoreau's reaction against readers' vicarious journeys abroad is exemplified by his statement that: 'I read one or two shallow books of travel in the intervals of my work, till that employment made me ashamed of myself, and I asked where it was then that *I* lived' (p.72). He observes that 'I had this advantage, at least, in my mode of life, over those who were obliged to look abroad for amusement, to society and the theatre, that my life was become my amusement and never ceased to be novel. It was a drama of many scenes and without an end' (p.80). He remarks: 'for the most part it is as solitary where I live as on the prairies. It is as much Asia or Africa as New England. I have, as it were, my own sun and moon and stars, and a little world all to myself' (p.91). He posits a dual sense of life, one that recognises and accommodates the natural and the so-called primitive: 'I found in myself, and still find, an instinct toward a higher, or, as it is named, spiritual life, as do most men, and another toward a primitive rank and savage one, and I reverence them both. I love the wild not less than the good'. It is a recipe for wholeness that prefigures Freud and also Graham Greene's *Journey Without Maps*, discussed in Chapter 7. Thoreau continues: 'He who is only a traveller learns things at second-hand and by the halves, and is poor authority. We are most interested when science reports what those men already know practically or instinctively, for that alone is a true *humanity*, or account of human experience' (p.143).

Thoreau's recommendation to focus on oneself and on one's immediate environment is voiced more strongly by his contemporary and fellow transcendentalist, Ralph Waldo Emerson, who, in his famous essay 'Self-Reliance', complains that 'It is for want of self-culture that the superstition of Travelling, whose idols are Italy, England, Egypt, retains its fascination for all educated Americans'.[47] Emerson sees no romance in travel. 'Travelling', he writes, 'is a fool's paradise'. He notes that whatever one's dreams of intoxication, one finds at one's destination 'the stern fact, the sad self, unrelenting, identical, that I fled from' (p.198). For Emerson, in this essay, to travel abroad (as he had done, in late 1832–33 to Malta and Europe and would again to Europe and Egypt in 1872) is to overlook one's own environs. In the context of a new nation, it is to value imitation of what one finds elsewhere over the cultivation of one's own country and arts. Thus, 'Insist on yourself; never imitate' (p.199). Imitation, he suggests, is the 'travelling of the mind' (198). For a proponent of U.S. literary culture and of a national identity independent of the old world in Europe, it is a profound concern. That question of the relationship between the old and new world informs, if not preoccupies, many U.S. travel texts and other literature that takes travel to or from Europe as its theme or setting.[48]

In another kind of looking-inward, the nineteenth century was also an age of social exploration. Most famously, in Britain the radical campaigner William Cobbett investigated conditions in the countryside in his *Rural Rides* (1830), a two-volume collection of articles published between 1822 and 1826 in the *Political Register*; Henry Mayhew's massive *London Labour and the London Poor* (published in three volumes in 1851, with a co-authored fourth in 1861) collected articles that resulted from interviews with members of the capital's underclass; Salvation Army founder William Booth's *In Darkest England* (1890) played on the title of Henry Morton Stanley's *In Darkest Africa* of the same year, bringing things full circle as Stanley's book had employed metaphors of crowded London in describing the Ituri Forest.

By the end of the nineteenth century, travel writing was approaching the shapes in which it would be familiar to us now. Mechanised flight was yet to come but the automobile was already altering perceptions. It would be the 1930s before Freud's ideas became sufficiently popularised to drive the interior journey in psychological terms, but he had begun to write, employing the language of racial imagery of his time, and the notion of the unconscious was spreading. Modernism was establishing itself and novelists such as Joseph Conrad were showing how the adventure narrative could be adapted into more complex forms, with ambiguity replacing imperial certainties; symbolism subverting single correspondences. The experimentations of modernism produced productive tensions with realism that led to some fascinating strains in the most intellectually and adventurous narratives of the twentieth century, as we shall see in our discussion in Chapter 5.

Chapter 5

1900–present

Comes over one an absolute necessity to move.
D. H. Lawrence[1]

I was no explorer.
Paul Theroux[2]

Motors of change

Three factors have been especially dominant in the shaping of travel writing since 1900. First, 'the Petrol Age', as Wyndham Lewis called it in his travelogue of North Africa, has changed people's sense of speed, their engagement with the landscape and their relationship with one another.[3] Second, intellectual and aesthetic movements have radically influenced ideas of the self, of truth and authority, and of artistic representation. The popularisation of Freud's concepts has resulted in the presentation of travel-narrators driven by unconscious desires and fears, producing the idea of the psychological inner journey, which will be examined in Chapter 7; and modernism and postmodernism have helped undermine the authority of a single narrative perspective. Third, the politics of 'race' and decolonisation, accompanied by the rise of liberation movements, have produced travel texts that challenge colonial stereotypes through the revision or reversal of colonial-era journeys.

In combination, these three phenomena contribute to the 'conscious inter- and metatextual reflection on the conventions of travel writing' that Barbara Korte claims is a particular feature of post-1900 travel writing.[4] This self-consciousness is not unique to the twentieth century: we saw in Chapter 3 that it is found in eighteenth-century texts too, and we should note that even in twentieth-century travel writing only a small minority of texts ever display this self-reflection. Nevertheless, it is with these more literary texts that we are mostly concerned here. The discussion that follows will examine how their handling of narrative structure and perspective takes travel writing in new directions.

Innovations in technologies of travel made people more aware of how their experiences were affected by the mode of transport. This in turn resulted in a narrative self-consciousness about how they travelled previously and now. Not infrequently, texts go beyond comment on the means of travel and reflect on the appropriateness of the literary vehicle itself.

Cars were first seen on the roads of Britain in the late nineteenth century. Narratives of travel by automobile date from those early years and accelerate in the first decades of the twentieth century. The introduction to J. E. Vincent's *Through East Anglia in a Motor Car* (1907) informs its readers that, 'A new method of travel ... brings ... the need for a new species of guide-book'.[5] It is not simply that new information is required, but that travel by motor car is different from other forms of travel. Most existing guidebooks,

> [e]xcept a small number of accounts of tours by horse-drawn carriages ... were compiled by men who travelled by train from place to place, obtaining no view of the country often – for deep cuttings destroy all joy of the eye for the railway passenger – and at best only a partial view, for the use of men and women condemned to the like method of travel. In them it is vain to seek for any appreciation of the pleasure of the road itself. The motor-car has changed all that. (p.xx)

The preference for automobile travel over journeying by rail is also expressed by the American Thomas Murphy (1866–1928), whose narrative is a record of a fifty-day, 5,000 mile trip around England and Scotland. Murphy tells his readers that 'I think it can be clearly demonstrated that this method of touring will give opportunities for enjoyment and for gaining actual knowledge of the people and country that can hardly be attained in any other way'.[6] He remarks of his experiences of travelling the British Isles: 'One seldom gets the real sentiment and beauty of a place in approaching it by railway. I am speaking, of course, of the tourist who endeavors to crowd as much as he can into a comparatively short time. To the one who remains several days in a place, railroad traveling is less objectionable'.[7]

In our own era of nostalgia for the steam train, this criticism of train travel may come as a surprise. Nowadays we are probably more familiar with early twentieth-century hostility towards the motor car for invading and ruining the countryside. Indeed, the introduction to Vincent's book aims to refute the anti-motorist's view that 'the motorist is a dust-raising, property-destroying, dog-killing, fowl-slaying, dangerous and ruthless speed maniac' (p.xx). Nonetheless, books like Vincent's remind us that there was enthusiasm for the new mode of transport and that it was seen as permitting a closer view of nature than that afforded by the train. The attractions for motor enthusiasts include a greater freedom to choose one's own route than was possible for rail passengers, and the ever-increasing distances that can be travelled while still motoring for pleasure (p.180).

Even greater distances were made possible by aeroplane. In her 1935 narrative of a flight from North America to Japan and China four years earlier, Anne Morrow Lindbergh writes of being the first white woman to arrive at Baker Lake after only three hours of flight from the modern port of Churchill; of flying over wild wastes south of Victoria Land but hearing through her earphones the 'noisy chatter of big cities over the edge of the world'; and of flying out of northernmost Point Barrow and seeing its supply ship stuck in ice.[8] These and other experiences she describes as 'a magic caused by the collision of modern methods and old ones; modern history and ancient; accessibility and isolation'. It is not only the juxtaposition that strikes her but her sense that this magic can occur only around this time: 'A few years earlier, from the point of view of aircraft alone, it would have been impossible to reach these places; a few years later, and there will be no such isolation' (p.4). She writes her story 'before it is too late' (p.6). The effect is to heighten the privileged status and uniqueness of her travel.

In explaining the fascination of their trip, Lindbergh quotes George Best's account of Frobisher's expedition from Hakluyt's *Voyages* on both the dangers but also the delight and profit of attempting new discoveries (p.13). She admits that she and her husband are not explorers in the Elizabethan sense but 'can sympathize with their point of view' and that 'Travellers are always discoverers, especially those who travel by air' as there are no signposts and no channels marked: 'The flier breaks each second into new seas' (p.13). Frequently, Lindbergh refers to early explorers and voyagers: she invokes Sebastian Cabot, Martin Frobisher and John Davis and the early search for a northwest passage to Cathay (pp.7–8). She mentions Magellan and the Portuguese and she quotes Cabot from Hakluyt (p.8). She writes: 'Our route was new; the air untravelled; the conditions unknown; the stories mythical; the maps, pale, pink, and indefinite, except for a few names, far to the east of our course, to show that someone before us pointed his ship, also, "North to the Orient."' (p.14). The aviators may literally transcend 'many of the difficulties that had beset the early surface travellers in search of a north-west passage' but whereas the sailors had a limitless supply of wind power, the pilots 'must plan and budget our fuel, arrange for its location along the route, sometimes sending it ahead of us by boat or train, sometimes using fuel already cached through the north'. The maritime adventurers had to cope with longer time; the aviators with greater space (pp.17–18). Of the Lindberghs' destination, part of the allure of the Orient is 'the syllables *Marco Polo*' (p.12).

Anomalous juxtaposition

For Britons, just as the Napoleonic wars limited continental travel, so during the First World War, 'The Defense of the Realm Acts of 1914 and 1915 effectively restricted private travel abroad', and even domestic travel was limited.[9] This, according to Fussell, was accompanied by a circumscription of vision, resulting in an imaginative and intellectual insularity. A reaction to this confinement was what Fussell terms the 'British Literary Diaspora' of the 1920s and 1930s, which saw many literary figures – with D. H. Lawrence in the vanguard – travel to Europe, the Far East, the United States and elsewhere. This diasporic movement, Fussell observes, was one of the signs of literary modernism.[10] Fussell is not the only critic to have recognised the centrality of travel to interwar writing. Philip Dodd has affirmed the travel book's status as 'the most important literary form of the 1930s' and remarked that it 'would appear to be the most appropriate form for writers … eager to "explore" and "discover" new allegiances'.[11] Likewise, Stan Smith has noted that, 'The 1920s and '30s were a boom time for travel writing in a specifically Modernist mode'.[12]

The impetus given to travel writing by modernism was profound and is still awaiting comprehensive assessment.[13] Many prominent modernist writers, better known for their other prose works or for their poetry, produced travel texts. Their number (in the Anglophone tradition alone) includes W. H. Auden, E. E. Cummings, D. H. Lawrence, Wyndham Lewis, Katherine Mansfield, John Dos Passos, John Steinbeck, Evelyn Waugh and Rebecca West. Besides recounting their own journeys in their travel books and essays, they explore the significance of journeys in their fiction, poetry and drama also.[14] Modernist travel writing reflects and reacts to the political as well as to the intellectual context. These were years of unstable borders between and within countries. The several conflicts of the 1930s generated many travel narratives. The Italian invasion of Abyssinia (1935–6) formed the basis of Evelyn Waugh's *Waugh in Abyssinia* (1936). The Spanish Civil War (1936–9), spawned works such as George Orwell's *Homage to Catalonia* (1938) and W. H. Auden's poem *Spain* (1937), which latter Stan Smith describes as in a sense, 'the most representatively symbolic piece of travel writing of the whole era'.[15] W. H. Auden and Christopher Isherwood's *Journey to a War* (1937) covers the Japanese aggression against China. The American Agnes Smedley's *China Fights Back* (1938) records the progress of the Eighth Route Army and her identification with it and with the communist cause. The Russian Revolution and its aftermath also provoked many visits and corresponding records, mainly by leftist sympathisers, some, but not all, of whom grew disillusioned with what they found.[16] In addition, well-known documentary travels appeared in the 1930s, including J. B. Priestley's *English Journey* (1934) and George Orwell's *The Road to Wigan Pier* (1937).

Political and social instability coincided with uncertain boundaries between the conscious and unconscious self (thanks to the popularisation of Freud's ideas), and – through artistic experiments – of a blurring of previously discrete perspectives. Glen MacLeod's remark that 'Modernist writers often patterned their literary experiments on parallels drawn from the visual arts' applies to authors of travel books also.[17] So does Pericles Lewis's comment that 'modernism called attention to the medium of the literary or artistic work, defined itself in contrast to convention, and radically altered the means of representation'.[18] Fussell has referred to the period as one in which the redrafting of frontiers has contributed to 'an awareness of reality as disjointed, dissociated, fractured. These actions of dividing anew and shifting around provide the method of collage in painting, and in writing they provide the method we recognize as conspicuously "modern," the method of anomalous juxtaposition'.[19]

The poets W. H. Auden and Louis MacNeice write in *Letters from Iceland* (1937): 'It is a collage that you're going to read'. Auden and MacNeice employ different forms. Their collage comprises, among other elements, verse, letters, 'photographs,/Some out of focus, some with wrong exposures,/Press cuttings, gossip, maps, statistics, graphs'.[20] Theirs is, as Stan Smith recognises, a book that 'plays deliberative games with the travelogue format'.[21] It is not alone in doing that. Modernist travel writing experiments with combinations of forms and with point of view, invites critical attention to its narrator, examines the relationship between observer and observed, questions the location and use of power, parodies its progenitors, plays with personae, and wonders about its own function. All of these features have the potential to undermine the authority both of traveller and travel book.

In his account of a visit to Soviet Russia, the U.S. poet E. E. Cummings breaks up the narrative even at word level, for example: 'vio(screa)lent(ming) ly'.[22] Imitating his hosts' pronunciation of his name, he represents himself in the third person as 'Kem-min-kz', and then modifies this to 'Kself'.[23] The device allows us to see what is normally hidden: that the 'I' in travel writing is a construction; not a straightforward correspondence with the author. Many interwar and modernist travel texts admit that they are partial, in the sense both of biased and incomplete. In his prefatory note to *The Lawless Roads*, Greene claims that 'This is the personal impression of a small part of Mexico at a particular time, the spring of 1938'.[24] Helen Carr observes that increasingly in the twentieth century travel writing became 'a more subjective form, more memoir than manual', and this is especially evident in modernist texts.[25] D. H. Lawrence confesses near the start of his *Mornings in Mexico* (1927) that: 'We talk so grandly, in capital letters, about Morning in Mexico. All it amounts to is one little individual looking at a bit of sky and trees, then looking down at the page of his exercise book'.[26]

But that focus on the particular and the individual means distinguishing oneself from others. For example, Wyndham Lewis's narrative goes on to exhibit the disdain for tourism that is characteristic of much modernism. His intention to plan a route that would avoid 'the stupefying squalor of anglo-american tourism about one, poisoning the wells and casting its baedekered blight' is typical of the growing feeling during the interwar years that tourism is making travel less authentic and less personal.[27] The search for the unspoiled – which is actually not nature in itself, but a culturally constructed idea of the authentic – is a part of this and will be discussed in Chapter 6.

When Lewis visits Oran, 'a stereotyped French city', he asks whether it is not enough that the people who live there (the 'Berbers') are as they have always been and he despairs that 'Our Machine Age civilization has pushed its obscene way into the heart of their country'.[28]

The flight from the modern was evident before 1900. It impelled nineteenth-century primitivism, for example, and found a positive site in the islands of the South Pacific, which attracted, among others, Paul Gauguin and Robert Louis Stevenson. However, the mechanised slaughter of the First World War produced a new reaction against industrialism. For Fussell, the 'fantasies of flight and freedom which animate the imagination of the 20's and 30's and generate its pervasive images of travel can be said to be begin in the trenches'.[29] There is the sense of a moral fall in what Robert Byron describes as 'an age of weapons that deal death from a distance'.[30] Certainly, this attitude is expressed directly by Lewis in his travelogue:

> [T]he atmosphere of our dying European society is to me profoundly depressing. Some relief is necessary from the daily spectacle of those expiring Lions and Eagles, who obviously will never recover from the death-blows they dealt each other (foolish beasts and birds) from 1914–1918 . . .
>
> Perhaps nothing short of the greatest desert in the world, or its proximity, would answer the case.[31]

Yet modernity is often embraced. One of the most cited examples is Auden's expression of his preference for industrial landscape: 'Clearer than Scafell Pike, my heart has stamped on/The view from Birmingham to Wolverhampton' and 'Tramlines and slagheaps, pieces of machinery,/That was, and still is, my ideal scenery'.[32] Another instance is in Robert Byron's *The Road to Oxiana* (1937), which opens with the author in Venice where he mischievously observes that 'the Doge's Palace looked more beautiful from a speed-boat than it ever did from a gondola' (*RO*, p.3). Byron's is one of the most influential of modernist travel texts, widely praised by authors and critics alike. William Dalrymple lauds it as 'a terribly funny and a brilliant book ... the great travel book of that period, certainly the greatest of the 1930s', and describes his own first travel book, *In Xanadu*, as in many ways a homage to it.[33] Sara Wheeler hails it as 'the greatest travel book ever written'.[34] Jonathan Raban, endorsing Paul Fussell's selection of it as 'the archetype of the entire genre', has gone so far as to proclaim, 'understand Byron and you understand the nature of travel writing'.[35] He salutes *The Road to Oxiana* as 'a brilliantly wrought expression of a thoroughly modernist sensibility, a portrait of an accidental man adrift between frontiers'.[36] The appeal of Byron's book lies in the combination of its prose, the narrative figure and the author's knowledge of art and architecture.

Byron's construction of an eccentric persona is immediately apparent. His second paragraph reads in its entirety: 'Lifar came to dinner. Bertie mentioned that all whales have syphilis' (*RO*, p.3). This paragraph, like others throughout the book, is in the form of a journal entry, prefaced with place and date. The impression is of spontaneity and immediacy. In fact, Byron crafted and reworked his prose carefully to create this effect. As Raban points out, '*The Road to Oxiana* was the product of three years of constant writing and revision. Its casualness is an elaborate fiction'.[37] That air of informality extends to the irreverent, iconoclastic narrator. In a rupture from the Grand Tour's public emphasis on education, the third paragraph tells us 'we took sanctuary from culture in Harry's Bar' (*RO*, p.3).

The Road to Oxiana displays another characteristic of much travel writing after 1900: national and individual self-deprecation. Byron jokes that 'even English occupation has been unable to change Greek cooking for the worse' (*RO*, p.13). The criticism extends beyond humour. Byron reports of an Air Force officer whose photographs taken near Mosul of corpses, many shot in the genitals, have been confiscated and who has been ordered to remain silent: 'He was furiously indignant, as anyone might be when it comes to saving British face by the concealment of atrocities' (*RO*, p.46). Byron holds the British liable for cultural destruction, too. In Herat he writes that 'the most glorious productions of Mohammadan architecture in the XVth century, having survived the barbarism of four centuries, were now rased to the ground under the eyes, and with the approval, of the English Commissioners' (*RO*, pp.98–9).

Such comments push the narrator forward, making his tone and personality as visible as the objects he describes. In keeping with this is the anti-heroic self-representation that will come to characterise many travel books of the twentieth century. Here is Byron reporting on a night-time visit to relieve himself in a courtyard that is used for the purpose by 'men and beasts alike': 'As I reached the outside staircase, I slipped. The lantern went out; my only garment, a mackintosh, flew over my head; and I found myself lying naked in a bed of snow and excrement, which clove to my body in the frost' (*RO*, p.120).

One might imagine this from Sterne but not from Livingstone, Stanley or other nineteenth-century explorer-heroes. This type of bumbler is recognisable in later travellers like Redmond O'Hanlon and Bill Bryson, but authors are in control of the embarrassment they choose to share. There is, paradoxically, an authority that accrues from the invitation to laugh at oneself.

Curious composite ideas

In his account of a visit with photographer Robert Capa to the Soviet Union three years after the end of the Second World War, John Steinbeck writes: '[W]e came to the conclusion that the world of Sir John Mandeville has by no means disappeared, that the world of two-headed men and flying serpents has not disappeared'.[38] The context of his remark is the scare-mongering of the U.S. media in which 'news has become a matter of punditry' (p.3), and hostility towards Russia is common. Steinbeck and Capa's trip is designed to be more objective and honest; and to record, in words and photographs, the private life of the USSR that they claim is never represented in the West. They aim to avoid the preconceptions that result in the dangerously negative stereotypes of the incipient Cold War. Steinbeck states: 'We shall write what we saw and heard', a practice he acerbically remarks is 'contrary to a large part of modern journalism' (p.8). Their journey leads them to the discovery that 'just as we [Americans] are growing horns and tails on the Russians, so the Russians are growing horns and tails on us' (p.7).

Like the modernist travellers previously discussed, Steinbeck undermines the idea of authoritative generalisations. Indeed, he refers to 'the *danger* of making general statements' (p.43, italics mine). In the very first chapter, he writes: 'This is just what happened to us. It is not the Russian story, but simply *a* Russian story' (p.8, emphasis in original). When he and Capa are asked by Ukrainian farmers about farmers and farms in the United States, they try to explain that there are many different types of farms in the United States, as there are in Russia, and 'it is difficult for our people to imagine Russia, with every possible climate from arctic to tropic, with many different races and languages'. From Steinbeck and Capa's knowledge of Americans' views on the USSR and from what they learn of Soviets' conceptions of the United States, 'it was clear to us that peoples have a curious composite idea of one another' (p.86). Likewise, they tell their hosts that the United States is 'a huge country' of which they themselves know only a little, and about which they would be unable to answer many of the questions put to them, 'but we would try' (p.107). Steinbeck as traveller functions as a mediating figure, aiming to dispel each side's illusions about the other. His text tackles stereotypes, rather than perpetuates them. When he and Capa are asked many questions about the United States, 'we began to realize that America is a very different country to explain. There are many things about it we don't understand ourselves' (p.57). This undercuts the traveller's authority as representative of and spokesperson for his or her nation, but clearly implies, too, that if one cannot even be sure about one's home society, one is unlikely to understand properly much of a foreign country on the basis of only a very short acquaintance. The consequence of this is a travel book that proclaims what it does *not* know as much as, if not more than, what it does. The unsettling of authority is characteristic of a strain of twentieth-century travel writing that seems to increase in prominence between the two World Wars and to continue in the postmodern period. Indeed, Blanton asserts that 'The most persistent characteristic of late-twentieth-century travel writing is the refusal of the authors to admit to knowing anything for sure'.[39]

Similarly, in *Travels with Charley* (1962) – John Steinbeck's account of a three-month, 10,000-mile trip through the United States, impelled by what he calls 'the virus of restlessness' (a phrase one might equally apply to Bruce Chatwin nearly a generation later)[40] – the author feels 'that there are too many realities' for there to be a fixed, definitive version: 'What I set down here is true until someone else passes that way and rearranges the world in his own style' (p.69). Steinbeck recalls how, long before, he visited Prague at the same time as the reporter Joseph Alsop, with whom he flew home:

> [H]is Prague had no relation to the city I had seen and heard. It just wasn't the same place, and yet each of us was honest, neither one a liar, both pretty good observers by any standard, and we brought home two cities, two truths. For this reason I cannot commend this account as an America that you will find. (p.70)

The admission of multiple perspectives, alternative truths and realities, is accompanied by a statement on the difficulty of reaching general conclusions: 'I thought how every safe generality I gathered in my travels was canceled by another' (p.141). It is likely that these caveats, common to many modernist and postmodernist travel texts, are connected also with the status of the protagonist as the old heroes of travel are replaced with more ordinary figures, a change that coincides (perhaps causally) with the loss of the old authority. To stay with the example of Steinbeck, at the end of his trip, he gets lost in New York on his way home and laughs at the absurdity of having driven all over the country only to lose his way in his adopted city. He is helped by a sympathetic policeman, and the book closes with the line: 'And that's how the traveler came home again' (p.246). His homecoming is an incompetent, anti-heroic affair.

In keeping with the comparison between older heroes and the modern condition, Steinbeck declares that Fargo, North Dakota is 'kin to those magically remote spots mentioned by Herodotus and Marco Polo and Mandeville' (p.122). It turns out to be bland when he visits it, but the experience does not disillusion him: romance wins over reality (pp.121–2). The same juxtaposition is apparent in his naming the camper truck in which he makes his journey Rocinante, after the horse of Don Quixote – the deluded mock-heroic protagonist of Cervantes's picaresque novel. Furthermore, the ordinariness of Steinbeck is emphasised by his companion: his dog.[41] Steinbeck uses Charley to criticise humans in general and white Americans in particular: 'Charley doesn't have our problems. He doesn't belong to a species clever enough to split the atom but not clever enough to live in peace with itself.... I've seen a look in dogs' eyes, a quickly vanishing look of amazed contempt, and I am convinced that basically dogs think humans are nuts' (pp.237–8).

The dog serves as a device through which Steinbeck makes some of his own observations. Paradoxically, it underlines the author's individuality by giving him a unique companion. It also lends distinctiveness to his travel book. Doing so becomes more important throughout the century. Once there are no blanks left on the map, attention is drawn more to the traveller and various gimmicks are employed to ensure this. The most interesting and enduring narratives, however, are those, like Steinbeck's, that use these devices to question the assumptions and test the conventions of the genre.

The woods are full of wardens

The emphasis on individuality is evident in the very title of beat writer Jack Kerouac's *Lonesome Traveler* (1960). The first full paragraph of the book begins: 'Less [Let's] begin with the sight of me';[42] words that direct the gaze of the readers onto its author-protagonist. The deliberateness of this strategy indicates Kerouac's knowledge that travel texts traditionally keep attention away from the seer in favour of the seen and that Kerouac wants to shift this perspective; to do something different. His prose style furthers this sense of distinctiveness. In the first chapter and several of the others, punctuation is sparse, conveying a sense of the rhythms of thought and speech. Dashes seem to be employed as frequently as commas. Like Cummings, he uses spelling and a mixture of upper and lower case letters to render others' accents and inflections, for example those of his buddy Deni Bleu, whom he records saying: 'Kerouac is a victim, a VIC timm of his own i ma JHI NA Tion' (p.7). Like the modernists, Kerouac makes his readers aware of the limits of his view: 'this gnashing huge movie of earth only a piece of which here's offered by me, long tho it is' (p.5).

In another respect, too, *Lonesome Traveler* resembles a modernist travel text: its sense of a freedom from restriction and sobriety when Kerouac crosses the border into Mexico. There, he writes, one experiences 'a great feeling of entering the Pure Land'. He goes on: '[Y]ou can find it, this feeling, this fellaheen feeling about life, that timeless gayety of people not involved in great cultural and civilization issues – you can find it almost anywhere else, in Morocco, in Latin America entire, in Dakar, in Kurd Land' (p.22). One senses D. H. Lawrence behind Kerouac's capital exclamation that: 'THE EARTH IS AN INDIAN THING' (p.22). Indians are used, as by Lawrence, to criticise aspects of white U.S. society.

Kerouac's final chapter, 'The Vanishing American Hobo', evinces the kind of nostalgia evident in contemporary travel writing. 'The Jet Age is crucifying the hobo because how can he hop a freight jet?' Kerouac asks (p.176). The complaint extends to one about authority as he attributes the current hard times for hobos to increased police surveillance (p.172). One can no longer be alone in the 'primitive wilderness ("primitive areas" so-called)' (p.182). The 'definite special idea of footwalking freedom' (p.173) that has always existed in the United States has now been trampled on, for, as the final words of the book solemnly have it, expressing the need to escape and the diminishing opportunities to do so: 'The woods are full of wardens' (p.183).

Living between categories

In her 1997 book on travel writing, Casey Blanton remarks that 'Most contemporary travel writers share a sense of themselves as exiles'.[43] That sense of displacement is one of the ways in which modern travel authors characterise themselves as individuals who are not at home in their current setting or, indeed, in the places they have left behind. Their identity is predicated on their lack of affiliation or on multiple affiliations. The figure of the nomadic or rootless traveller has become a popular one in recent years and was exemplified by

Bruce Chatwin. Pico Iyer's *The Global Soul* (2000) adopts it almost to the point of self-parody. He writes:

> I'd often referred to myself as homeless – an Indian born in England and moving to California as a boy, with no real base of operations or property even in my thirties. I'd spent much of the previous year among the wooden houses of Japan, reading the "burning house" poems of Buddhist monks and musing on the value of living without possessions and a home.[44]

The occasion of these remarks is the destruction by fire of Iyer's California home, but the unfortunate event emphasises the mobility and lack of belonging that he self-advertises. 'Those of us who live between categories' (p.11), is how Iyer, 'a person with an American alien card and an Indian face and an English accent, on his way to Japan' (p.10), refers to himself; an 'in-betweener' (p.19), complementing the status of the genre in which he writes. It is, Iyer asserts, the speed of things that distinguishes contemporary developments from ancient movements. 'The two great engines of our age – technology and travel (now the largest industry in the world) – give fuel to each other, our machines prompting us to prize speed as an end in itself, and the longing for speed quickening a hunger for new technologies' (p.12).

Iyer seems attracted to the idea of not having a fixed identity, just as Chatwin liked not to be settled in a fixed place. Iyer recalls as a child travelling three times a year between his parents' California home and his boarding school in England, 'realizing that as a member of neither culture, I could choose between selves at will'. Indeed, he boasts that with any of his 'potential homes', he could 'claim or deny attachment' as he wished (p.21). He frequently parades his free-floating status, maintaining some knowledge of the Global Soul, in part because of his having 'grown up simultaneously in three cultures' (p.23). His determination to appear unique has him rejecting even the categories of other actual or self-proclaimed marginal figures. He refuses as inappropriate the labels of exile, expatriate, nomad and refugee; instead, 'the Global Soul is best characterized by the fact of falling between all categories' (p.23). Yet Iyer's is not such a unique position. His travels show him to be engaged in exactly the same process as predecessors who waved the flag of their nations; that is, he defines himself against those whom he encounters.

The lucidity of loneliness

Paul Theroux, one of the figures responsible for the revival of the popularity of travel writing in the last quarter of the twentieth century, states in probably his best-known work: 'Travel is at its best a solitary enterprise: to see, to examine, to assess, you have to be alone and unencumbered'.[45] Other people, he explains, can mislead one, interfering with one's thoughts and impressions. He prefers to travel alone: 'it is discovery, not diversion, that I seek. What is required is the lucidity of loneliness to capture that vision which, however banal, seems in my private mood to be special and worthy of interest' (p.183). Later, near the end of the book, on arrival in a largely empty Patagonia, Theroux thinks to himself: '*It's perfect*'. He muses that if one of the aims of travel is to experience the explorer's thrill of being alone on a 'solitary mission of discovery in a remote place, then I had accomplished the traveller's dream'. He remarks that 'In the best travel books the word *alone* is implied on every exciting page' (p.416). Theroux confesses to missing his wife and children and to hating travel without companions, which he finds depressing, but he insists that if he is alone he sees more clearly because companionship distorts one's perception, causing one to view things through another's eyes (pp.188–9). It would also detract from his individuality. Similarly, but with less self-absorption, Patrick Leigh Fermor, recalling his own trip across Europe en route to Constantinople, writes: 'I knew that the enterprise had to be solitary and the break complete. I wanted to think, write, stay or move on at my own speed and unencumbered, to gaze at things with a changed eye and listen to new tongues that were untainted by a single familiar word'.[46] Of course, it is not complete isolation. Theroux contrasts himself with fellow passengers and tourists; Leigh Fermor compares himself with Ulysses (p.20) and eagerly affirms the truth of a German's suggestion that '"You are travelling about Europe like Childe Harold?"' (p.42). The invocation of these past models is meant both to trace a lineage and to establish the narrator's present peerlessness.

Twentieth-century travel writing is characterised by this emphasis on the lone traveller whose observations are made to carry more force by the weight of personality. Being alone is esteemed by some as a valuable and enriching condition of travel. The prolific travel writer Eric Newby bemoans the loss of quiet places to tourism and the bulldozer, but warns that 'Even worse will be the day, which has not yet come, when the desire to be alone has finally been extinguished from the human heart'.[47] Theroux's strategy is to make himself seem alone in the midst of other travellers. He devotes more space to an examination of the people he encounters – other travellers and local inhabitants – than to foreign landscape or cultures. To him, fellow passengers and the residents of the places through which he passes *are* the landscape. The terrain he explores is other people, from whom he is constantly marking his difference. His loneliness may be highlighted through this process but so, too, is his individuality. In that sense, ironically, the Anglo-American Theroux serves as a symbol of the late twentieth-century male travel writer: an individual figure with no obvious affiliations. For the Global Soul, as Iyer phrases it, 'all notions of affiliation are hazy' (p.258). By contrast, women, and especially women of colour, are often concerned to seek out affiliations as Chapters 8 and 9 show.

Theroux also testifies to the break from the hero figure we have met with in earlier times. Even though he admits that 'Travel is pointless without certain risks' (p.154), and that he craves 'some danger, an untoward event, a vivid discomfort' (p.183), he writes: 'I was no explorer: this was supposed to be enjoyment, not a test of stamina or patience. I did not take any pleasure in suffering the torments of travel merely so that I could dine out on them' (p.99).

For many, the age of exploration is over or requires redefinition. Theroux's contemporaries tend either to reject or to parody the label. Theroux is also keen, however, to refuse the tag of tourist (e.g., p.109). He distinguishes his travels from those of others and his activities from those of locals. As one of many instances, when a hotel owner advises him to visit the market at Chichicastenango because 'That's what everyone does', he thinks to himself, 'And that's why I don't want to do it' (p.123).

Re-mapping

The later twentieth century sees the stronger emergence of a postcolonial sensibility in travel writing. This will be discussed more fully in Chapter 8, but we can note here one of the most interesting and striking examples of such a text. *Maps and Dreams* (1981), by anthropologist Hugh Brody, recounts the author's eighteen months with the Dane-zaa people (or by their European name, Beaver Indians) of northern British Columbia.[48] Brody had worked on Inuit studies in the Northwest Territories and Labrador before being asked by the Union of British Columbia Chiefs 'to design a similar study of the northeast corner of their province' (p.xxiii), including land use and occupancy projects, in the face of the possibility of a natural gas pipeline being run through their territory. He explains that: 'Their primary aim is to map and explain all the ways in which Inuit and Indian peoples have used their lands within living memory' (p.xxiii).

Brody's text is remarkable for its author's anger at the effects of colonialism, his rejection of stereotypes, his sophisticated strategies for challenging them and his deliberate structuring of his narrative to try to do justice to his subjects. He tells us that 'Indians have suffered attempted genocide, dispossession on a mass scale, the white man's persistent blindness to injustice, and our dismaying indifference to the possibilities for radical change that now stare us in the face' (pp.ix-x). Noticing that 'The victims themselves ... are inclined to be gentle and self-effacing', Brody writes that 'I feel my own need to be clamorous on behalf of Indians – indeed, of all the peoples of what the great Indian leader George Manuel called the Fourth World'. He declares that European colonists have waged a war against 'the original occupants of Europe's new-found lands ... killing millions', and that 'the undeclared objective of this war has always been to deprive the indigenous inhabitants of their resources: territory, water, wildlife, fish, language, religion, even their children' (p.x). It might be charged that in assigning to himself the role of angry spokesperson for the gentle-mannered peoples of the North and deciding for them what are appropriate and inappropriate self-designations, Brody is, despite his professed stance, placing himself above them, acting as arbiter of their best interests. Elsewhere, however, he is powerfully and perceptively critical of whites' attitudes. In particular, he critiques the stance of those who like the primitive to remain in a timeless state immune from change. He notes that 'some urge the preservation of pure forms of tribal life in forest sanctuaries, where our idea of "tradition" is the formaldehyde in which to preserve what *we* like about *them*' (p.xi). Brody realises that pre-industrial culture is not static: 'The surviving aboriginal societies ... are not frozen in some archaic condition, but are our contemporaries. Their existence may be different, but they are modern; they live now, and – like us, like everyone – have to make accommodations between their pasts and their present' (p.xiv).

Brody's representation of the people and their situation and of his own activities is not conveyed merely by theme but through an innovative dual structure too: he informs us that the odd-numbered chapters are about the eighteen months he spent on the Reserve, and 'attempt to do justice to the way that the Indians of one reserve answered questions about a research project'. They take him on a series of journeys, showing and explaining to him 'far more than I could see or understand' (p.xix). He refers to 'how much prejudice and misconception I had to shed' (p.xxiv). They show him aspects of their way of life 'on their own terms'. And so, 'The odd-numbered chapters try to follow a route selected by the people' (p.xx). By such methods, Brody aims to reverse the direction of power in traditional ethnographies and travel texts and to restore power to the indigenous subjects. The even-numbered chapters 'give the detailed, at times technical, findings' and 'Above all, they seek to show the extent to which Indian economic life is modern, resilient and viable' (p.xxii).

Another feature of contemporary travel writing – not unique to it, but characteristic of it – is bathos; a rejection of the picturesque and the sublime. The hapless, comic protagonist moves through a landscape that is much less inspiring or sustaining than, say, in the eighteenth century. So, for example, in *Notes from a Small Island*, the record of a tour around Britain undertaken in valedictory fashion before the author moves with his family back to the United States, the best-selling travel writer Bill Bryson gives his take on going to see a famous monument:

> Impressive as Stonehenge is, there comes a moment somewhere about eleven minutes after your arrival when you realize you've seen pretty well as much as you care to, and you spend another forty minutes walking around the perimeter rope looking at it out of a combination of politeness, embarrassment at being the first from your bus to leave and a keen desire to extract £2.80 worth of exposure from the experience.[49]

Along with this and other instances of self-deprecation in the book are displays of middlebrow taste, quite in contrast to earlier demonstrations of learning. Thus, for example, Bryson refers to Tintern Abbey as 'made famous, of course, by the well-known Wordsworth poem, "I Can Be Boring Outside the Lake District Too"' (p.149). This is accompanied by another anti-intellectual dig as he remarks of the University of Oxford that although 'I have the greatest respect for [it] . . ., I'm not entirely clear what it's *for*, now that Britain no longer needs colonial administrators who can quip in Latin' (p.153). Obliquely and probably unintentionally, this suggests the question that underlies many post-war British travelogues: what is Britain for? The inevitable follow-up question for the British travel writer (and for travellers from other former colonial powers) is: what am *I* for? The need for an answer impels some of the quests that are discussed in Chapter 6.

Part II

Continuities and departures

Chapter 6

Quests

We're always leaving home because we're partly looking for something else.
Raphael Kadushin[1]

Quests of different sorts have motivated travellers for millennia. They may be spiritual or material, pacific or martial, solitary or collective, outward into the world or inward into the self. Travellers strive for victory – over aspects of themselves or over others. They search for enlightenment; for knowledge of other people, societies and culture, of flora, fauna and geology; they look for financial profit for themselves, their companies or their countries; they seek new homes, temporary or long-term, through choice or necessity; they pursue leisure, sex, self-improvement; they aim to find spiritual reward or psychological repair in enactments of the inner journey (the subject of Chapter 7).

In the course of the quest, challenges have to be confronted and overcome. The obstacles to be surmounted may be human, animal, topographic or facets of one's own psyche. Triumph over these endows the traveller with authority and status and reduces the standing of the antagonist.

Elsner and Rubiés write that 'The importance of the modern theme of travel as a quest – often a negative, pointless one – and of travel literature as a fundamental part of a system of empirical narrative practices is best understood historically, in the light of the traditions that have defined Western culture through Antiquity and the Middle Ages'.[2] Some idea of the emergence and development of this theme has been provided by the historical overview in Part I. A critical text in this regard is Cervantes's picaresque novel *Don Quixote* (1605–14), a monumental work that mocked the chivalric delusions of its titular quester. The puncturing of fantasy and the injection of realism applied beyond the Spanish borders, but it would be wrong to imply that realist, secular narratives have supplanted the sacred. Narratives of religious quest that provide solace or fulfilment to their protagonists continue to be produced.

Most journeys are quests of some kind. The quest is not merely a part of the content of travel accounts; it influences their very structure and it endures because of its flexibility as metaphor. The protagonist embarks on a mission, encounters impediments, removes them (more often than not), attains his or her goal and sets out on the return voyage, having increased his or her (usually his) own worth through the successful completion of the objective (unless the nature of the quest precludes return).

This chapter will focus on quests since 1850, allowing us to examine the survival and adaptation of ancient models. The ways in which these are modified – how they are told, what is preserved, what has changed, what is omitted – tell us something of the society that reproduces them, but also something about how we want to view that society.

Many explorers deliberately invoke the figure of Odysseus or other classical questers. Such comparisons underline the masculine ethos of the quest, for if the male protagonist compares himself with Odysseus, so the woman (if mentioned at all) occupies the role of Penelope, staying faithfully at home waiting patiently for his return. In his *In Darkest Africa* (1890) – subtitled *Or The Quest, Rescue, And Retreat Of Emin Governor Of Equatoria* – Henry M. Stanley suggests a connection with Xenophon, whom we met in Chapter 2, when he writes of leading Emin's thousands of followers to the safety of the coast. This was a quarter of a century after Stanley's successful quest was triumphantly announced in the very title of the book that made him famous, *How I Found Livingstone* (1872). In his modernist novel *Ulysses* (1922), James Joyce modelled the mundane activities of protagonist Leopold Bloom in Dublin on 16 June 1904 on the structure and events of the *Odyssey*; John Steinbeck's *Tortilla Flat* (1935) transfers Arthurian structures and settings to the drink-centred adventures of jobless *paisanos* in post-World War I California; Derek Walcott's epic poem *Omeros* (1990) adapts Homer and Dante in its rendition of the lives of St. Lucia fishermen. Just as in literary fiction and poetry, so in travel writing: the capacity for heroism in the modern world has changed; it has become diminished or democratised, depending on one's point of view. In Chapter 5, we saw how, in the twentieth century, travel writers such as Robert Byron construct comic personas for themselves, reflecting the altered status of the traveller after the age of so-called heroic exploration has passed. In keeping with the fallible, bumbling, protagonist of many contemporary travel texts, the quests they undertake have become more ordinary, ironic or bathetic. The old heroes and their adventures survive as reference points against which latter-day exploits fall funnily short, contributing to the comic potential of the modern protagonist and to the often quirky attraction of the author's public persona. Marketing considerations play an important part in this phenomenon, with publishers needing to attract and retain the attention of potential readers. For this they rely on the author's celebrity or on the eccentricity of the trip. It is not altogether a new development. Mark Twain's *The Innocents Abroad: or The New Pilgrim's Progress* (1869), which has been discussed in Chapter 4, wittily charts the descent from an heroic to a commercial age, offering in its humorous narrative voice a mode of telling travel stories in a world of mass tourism and, paradoxically, of marking the individuality of both author and narrator.

We might wonder what there is left to find in the modern world; what quests remain to be embarked upon now that the 'age of discovery' is over. The presence of the phrase 'in search of' from the titles of modern travel narratives indicates the range of types. H. V. Morton's best-selling book, *In Search of England* (1927), is an account of the author's travels in a Morris motor car. It was followed by other volumes in search of Scotland (1929), Ireland (1930), Wales (1932), South Africa (1948) and London (1951). John Steinbeck's *Travels with Charley* (1962), discussed in Chapter 5, is, its subtitle announces, a journey *In Search of America*. John Lazenby's *Test of Time: Travels in Search of a Cricketing Legend* (2005) sees the author travelling to some of the places in Australia visited by his grandfather, the England cricketer J. R. Mason, during the Ashes tour of 1897–8. Lazenby's is one of very many modern quests performed under the label 'in the footsteps of', searching for the spirit of one's ancestors or for the surviving signs of former times. The justification of such books rests on their association with a forebear, usually a more illustrious one. They unwittingly suggest a lack of originality, a dependence on more worthwhile predecessors, that heightens the sense of belatedness; of living in a less interesting period with fewer and smaller accomplishments. Gavin Bell, the subtitle of *In Search of Tusitala* (1994) informs us, performs his *Travels in the Pacific after Robert Louis Stevenson*, while Gavin Young journeys to Asia *In Search of Conrad* (1991). More musically, Jason Webster undertakes *A Journey in Search of Flamenco* in *Duende* (2003), Marybeth Hamilton goes *In Search of the Blues* (2007), and, more specifically, Michael Gray goes *In Search of Blind Willie McTell* in *Hand Me My Travelin' Shoes* (2007). Christopher Robbins is *In Search of Kazakhstan* (2007); Michael Moran writes in *A Country in the Moon: Travels In Search of the Heart of Poland* (2008); Decca Aitkenhead goes clubbing in *The Promised Land: Travels in Search of the Perfect E* (2002); Christopher Ross *Travels in Search of a Samurai Legend* in *Mishima's Sword* (2006); Mirabel Osler undertakes *Travels in Search of the Legendary Food of France* in *The Elusive Truffle* (2010); Stuart Maconie is *In Search of the North* [of England] in *Pies and Prejudice* (2008); and William Dalrymple, whose first book was *In Xanadu: A Quest* (1989), which saw him in search of the remains of Kublai Khan's pleasure dome, has more recently been *In Search of the Sacred in Modern India* in *Nine Lives* (2009).[3] And so on. Of course, some pre-twentieth-century travel texts also employed 'in search of' in their titles. Elisha Kent Kane's *The U.S. Grinnell Expedition in*

Search of Sir John Franklin, A Personal Narrative (1854) was one of many narratives to result from the several expeditions dispatched to look for the missing Arctic explorer. But it seems the market for individual searches has grown now, and in general there appears to be a greater air of confidence and assuredness in the quests of the nineteenth century. While it would be wrong to draw too sharp a separation between pre- and post-1900 narratives, the twentieth century sees a weakening of certainty and of affiliations around class, national, religious and even gender identities. Totalitarian attempts to solidify these are testament to the sense of slippage. Elsner and Rubiés's judgement that 'Modern travel writing is a literature of disappointment' arises from their view that a continued desire for a sacred vision might not result in spiritual fulfilment and that there is a 'desire for a past in which the fragments inherited by the present were once available in an ideal wholeness'; a secular as well as religious longing (ER, p.6). There is, they write, a 'modern condition of sensing an absence – richer, fuller, more resplendent than the present' (ER, p.7). That sense of loss, of something missing, permeates many contemporary narratives and drives their protagonists to discover it. 'There I slept, more safely than in Chicago, a wanderer not only in space but in time also, living a life that most of the world has now forgotten', writes Freya Stark in her travelogue of Luristan, the mountainous region between Iraq and Iran.[4]

In addition, there is the instability of the self diagnosed by Freud, which informs Chapter 7. This is another factor that contributes to the figure of the individual travelling in search of meaning, purpose or belonging, in contrast to the more confident and strident expansionism of earlier ages; for example, in the early modern period and the later nineteenth century. This is not to say that there was no individual travel in those years or that there has been no group or service travel since 1900. Rather, there has been a change in the dominant characteristics of Anglophone travel writing. The differences are to be found mainly in a personal search for meaning in place of the older certainties of group identity. Often, the simple fact of the search or the questions posed along the way are more important than the results: there may not be any answers. So, for example, John Steinbeck, writing of his journey around the United States, asks himself if he is learning anything about his country and responds: 'If I am, I don't know what it is'.[5] He remarks: 'I came with the wish to learn what America is like. And I wasn't sure I was learning anything'.[6]

To be a pilgrim

Amid the changes, an enduring type of quest is the pilgrimage. It takes many forms, which contributes to its longevity. We met with some of its early

Christian manifestations in Chapter 2. Mary Baine Campbell writes in her study of European travel writing between 400 and 1600 of how 'Pilgrimage became crusade; the search for Marco Polo's Cathay ended in the conquests of Mexico and Peru. Many pilgrims were soldiers, many missionaries were military spies, most early explorers were conquistadores'.[7] In more recent times, pilgrimage has taken on an increasingly secular and metaphorical connotation. The nineteenth-century British traveller and long-time resident in India, Fanny Parkes, published her journals in 1850 as *Wanderings of a Pilgrim in Search of the Picturesque*. She ends them plaintively, pointing to the difference between her past adventures in India and her retirement in Sussex:

> And now the pilgrim resigns her staff and plucks the scallop-shell from her hat, – her wanderings are ended – she has quitted the East, perhaps for ever: – surrounded in the quiet home of her native land by the curiosities, the monsters, and the idols that accompanied her from India, she looks around and dreams of the days that are gone.[8]

One should not infer from this valediction, and from the common perception of our move to a more godless age, that religious pilgrimages are confined to the past. Besides pilgrimages by Hindus to Benares and by Muslims to Mecca, for example, Christian pilgrimages survive and one, in particular, has flourished. That is the pilgrimage to Santiago de Compostela in northwest Spain, which Paul Genoni has described as 'arguably the most significant and popular of the remaining medieval Christian pilgrim routes in Europe'.[9] Genoni notes that this pilgrimage, which people had begun to undertake in large numbers by the start of the tenth century, underwent a gradual decline in the thirteenth century although its routes were still travelled, before undergoing a major revival after the Second World War. Nearly 150,000 pilgrims travelled at least 100 kilometres on foot or 200 kilometres by bicycle in 2009 and more than 270,000 in 2010, a 'Holy Year' (158).[10] Genoni observes that some of the medieval pathways to Santiago are still used, the most popular being the *Camino Frances* that runs westward from the French-Spanish border and covers a distance of nearly 800 kilometres, which usually takes thirty to thirty-five days to walk (159). Citing Nancy Frey's observation (pp.237–54) that the pilgrimage 'really gathered pace in the 1980s as the pilgrim path was increasingly recognised as one of Europe's great "walks"', Genoni suggests that for the modern pilgrims, 'this anachronistic mode of travel ... creates a powerful link to the pilgrimage's medieval past' (159). The point that Genoni makes about this has a much broader relevance, applicable to all those who journey along historic routes: '[T]he disrupted sense of time in Santiago narratives', he argues, 'is a rhetorical device deployed to suggest a particular effect of travel – that is, its capacity to induce in the traveller the sense that time has been transcended or "crossed", and that the traveller has undergone an experience that is seemingly of another, earlier epoch'. He reads 'This "crossing of time" in pilgrim narratives ... as an example of the negotiation of the relationship between past and present that is common in contemporary travel literature, whereby travel is narrated as a nostalgic encounter with a past made desirable by the crippling effects of modernity' (157). In other words, there is a dual or overlapping sense of time, with the modern pilgrim seeking a connection with an earlier epoch. That association complements the meaning of the pilgrimage: the invocation of pre-industrial society grants the pilgrim an air of purity and simplicity. As Genoni expresses it: '[T]he accounts of "pilgrim time" are both essential to the expression of a successful pilgrimage and deeply reflective of contemporary anxieties about many aspects of modernity' (158). 'A sense of quiet life, unchanging, centuries old and forgotten, held our pilgrim souls in its peace', writes Stark of Luristan.[11] There is, in people's minds, a correlation between complexity and corruption. In this respect, then, there is a double-layered journey. On the surface, there is the straightforward fact of treading for oneself a well-worn path. In Genoni's words, 'By virtue of its long, unbroken history, anyone who walks to Santiago as a pilgrim cannot help but be aware they are entering an association with the past, by undertaking an activity that has remained remarkably unchanged for over a millennium' (158). On a deeper level, this desire for what is posited as a more essential, direct experience is a symptom of the larger cultural yearning for what is perceived to be a less complicated existence. This is borne out by the fact that, 'A notable characteristic of contemporary Santiago narratives is their frequently expressed nostalgic and romantic attachment to an earlier time, closely coupled with a distrust of modernity' (p.160).

There are similarities to be drawn with primitivism, New Age travels and related spiritual quests, although the pilgrimages of the major religions derive much of their meaning from community whereas New Age and associated travels are often solitary affairs, depending on lone or small-group encounters with indigenous peoples from whom it is thought there are vital lessons to be learnt.[12] Such ventures are self-serving. Robert Clarke notes the proliferation of New Age travel books in the 1980s and 1990s that 'justifiably were criticised as examples of contemporary cultural colonisation and appropriation for their representations of Aboriginal Australian cultures'. Among the titles Clarke cites are Harvey Arden's *Dreamkeepers* (1994), Marlo Morgan's *Mutant Message Down Under* (1994), Lyn Andrews's *Crystal Woman* (1987), Benedict Allen's *The Proving Grounds* (1991) and Monica Furlong's *Flight of the Kingfisher* (1996). Clarke observes:

> Generally presented as works of non-fiction, the narratives of these books are usually structured around a quest for *sacred heritage*, whereby

> a spiritually-alienated, and religiously nomadic Western traveller seeks and experiences the vestigial and primordial spiritual wisdom of Aboriginal cosmology generally through the medium of an Aboriginal guide, and is empowered to communicate a message of spiritual rejuvenation to the rest of humankind.[13]

In such literature, as in literary examples of primitivism, the narrator is a mediating figure, travelling between existences, imparting knowledge to invigorate us in our mechanical lives.

There is a kinship here with Robyn Davidson's remarkable travel book, *Tracks* (1980), in which her journey across the Australian desert has her 'escape the motorized post-modernity at the urban edges of Australia's coastal region and with it the constitutive constraints of disabling femininity in metropolitan centers'.[14] Davidson writes that one of her reasons for wanting to travel in the desert was that she had 'read a good deal about Aborigines' and it would be 'a way of getting to know them directly and simply'. Her very next paragraph constitutes a telling juxtaposition: 'I had also been vaguely bored with my life and its repetitions – the half-finished, half-hearted attempts at different jobs and various studies; had been sick of carrying around the self-indulgent negativity which was so much the malaise of my generation, my sex and my class'.[15] Although she tells us that she made her decision about the trip 'instinctively, and only later had given it meaning' (p.50), the link is apparent. She accomplishes what Smith terms her renegotiation of her 'identity as feminized woman',[16] but what is also a renegotiation of her Australian identity, through encounters with Aborigines. In particular, the understanding she claims to reach with an elderly Aborigine man, Eddie – one that she represents as transcending language barriers – has great significance for her: 'After two weeks with Eddie I was a changed person' (p.180). In previous centuries, change might be feared or resisted (as testified by whites' narratives of captivity by Native Americans or Barbary pirates[17]) but now transformation is often an aim of the quest. Indeed, responsiveness to one's travel experiences – an openness that results in a change of outlook – is lauded by one theorist, Syed Islam, as a marker of a worthy ethical approach to travel. Islam designates this nomadic, as opposed to sedentary, travel.[18] Such usage of the indigene to effect this transformation, however, lays Davidson open to the charge of exploitation or, to use Holland and Huggan's term, 'cultural voyeurism', but Holland and Huggan largely absolve her of this. They argue that unlike Bruce Chatwin's romanticised treatment of Dreamtime in his book *The Songlines* (1987), *Tracks*, which does attend to Aborigines' living conditions and lack of political power, 'is based on an understanding of their material situation'.[19] Yet even texts that appear radical in their politics are at risk of using the Other exploitatively to the advantage of the self. The quest may be for the benefit of the protagonist, for even where a rescue or relief is concerned, it redounds to the quester's credit.

The quest narrative has bequeathed to travel writing its uneven vision. The focus is on the searcher, and the tale is told from his or her perspective. When landscape, wildlife or people impede the hero's progress, these are represented not as neutral but as hostile, or a test of faith, or as immoral; even evil. They are seen to obstruct the hero's rightful progress, the continuation of which is often ascribed to divine providence. Listeners to and readers of the tale are positioned into sharing the hero's perspective. They accept that the importance of the goal overrides the interests of those whom he or she encounters along the way. Questers use the lands through which they pass for their own purposes. The places and the people they meet on the way are subordinated to those and exist in relation to the quest, aiding or hindering its accomplishment. The landscape functions symbolically, a fact that helps instate what may be seen as the fundamental inequality and self-serving nature of travel writing: quests are for the benefit of the self. They reinscribe oppositions of self and Other and they do not allow for the direct representation of the Other's point of view. The Nigerian writer Chinua Achebe's criticism of Joseph Conrad's novella *Heart of Darkness* (1902) for its use of 'Africa as setting and backdrop which eliminates the African as human factor' is relevant here. Achebe accuses Conrad of using 'Africa as a metaphysical battlefield devoid of all recognizable humanity, into which the wandering European enters at his peril'.[20] In that novella's quest, which is at once both internal into the psyche and external into the unnamed Belgian Congo, Marlow proceeds from the Thames, which 'had known and served all the men of whom the nation is proud, from Sir Frances Drake to Sir John Franklin, knights all, titled and untitled – the great knights-errant of the sea' to the company station where the men, with 'their absurd long staves in their hands' are 'like a lot of faithless pilgrims' whose whispering of and sighing for ivory, as though 'they were praying for it' produces a 'taint of imbecile rapacity'.[21]

Perhaps one of the things to have changed in more recent times is the identity of the type of person undertaking quests. Women and people of colour have always quested, of course, but their presence in Anglophone travel writing is now greater and will be examined in Chapters 8 and 9.

'Simplicity is the whole secret of well-being'

One of the most lyrical and celebrated of texts to move between the spiritual and the inner quest is Peter Matthiessen's *The Snow Leopard*. It narrates its author's expedition to the Crystal Mountain in Nepal from late September to early December 1978 with zoologist George Schaller, whom he first met in 1969. Schaller ('GS') is going to study the bharal or Himalayan blue sheep. 'And where bharal were numerous, there was bound to appear that rarest and most beautiful of the great cats, the snow leopard.'[22] Schaller, writes Matthiessen, knows of only one Westerner besides Schaller himself who has seen the creature in the previous twenty-five years. For Matthiessen, 'the hope of glimpsing this near-mythic beast in the snow mountains was reason enough for the entire journey' (p.13). Matthiessen had seen the Crystal Mountain on a visit to Nepal twelve years before, but now, 'to close that distance, to go step by step across the greatest range on earth to somewhere called the Crystal Mountain, was a true pilgrimage, a journey of the heart' (p.13). It also offers the opportunity to visit the Land of Dolpo, 'all but unknown' since 'the usurpation of Tibet by the Chinese' and 'said to be the last enclave of pure Tibetan culture left on earth' (p.13). Quoting from Lama Angarika Govinda's *The Way of the White Clouds* (1973), Matthiessen writes that Tibetan culture 'was the last citadel of "all that present-day humanity is longing for, either because it has been lost or not yet been realized or because it is in danger of disappearing from human sight: the stability of a tradition which has its roots not only in a historical or cultural past, but within the innermost being of man"' (pp.13–14). This sense of catching things just before they vanish is typical of a strong undercurrent in modern travel writing: the idea of having arrived in time to witness a sight that will be gone before one's readers get the chance to see it, or even too late to experience the authentic oneself.[23] It has similarities to what anthropologists call salvage ethnography. It is evident, too, in Matthiessen's statement that 'This wilderness will be gone by the century's end' (p.53). The identification of an endangered state or situation with our 'innermost being' illustrates the sense of post-industrial alienation from the modern that suffuses twentieth-century literature.

As Raymond Williams in his book *The Country and the City* (1973) has observed, there has long been a tendency to idealise previous generations and their existence, especially when we look back from this side of the Industrial Revolution and contemplate pre-industrial, pastoral worlds in order to criticise or come to terms with our own. Early on in his journey, Matthiessen writes: 'In the clean air and absence of all sound, of even the simplest machinery … in the warmth and harmony and seeming plenty, come whispers of a paradisal age' (p.26). Matthiessen's narrative, which also records his coming to terms with the death of his wife Deborah from cancer the previous winter, turns to the spiritual and the natural world, associating each with the other, for relief and insight. Both Matthiessen and Deborah had become students of Zen Buddhism.

For Matthiessen, the absence of the modern allows for a more direct realisation of the self, especially in relation to nature. The stripping away of material goods discloses the essential; the elemental. In the hill village of Naudanda, Matthiessen tries out 'my new home, a one-man mountain tent, in poor condition' (p.30). Surveying the land to the east below, he seems contentedly to remark, 'There are no roads west of Pokhara, which is the last outpost of the modern world; in one days [sic] walk we are a century away' (p.30). This flight from modernity, discussed in Chapter 5 of the present volume, represents a quest for a pre-industrial self closer to nature. Matthiessen refers to 'the holistic knowledge shared by so many peoples of the earth, Christians included, before the advent of the industrial revolution made new barbarians of the peoples of the West' (p.64).

Matthiessen's is not altogether a naive vision of an unspoilt or threatened idyll. He knows that the area through which he travels is subject to change, not only from tourism but from its own inhabitants. Of a boy who escorts him and Schaller through a village, he writes: 'One day this boy and others will destroy that forest, and their sheep fields will erode in rain, and the thin soil will wash away into the torrents, clogging the river channels farther down so that monsoon floods will spread across the land.... Nepal has the most serious erosion problem of any country in the world' (p.31). In a sense, though, this acknowledgement of inevitable change owing to deforestation leads to criticism that the Nepalese fail to do enough to keep things as they are or as they were: 'In GS's view, Asia is fifteen to twenty years behind East Africa in its attitudes towards conservation, and the gap may well prove fatal' (p.32).

There is an ascetic aspect to Matthiessen's journey ('GS and I love to travel light' [p.39]). There often is in quests, at least in those that possess a spiritual element and which frequently posit an elemental testing of physical and mental strength unencumbered by superfluous accoutrements. Signs of hardship on the trip become proof of the value of the quest: 'It relieves me that GS is mortal, prey to the afflictions of the common pilgrim' (p.33). Physical suffering and mental anxiety are antidotes to the ease of a superficial life of modern-day comforts in the United States. They reaffirm life.

As we saw with the Australian New Age narratives, that antidote delivers a cure at the expense of others. Matthiessen's expressions of attraction to the sherpas' Buddhism are packed with patronising platitudes, albeit positively meant: 'These simple and uneducated men comport themselves with the wise calm of monks, and their well-being is in no way separable from their religion' (p.41); 'their dignity is unassailable', they are 'tolerant and unjudgmental' and their outlook 'open and generous', constituting a 'kind of merry defencelessness' (p.40). Peter Bishop claims that: 'Tukten, the Sherpa, moves very close to becoming a ridiculous stereotype of the Eastern Wise Man'.[24] In a later interview, Matthiessen confesses his ignorance of Tukten:

> Unfortunately, his life didn't last very long [after Matthiessen's journey] – he died of, I think, TB and drink. Turns out he was a Tibetan, I didn't even know that. He was a Gurkha soldier for a long time. He even was in Singapore for a while; he was a well-traveled fellow. He spoke Malay – I didn't know any of that.[25]

The search for purity takes precedence. 'Simplicity is the whole secret of well-being', Matthiessen exclaims (p.109). It is a late twentieth-century utterance of a sentiment known to those modernists who sought to escape (if briefly) the complexities of modern life. In the entry for 14 October, Matthiessen records Schaller asking him, '"Do you realize we haven't heard even a distant motor since September?"' (p.93). Matthiessen affirms this, adding that, 'No aeroplane crosses such old mountains' and 'We have strayed into another century' (p.93). Whereas many earlier travellers wanted to pull indigenous peoples into what they saw as the modern world, Matthiessen (and many of his readers) want to flee their own time. In doing so, Matthiessen hopes to find an essential self that has been buried and distorted by the weight of the post-industrial, mechanised world. Before, other 'races' had generally been reviled; now they are embraced as offering a purer and more natural existence from which the modern world could learn. For Matthiessen, follower of Zen Buddhism, the ideal lies in the obliteration of the ego and 'intuiting the true nature of existence', a condition he believes 'has appeared, in one form or another, in almost every culture known to man'. These versions or equivalents of meditation have 'nothing to do with thought of any kind – with anything at all, in fact' (p.90). And he compares this process with the practices of the 'Bushman', the 'Eskimo', the dervish, the 'Pueblo sacred dancer', Hindus and followers of Tantra (p.90). He explains that 'in Zen, one seeks to empty out the mind, to return it to the clear, pure stillness of a seashell or a flower petal'. When body and mind become one, ego diminishes and:

> The weary self of masks and screens, defences, preconceptions, and opinions that, propped up by ideas and words, imagines itself to be some sort of entity (in a society of like entities) may suddenly fall away, dissolve into formless flux where concepts such as "death" and "life", "time" and "space", "past" and "future" have no meaning. There is only a pearly radiance of Emptiness, the Uncreated, without beginning, therefore without end. (p.91)

Matthiessen writes that 'meditation represents the foundation of the universe to which all returns ... In this "void", this dynamic state of rest, without impediments, lies ultimate reality, and here one's own true nature is reborn, in a return from what Buddhists speak of as "great death"' (p.91). It seems a retreat from all that travel writers except pilgrims have traditionally written themselves into; a withdrawal from the world into which they have moved and on which they have sought to impose themselves.

Matthiessen's elegiac book has rightly attracted much praise but this illusory stripping of the self, while a reaction against the processes of expansion and materialism that helped drive travel writing in earlier centuries is not so much in opposition to it as it appears. The foreign territory remains the site for the fulfilment of the self, even if that fulfilment purports to rest on the self's erasure. After all, Matthiessen has fashioned a full-length book from the idea, furthering his reputation and sales. In that regard, his travel is as much about self-affirmation as other and earlier forms of travel writing, whatever its innovations in presenting a search that is both fulfilling and a failure.

Casey Blanton observes that 'Matthiessen's spiritual and scientific quest … becomes, in Western terms, an anti-quest, mirrored by the search for Tukten at the end'.[26] That is, not only does Matthiessen fail to see a snow leopard, but Tukten fails to appear for the meeting Matthiessen has arranged at the end of the book. 'What Peter Matthiessen brings back in *The Snow Leopard* is the message that the quest does not necessarily have to involve dangerous treks to fabled monasteries. What Tukten teaches is that our quest can be found in life itself among its day-to-day events, both painful and pleasurable, that make up the eternal now'.[27]

The contemplation of the self, alongside that of existence that pilgrimage entails, is fascinatingly evident in the following passage, written of daybreak at a time when the moon is still visible: 'How strange everything seems. How strange everything is. One "I" feels like an observer of this man who lies here in sleeping bag in Asian mountains; another "I" is thinking about Alex [his eight year-old son]; a third is the tired man who tries to sleep' (p.46). These lines indicate effectively, if inadvertently, the different selves at play in travel writing: the traveller, the traveller's contemporaneous thoughts of elsewhere and the author who subsequently contemplates and writes about the traveller.

A pilgrim without a point

As *The Snow Leopard* suggests, modern quests may be a search for the meaning of a quest, rather like that of Oedipa Maas's search for significance in Thomas Pynchon's postmodern picaresque novel, *The Crying of Lot 49* (1966), or they may prove elusive and focus attention on the person undertaking them as in Bruce Chatwin's bold and influential mixture of fact and fictionalising, *In Patagonia* (1977). The condition of the modern search is represented by gay writer Mitch Cullin's reflection that 'In hindsight, I was probably a pilgrim without a point, seeking needed information but not knowing what questions to ask or what kind of answers should be sought'.[28] The qualifying opening to that sentence – 'In hindsight' – may strengthen the impression of aimless travelling but it signals a paradox: Cullin's statement about a pointless pilgrimage discloses self-knowledge about his condition.

A prominent theme of the twentieth- and twenty-first century quest is the inward voyage, the subject of Chapter 7. Susan Fox Rogers writes of how 'Going to Alaska was to be a sort of pilgrimage, a journey into land and self that I had always envisioned as a solo venture'.[29] Rogers's solo trip is threatened by the presence of her father, who has decided to join her. Despite her initial desire to be alone, she finds herself growing closer to her father from whom she has felt distant both since and before coming out as a lesbian. She discovers that 'I no longer wanted to compartmentalize myself, my lesbian self not communing with family, my love of the outdoors not mixing with the rest. Alaska was giving me not just distance and perspective but dimension'.[30] After having their first-ever conversation about sex (p.165), Rogers recognises his facial features in herself and, although they 'never came to an agreement' (p.166), she regards that as unimportant. She experiences a feeling like freedom and has a sense of purpose. When her father leaves Alaska three days later, Rogers is 'suddenly deeply unhappy to be alone', having

> come to treasure the pace of our lives together, the comfort of his presence and the surprise of our conversations. But I knew that I needed to keep moving, into the interior of Alaska, where I would begin the journey I had originally set out to take. Now there was a difference: this journey was no longer a running away, a rejection of where I came from. It was more a running to (or running into). And somewhere around Denali I shed my old skin and emerged: lesbian, Rogers; desire and family.[31]

Rogers's short travel piece exhibits the core features of the modern quest: a search for individual identity conducted against a natural landscape that leads to a self-knowledge. That in turn leads to a rebirth – here signified by the shedding of Rogers's old skin – which prepares one for a more fulfilling re-entry into society.

However, it would be a mistake to think that modern travel writing is predominantly inward-looking. It can be accused of being solipsistic, but the charge would be unjust. It is often purposefully and campaigningly outward-looking. Given the close links between reportage and travel writing, it is not surprising that journalistic investigations involving travel also often take the form of quests. These may be inquiries into the state of affairs in one's own country or abroad. Many visited Russia after the 1917 revolution to see for themselves the soviet experiment; others to witness or take part in the Spanish Civil War, perhaps most famously related in George Orwell's *Homage to Catalonia* (1938). The poet Lawrence Ferlinghetti goes to Nicaragua on what he sees 'as a voyage of discovery, hoping to discover the Sandinistas are in the right, and that I might take some public stand in their favour, rather than the political silence maintained by many U.S. writers today'.[32] Joan Didion reports in 1982 on El Salvador, where 'The dead and pieces of the dead turn up ... everywhere, every day, as taken for granted as in a nightmare, or a horror movie',[33] and where 'Body dumps are seen ... as a kind of visitors' must-do, difficult but worth the detour' (p.20). There, 'In the absence of information (and the presence, often, of disinformation) even the most apparently straightforward event takes on ... elusive shadows, like a fragment of retrieved legend' (p.67). Didion relates her recent realisation that 'the texture of life in such a situation is essentially untranslatable' (p.103). George Monbiot embarks on 'An investigative journey through Indonesia', as the subtitle to his book *Poisoned Arrows* (1989) puts it. At the end of his trip, he writes: 'While much of what I'd seen was in all ways wrong, for other things there were many different truths: the government's truth, the transmigrant's truth, the local people's truth, my truth'.[34] He realises that 'there were no snap answers to my own frustrations. My search for something more real than my job in London had led me round full circle: to see that there were indeed no end points'.[35] Monbiot's hunt for meaning in his life is typical of individuals' quest for significance in their twentieth- and twenty-first century lives.

Pilgrimages now are often made to secular, tourist sites. Bill Bryson takes the Granada Studios Tour of the soap opera *Coronation Street*. It seems that he is joined by 'nearly everyone else in the North of England';[36] and that 'for millions of us it is a near-religious experience' (p.228). The attraction of the soap to Bryson (and to other fans) is its ordinariness: 'Where I came from, soap operas were always about rich, ruthless, enormously successful people ... And here was this amazing programme about ordinary people living on an anonymous northern street, talking a language I could barely understand and never doing much of anything.... I was a helpless devotee' (p.228).

Indeed, to bring things full circle, travel writers have themselves become the object of quest and homage. Nicola Watson has charted nineteenth-century examples of this phenomenon and Michael Shapiro, in the Afterword to his volume of interviews with some of the leading practitioners of the genre, conducted in or near their homes, remarks: 'The travels for this book *became a pilgrimage*, and a way to honor the writers who have expanded my horizons, stoked my hunger for exploration, and enhanced my appreciation of this wonderfully diverse world'.[37]

We have seen, then, that the quest is central to the travel narrative. It is probably the single most important organising principle of travel writing. Most journeys involve a quest of some kind and there can be no quest without a journey. Over the centuries, the object of the quest and the way that the quest story is told may have changed, but the basic structure of subject, object, passage and obstacle remain. It would be wrong to reach too firm conclusions about the character of any age from its quest narratives – there are always plenty of counter examples that do not fit the generalisation one is making – but a characteristic of the twentieth- and twenty-first century quest is that its object may be elusive, its success difficult to judge, and its conduct seen from different points of view. It may also entail an interior journey, as we shall see in Chapter 7.

Chapter 7

Inner journeys

Journeys rarely begin where we think they do.
Colin Thubron[1]

The most foreign territory will always lie within.
Sara Wheeler[2]

The journey into the self is often identified by critics as a feature that distinguishes modern travel from its precursors. There are three main reasons for this view: the focus of Romanticism on inner consciousness and its relationship to the external world, the introduction of psychoanalysis in the late nineteenth century, and the perception that there are few or no places in the world left to discover. These developments, it is often said, impel the interior voyage into the self and provide the conceptual framework and metaphors for the expression of that voyage. In fact, the inward journey is not in itself new. For millennia, pilgrimage depended upon a correlation between one's inner state and a ritual physical movement to a sacred destination, often along prescribed routes. Nor is self-exploration a modern innovation. What has helped bring about a change in the direction of travel writing since the late nineteenth century, however, is the influence of Sigmund Freud's concept of a divided self driven by unconscious fears and desires. Freud's ideas unsettled the belief in an authoritative and stable author-narrator. They also ushered in the theme of psychological examination, which became as important in some narratives as the actual travel that produced or accompanied it. In the 1930s, in particular, 'the teachings of Freud and Jung ... were becoming sufficiently widely popularized to form part of the idiom of artists and writers'.[3] One of the most prominent examples of this in the travel writing of the decade – indeed, of the century – is Graham Greene's *Journey Without Maps* (1936), which will be discussed in this chapter.

Another type of inner journey to be given new shape in the twentieth and twenty-first century is that of self-investigation on a national level. In Britain, this takes two main forms. First, the 'condition of England' genre in which concerned travellers document the poverty and deprivation they discover in their own country. Well-known examples of this kind of writing, which straddles travel and reportage, include George Orwell's *Road to Wigan Pier* (1937) and J. B. Priestley's *An English Journey* (1934). This sub-genre follows in the tradition of earlier investigations, such as those by William Cobbett (1830), Henry Mayhew (1851, 1861) and William Booth (1890), but is given fresh impetus in the 1930s by the continued effects of the great depression. It sees a later revival with post-Thatcher works such as Nick Danziger's *Danziger's Britain: A Journey to the Edge* (1996) and Nik Cohn's *Yes We Have No: Adventures in Other England* (1999). The second form of this national type of inner journey arises from the self-questioning provoked by the end of formal empire. The success of independence struggles, especially in Africa and Asia, helped force on the British an introspection that contrasted with the predominantly outward-looking movement of previous years. Britain is still coming to terms with its post-imperial role, often in denial of, or trying to compensate for, the loss of its former status. This troubled adjustment, too, is reflected in many of its travel texts as they oscillate between judgmental pronouncements and jokey nervousness about one's dignity. Following modernism's presentation of alternative and multiple perspectives, discussed in Chapter 5, the shift in political power further unsettles narrative authority in travel writing and is accompanied by an increased emphasis on the personal over the collective, and on the individual over the national, as group identities and affiliations become unsettled and confused.

Both the unsettling and the individuation are prefigured in Graham Greene's comment that 'if there are fallacies into which the passing visitor falls, there are fallacies too which come from a close acquaintance'; a remark that illustrates the attention to differences in point of view that is characteristic of modernism.[4] Greene's observation implies that he is trying to find for himself an appropriate distance that will avoid the fallacies of either the fleeting or the intimate observer, while encouraging us to watch him attempting to find a satisfactory position.

The present chapter focuses on the inner journey as a voyage into the self but it views contemporary introspection as a response to modern political and cultural developments. It turns now to a discussion of *Journey Without Maps* to show the construction of the inner journey and to consider events that helped propel it.

Something of importance to myself

Paul Fussell has written of how Greene spent his publisher's advance on a trip to Liberia in 1934 and then struggled to produce an engaging narrative from the experience.[5] In Fussell's words, the solution Greene found:

> ... was to conceive the journey as a metaphor for something else. "The account of a ... slow foot-sore journey into an interior virtually

> unknown – was only of interest if it paralleled another journey. . . ." Thus, he [Greene] says, "I rashly proposed to make memory the very subject of this book", specifically, memory of the complicated delights of fear in infancy.[6]

Freudianism had much of its foundation on the interpretation of infantile fears and desires. Greene mapped his childhood instincts and emotions onto the interior of Africa, purporting to find there a vitality that European civilisation had repressed in itself. Comparing psychoanalysis with physical (more specifically, African) exploration, Greene writes of how:

> Freud has made us conscious as we have never been before of those ancestral threads which still exist in our unconscious minds to lead us back. The need, of course, has always been felt, to go back and begin again. Mungo Park, Livingstone, Stanley, Rimbaud, Conrad represented only another method to Freud's, a more costly, less easy method calling for physical as well as mental strength. (p.252)

Greene, who describes himself as 'a Catholic with an intellectual if not an emotional belief in Catholic dogma' (p.15), finds in the Republic of Liberia an attractive 'seediness' that cannot be found elsewhere. This seediness, and even the version of it he finds in civilisation, 'seems to satisfy, temporarily, the sense of nostalgia for something lost; it seems to represent a stage further back' (p.17). Greene combines two ideas of the past, which serve to link two different ideas of the interior. He joins his (and the reader's) individual past to the concept of a racial past. Thus his (and his compatriots') childhood is associated with African life. The latter is seen as primitive, existing in a state prior to the one the West enjoys now. Whereas in the nineteenth century this would be a cause for missionary zeal, Greene views as positive the opportunity to rediscover things from his childhood that he has forgotten or suppressed. In this respect, his journey follows Freud's thesis, published six years before, that 'it is impossible to overlook the extent to which civilization is built upon a renunciation of instinct, how much it presupposes precisely the non-satisfaction (by suppression, repression or some other means?) of powerful instincts'.[7]

In contrast to announcements by others of their expeditions, Greene writes that: 'The motive of a journey deserves a little attention. It is *not the fully conscious mind* which chooses West Africa in preference to Switzerland' (p.18, my emphasis). To him, 'Africa has always seemed an important image' (p.18) and represented more than he could say. While particular areas of Africa (such as Kenya and South Africa) evoke specific images, the continent as a whole produces indefinable but powerful impressions. Greene states that not all of Africa has such a powerful effect on the unconscious. In his view, those parts that have been settled by whites who have reproduced their own society and culture will not impact on the unconscious in anything like the same measure. According to Greene, 'A quality of darkness is needed, of the inexplicable' (p.18).

What is wanted is mystery. In the previous century, Henry Rowley may have shared the urge of his contemporaries in presenting us with *Africa Unveiled* (1876), but Greene wishes for the return of obscurity. Expending effort to discern will restore to the spectator a purposeful role, making of the onlooker an investigator. 'This Africa', Greene exclaims, 'may take the form of an unexplained brutality' (p.18), and he quotes from Joseph Conrad's diary to show it. Greene writes that an old man being beaten outside a prison, naked widows 'covered with yellow clay squatting in a hole, [and] the wooden toothed devil swaying his raffia skirts between the huts seem like the images in a dream to stand for something of importance to myself' (p.19). The dream imagery belongs to the unconscious; the uncertainty of its meaning is a departure from the confident knowingness of nineteenth-century pronouncements on Africa. Yet Greene's suggestion that the images of Africa stand for something important to himself is an act of appropriation similar to that for which the Nigerian writer Chinua Achebe has attacked Conrad.[8] That is, Africa is of value for what Greene believes it tells and can teach him about himself. This textual and conceptual exploitation of the 'native' has been criticised by Abdul JanMohamed, who asserts that 'Just as imperialists "administer" the resources of the conquered country, so colonialist discourse "commodifies" the native subject into a stereotyped object and uses him as a "resource" for colonialist fiction'.[9] JanMohamed makes a direct connection between the textual and the external:

> we can observe a profound symbiotic relationship between the discursive and the material practices of imperialism: the discursive practices do to the symbolic, linguistic presence of the native what the material practices do to his physical presence; the writer commodifies him so that he can be exploited more efficiently by the administrator, who, of course, obliges by returning the favor in kind.... In fact, at any given point within a fully developed dominant imperialism, it is impossible to determine which form of commodification takes precedence, so entirely are the two forms intertwined.[10]

There may be a risk in so equating the metaphorical with the actual, but JanMohamed's argument is that the one enables the other and that the literary is therefore not innocent. To colonialist fiction we can add travel literature.

Greene moves metaphorically back and forth between Africa and the West, observing that 'Today our world seems peculiarly susceptible to brutality';

that 'We, like Wordsworth, are living after a war and a revolution' and that 'when one sees to what unhappiness, to what peril of extinction centuries of cerebration have brought us, one sometimes has a curiosity to discover if one can from what we have come, to recall at which point we went astray' (p.19). Underlying the air of threat and despair is the prospect of another conflict. For example, recalling a flight to Berlin, Greene remembers the quick, happy impression on approach and landing, 'but on the ground, among the Swastikas, one saw pain at every yard' (p.34). He refers to the world of the Nazis coming to Africa.

In utilising Africa in order to establish a correlative between the instinctive life there and the darkness at the heart of civilisation while suggesting that Africans deal with the primal less destructively, Greene treats Africa for his own purposes, illustrating the truth of Philip Dodd's later remark that 'Africa is less the property of those who live there than of the European writers who have made it theirs'.[11] And Africa remains – for the West – in a condition of infancy. For all Greene's stated desire to regard Africa again as a mysterious land, it is rendered strangely recognisable by its resemblance to a state through which 'we' have passed. This belief in what was termed recapitulation theory had been popularised by anthropology in the second half of the nineteenth century, and in particular by sociologist Herbert Spencer. As George Stocking explains, by the beginning of the twentieth century, 'The idea that the mental processes of savage man were similar to those of civilized children had long been and still was a commonplace. So also was the related notion that mental development in the "lower races" came to a gradual halt in early adolescence'.[12] Observing a masked dance, Greene muses: 'Here in Liberia again and again one caught hints of what it was we had developed from.... One had the sensation of having come home, for here one was finding associations with a personal and a racial childhood, one was being scared by the same old witches' (p.93).

There is a sense here, as he encounters the strangely familiar, of what Freud called the *unheimlich*; the uncanny.[13] Africa allows Greene to recognise, confront and come to terms with the things that caused him fear in infancy and that he now recognises correspondences of in the 'dark continent'. He compares his physical travel there with the investigation of one's past that is undertaken in therapy in which psychoanalysis returns patients to the idea they have been repressing. This Greene describes as 'a long journey backwards without maps' that involves the picking up of clues until one confronts 'the general idea, the pain or the memory' (p.97). Africa, Greene suggests, makes one face what one has been avoiding. There, one cannot escape one's fears.

Whereas much previous writing on Africa aimed to shine a light on the 'dark continent', as Stanley had called it, Greene wishes to retain some darkness that may match his own and his readers' shadows. Of course, there is an irony in that his exploration of his unconscious fears (and desires) is highly crafted. The paradox of Greene's text is that it gives form to the unconscious. Despite its title, it charts its parallel narratives deliberately. As with all representations of the unconscious, then, it is an artifice - a contrivance to give the appearance of the spontaneous and instinctive. Greene is aware of what he is doing and why. He claims to lack the confidence to 'see the journey as more than a smash-and-grab raid into the primitive'. He tells of a dream of a witch that he used to have as a small child nearly every night. Greene would be walking along a dark passage to the door of his nursery. In front of the door there would be a cupboard with the witch waiting inside. He compares the witch to 'the devil in Kpangblamai, feminine and inhuman'. He would be unable to reach the safety of the nursery until, after several years, he attained it by 'running blindly' past her. The dream disappeared from his life but now he seems to have returned to the dark passage: 'I had to see the witch: but I wasn't prepared for a long or careful examination' (p.120).

Greene explains that he had been afraid of the primitive but after coming across it in Duogobmai, lower than which he is sure one could not get, he suddenly felt carefree and relieved. The shock had come in an instant as they made their way 'through the dung and the cramped and stinking huts to our lampless sleeping place among the rats'. This was 'the worst one need fear, and it was bearable because it was inescapable' (127).

Such descriptions reinforce an association of Africa with darkness in all its senses. Greene may be asking his readers to look again at the primitive but his finding something of value in it intensifies the negative qualities that are often attributed to it. *Journey Without Maps* includes familiar derogatory comments on Africa. For example, Greene writes of a 'truly horrible village', in which there was nothing to do but get drunk. Its inhabitants had never seen whites close-up. Their stares irritate him. And they were so ugly, so diseased' (129). Greene is far from the first traveller to be discomfited by the return stare of the people whom he encounters, but his outspokenness is presented as the symptom of someone who is not sure of himself. Later, in Galeye, where most of the younger people had never seen a white person, they stand all day in the doorway. Greene confesses to being made nervous by the persistent stares but, in keeping with his use of Africa to unsettle the attitudes of his readers, he invites them to 'recognise the superiority' of the Africans in their conduct towards the strange. The Africans, he remarks, may have found their visitors as novel as Britons would a circus, but they 'had no wish to stuff us or skin us or put us in cages' (p.155).

That dig at the customs of his home country is an example of how Greene, like his contemporary, Evelyn Waugh, combines an impatience towards and intolerance of Africa with criticism of aspects of British life. The ambivalence may have been manifested by nineteenth-century explorers of Africa, but Greene's combination of the negative and positive marks a distinctive departure. He is more explicit about the qualities of the females he observes, too. He complains about the monotony of the nakedness but discloses that a small girl he sees with a turban and Oriental features and 'small neat breasts ... did appeal to a European sexual taste even in her dirt'. Attraction coexists with repulsion however. He finds something 'shifty and mean' about the dirty village of Duogobmai. It is, he tells us, the only place he finds 'nothing to admire' in until he arrives in 'Bassa country where the coastal civilisation had corrupted the natives' (p.130). Again, there is nothing to do but drink, and to rush to get drunk before darkness falls. Greene fears rats and most of the night he lies awake listening to the vermin. He learns that the cockroaches and rats will eat anything left outside a case: 'shirts, stockings, hair-brushes, the laces in one's shoes' (p.131).

This impression of Africa as a place that corrodes one's possessions at the same time that it saps oneself is common in travellers' (especially explorers') accounts of the continent, and of its interior in particular. Conrad had realised the value of these symbols to a writer, and so does Greene. In addition to rats, Greene is worried by the diseases that he has read about in England: leprosy, yaws, smallpox. Although he knows that leprosy is barely contagious, he feels that 'even the dust in the cramped dirty town was poisonous'. He then operates on another level, bringing the physical and symbolic places closer together. Beneath the 'fear and the irritation', he is aware of 'a curious lightness and freedom'. He writes of having 'crossed the boundary into country really strange; surely one had gone deep this time' (p.133). This is travel as physical act and as metaphor. It works as allegory also: watching 'not a lovely dance' by unattractive 'emaciated old women', Greene reports that the women and his party were cheerful and happy. The 'timelessness, the irresponsibility, the freedom of Africa began to touch us at last' (p.135). The correlation between the external world and the inner self that we witness here is not new. We have seen it in the Romantic literature discussed in Chapter 3. Nor is the individual journey related by Greene any less laden than the adventures of the explorers who preceded him to the continent. He describes the fascination as:

> more than a personal fantasy, satisf[ying] more than a personal need. Different continents have made their call to different ages, and people at every period have tried to rationalise in terms of imperialism, gold or conquest their feeling for an untouched land, for a country "that

> hath yet her maidenhead, never sacked, turned, nor wrought, the face of the earth hath not been torn, nor the virtue and salt of the soil spent by manurance; the graves have not been opened for gold, the mines not broken with sledges, nor their images pulled down out of their temples." (p.135)

That last is, of course, a quotation from Ralegh and it is another example of the intertextuality of travel writing – made more explicit here than is often the case – but our recognition of it should not distract from Greene's insistence on the more than personal.[14] Fascination there may be, but we have also noted the references elsewhere in the text to Nazis. Greene, who was to work for British intelligence in the war and for whom, Tim Butcher claims, this trip was a 'dress rehearsal for his later career as a spy for MI6', would have been well aware of the political tensions in Europe.[15] Schweizer suggests that 'In a sense ... cultural anxiety, imperial anxiety, and ideological anxiety are all related to one another, and it is precisely this compound of anxiety-producing elements that marks the 1930s and its popular literary genre, the travel book'.[16] We might add to this list personal anxiety, though one should view that in its social context. While it is easy retrospectively to overdo the anxiety, it does exist. Greene himself, in the passage quoted above, invites us to take a collective rather than only a personal view of things. It is more than an individual tale, even in its psychoanalytic conceit.

While a little drunk, Greene muses that the journey was worthwhile because it re-awoke 'a kind of hope in human nature. If one could get back to this bareness, simplicity, instinctive friendliness, feeling rather than thought, and start again ... [sic]' (pp.194–5). His journey backward or forward to seediness reinforces 'a sense of disappointment with what man had made out of the primitive, what he had made out of childhood' (p.228). That goes for what those in the West have made of their condition and possibilities also. He asks: 'There was cruelty enough in the interior, but had we done wisely exchanging the supernatural cruelty for our own?' (p.228).

As that question illustrates, Greene is, in part, writing a popular version of ethnographic allegory, exploiting his observations on African cultures to judge – usually unfavourably – his own. He declares the beach to be the most dangerous place for travellers in Liberia 'because its people have been touched by civilisation, have learnt to steal and lie and kill' (227). Like his modernist contemporaries, he entertains alternative points of view to the one he would be expected to hold: 'Everything ugly in Freetown was European' (37). Others before him had also found coastal areas, with their European influences, unattractive because their displays of hybridity created incongruity and contaminated what some visitors wanted kept pure, but Greene deploys the new theories of psychoanalysis to give added texture to his narrative. Perhaps its overt symbolism simply makes explicit what some would hold to be a truth of travel writing in general: that it always depends upon an actual or imposed correspondence between the traveller's inner self and the terrain that he or she covers. If Freud had helped change the conception and representation of the inner landscape one should not assume that the psychological interior is a private affair. It is shaped by the world with which it interacts. Indeed, the iconic status that Greene's text has now assumed in discussions of the inner or parallel journey testifies to our continued fascination in the twenty-first century with the primitive, even if we justify this on the grounds of a greater alertness to how the primitive is constructed. In a world of satnavs a journey without maps is more intriguing than ever.

No bank managers

Introducing *Temperamental Journeys*, a collection of essays on the *Modern Literature of Travel*, Michael Kowaleski explains that the title of his volume:

> comes from Norman Douglas's suggestion that "the reader of a good travel-book is entitled not only to an exterior voyage, to descriptions of scenery and so forth, but to an interior, a sentimental or temperamental voyage, which takes place side by side with the outer one". The most successful travel narratives generally blend outward, spatial aspects of travel (social observation and evocations of alien settings and sensibilities) with the inward, temporal forms of memory and recollection.[17]

Kowaleski warns against the danger of 'the solipsistic attraction of turning a travel account into merely a personal diary, a kind of therapist's couch' (p.9). 'For the best travel writers,' he suggests, 'the problems of perception, knowledge, and communication initiate a humbling but not paralyzing self-examination' (p.10).

The interior voyage has become so established in the years since Greene's travelogue that at the end of the twentieth century Dea Birkett and Sara Wheeler could claim that 'the writer's inner journey is the most important part – and certainly the most interesting part – of any travel book'.[18] In their view, it is one's interpretation of a place rather than the destination that matters. Creative imagination, they observe, has always been vital to successful travel writing, and 'now that writers have been everywhere, this feature – the inward-looking eye – is more important than ever. More important than anything else'.[19] In what they term (with debatable accuracy) the 'New Travel Writing', in which, they believe, fiction and creation play a larger part than before, 'it is the psychological journey that is paramount'.[20]

Whereas an early form of travel account was the pilgrimage, which combined outward observation with inner reflection, and while, as we have seen, landscapes have at later times been written of symbolically (for example, in Romantic-period writing), it is only really since the early twentieth century that protagonists have been depicted as divided in their inner selves. This, as we have noted, has its origins in Freudianism and psychoanalysis. A consequence for travel writing is the possibility it provides of a journey into the self. Nigel Leask has referred to the 'aesthetics of distance – the traveller's *desire* for the distant – which is crucial to the literary interest of travel writing'.[21] The postulation of the unconscious as a remote hinterland meant that this hidden territory could be approached in similar ways but with newly developed literary techniques and tropes. Whether this is entirely a twentieth-century phenomenon is arguable: Dennis Porter remarks in the introduction to his study of texts from the eighteenth century to the present that the main premise of his work is that 'the most interesting writers of nonfictional travel books have managed to combine explorations in the world with self-exploration'.[22] But inner voyages have become more prevalent since Freud and often make explicit reference to his ideas.

In texts like Greene's, the inner journey may be presented or interpreted as parallel to the external one, but sometimes the two intersect. For example, Wayne Koestenbaum wonders: 'What does one ever feel, visiting a city for the first time, but transference? Am I seeing Vienna, or my own phantoms?'[23] Appropriately, the catalyst for this reflection is a visit to the Freud museum. In *Skating to Antarctica* (1997), Jenny Diski combines a cruise to Antarctica in late 1995 with an inward journey into her troubled past. The whiteness of the Antarctic complements the wish for blankness, for whiteout that she experienced during periods of depression in her adolescence and early adulthood. The austerity that Diski craves is symptomatic of a type of quest often associated with travel: for the discovery of a self unencumbered by obtrusive materialism.

According to Geoffrey Moorhouse, 'In making the double journey, the trick is to get the balance right between the reality of events, and the author's imaginative response to them'.[24] He gives as examples Sara Wheeler's book *Terra Incognita* (1996) and as an unsurpassed case, Peter Matthiessen's *The Snow Leopard* (1978), which we examined in Chapter 6. Moorhouse's reference to the interior is more to the imagination than to the psychological, but both reside within, if in response to external stimuli.

Of course, the inner space, like the outer world, is gendered. Mary Morris, who has noticed the lack of a picaresque tradition among women novelists, has linked this with the paucity of opportunities allowed women to journey and observes that 'Denied the freedom to roam outside themselves, women turned inward, into their emotions.'[25] For Morris, 'Because of the way women have cultivated their inner lives, a journey often becomes a dialogue between the inner and the outer, between our emotional necessity and the reality of the external world'.[26] Ironically, Morris's comments are inspired by an observation in male author Henry Miller's *The Colossus of Maroussi* (1941) that all voyages are inward and the most difficult are made without moving. This, Morris asserts, sums up the inner dialogue felt by women who travel.

In Japan, the gay writer Mitch Cullen 'began sensing in the Japanese something that I felt was lacking in myself: a kind of wide, personal inward space – a place where the self could take refuge when faced with so many people and so little outward space'.[27] Contrasting this with Americans, especially those like himself from the desert Southwest, whose 'sense of inward space is usually determined by the amount of outward space that is available to us', Cullin writes: 'I craved for such space inside myself – rather than the tangled, narrow confines of my psyche – and I believed I might discover it somewhere along my travels'.[28]

In the discussion of *Journey Without Maps*, we read about Greene's sense of having come home when he was in Liberia; of having returned to a racial and personal childhood from which one has grown up and moved away. A similar feeling is expressed by Sara Wheeler in a travel book written sixty years later: 'In some bizarre way I had an atavistic sense that I had come home' (p.28). The scene of Wheeler's homecoming is not Liberia but Antarctica. Her encounter is with a very different land: one that has no indigenous human inhabitants or culture, yet it affords her, no less than West Africa did Greene, the experience – or at least the metaphor – of an interior journey. Wheeler's destination is 'the perfect *tabula rasa*', not only because of its barren landscape (it is, she points out, the highest, driest, coldest and windiest continent), but because, with international treaties protecting it from exploitation and with international scientific cooperation, it 'blunts the edges of nationality'. Other facts about Antarctica that appeal to Wheeler are that 'nobody owns it' (p.2) and 'The landscape drew my thoughts away from worldly things, away from the thousand mechanical details of my outward life' (p.68). Like Matthiessen in Nepal, she seeks an escape from the materialism of her own society. At her destination there will be 'No cities, no bank managers, no pram in the hall' (p.1). Quoting Ernest Shackleton on Antarctica as metaphor ('We all have our own White South') she admits that the continent was, and remains, 'a space of the imagination' for her (p.1). Despite their very different conditions, West Africa and Antarctica perform similar functions in Greene's and Wheeler's narratives. Each offers its visitor a blank space onto which preconceptions, fears and desires are projected. Each reflects something of the visitor's own state. In both cases, as in Matthiessen's *The Snow Leopard*, the removal from the clutter of materialist society allows a view of a more essential existence. Both Greene and Wheeler reach this perception through the conceit of an inner journey: the former, psychological; the latter, spiritual. In the Antarctic, 'loosed from my cultural moorings, I could find the space to look for the higher power, whatever it was, that loomed over the snowfields' (p.68). Writing in an age that is often said to be more secular, Wheeler's narrative has its epiphany in the spiritual: 'I called what I sensed there God ... but you could give it many names. It was more straightforward for me than it had been for some, as I brought faith with me' (p.162). Wheeler remarks of her attitude towards and dialogue with God that 'The inner journey, like my route on the ice, was not a linear one. It was an uncharted meandering descent through layers and layers of consciousness, and I was intermittently tossed backwards or sideways like a diver in a current' (p.163). Although she and Greene both recall their younger selves, they do not, despite Wheeler's account of the process, disrupt linear narrative to the extent of switching the timeframe of their stories: memories are clearly presented as such and embedded in the narrative present.

Near the end of her residence in Antarctica, Wheeler dreams vividly, without panic, fear or sadness, of her death at home. Awake, she recalls conversations with a friend who had recently become a Buddhist: 'I realised that my fear of losing my faith was based on another, more primeval fear. It was my own death that was haunting me, of course. Faith enabled me to cope with the concept of mortality, but if I lost faith, how would I live with the treacherous knowledge that I was going to die?' (p.288).

She had avoided facing this question. Unlike Buddhism, 'western culture strives to divert these thoughts and mask the concept of mortality so we don't have to confront it' (p.288). She suggests that if not addressed, it will resurface elsewhere, 'unresolved and in disguise' (p.289), perhaps through alcohol abuse. Like many others before her and since, she uses the distance she has gained from her homeland to reflect on and criticise its repressive culture. In the 'cultural void', the 'space in the imagination' of Antarctica, she is 'forced to begin confronting a fear I had barely acknowledged. Despite everything I had gone through to get where I was – the years of preparation and anxiety – it seemed to me then that the external journey meant nothing at all' (p.288). It is, she implies, the interior journey that matters. Read alongside *Journey Without Maps*, Wheeler's book shows that whatever the clime, the traveller's self-contemplation proceeds regardless. The particularities of landscape or culture may affect the type of symbol employed to advance the theme, but the similarities of subject outweigh the difference of location.

Whereas Diski and Wheeler utilise the idea of the whiteness and the emptiness of Antarctica to convey the theme of a blank space on which they can project their inner consciousness, Greene's use of Africa reminds us that Freud's notion of the unconscious itself deploys racial imagery. In Chapter 8, we will see that postcolonial writers have had to contend with the legacy of such symbolic constructions.

Chapter 8

Travelling b(l)ack

My sympathies were with the pagans.
Richard Wright[1]

Accounts of great travels never included black people, so I had no role models.
Colleen J. McElroy[2]

Earlier chapters have referred to the widespread contemporary critical view that, 'By producing knowledge about the other and circulating colonial stereotypes, travel writing is implicated in the reproduction of colonialism',[3] an argument that leads some critics to 'consider the travelogue an essentially imperialist mode of representation'.[4] The present chapter will examine some of the consequences of, and challenges to, the colonial legacy.

Writing at the end of the twentieth century, Patrick Holland and Graham Huggan stated: 'Travel writing today is beginning to take on a multicultural ethos. It is becoming increasingly difficult to justify the traveler's "one-way" vision – his or her perception, regulated from the imagined safety of the metropolis, of people, places, and cultures seen as alien or remote'.[5] We saw in Chapter 5 that modernism helped introduce into travel literature an appreciation of other perspectives, just as it did in other cultural forms. The limitations of a single point of view have been apparent for many years. Barbara Korte rightly acknowledges that 'Reversing the colonizer's direction of travel ... is a travel pattern encountered long before the emergence of postcolonialism',[6] although the practice predates by centuries the examples given by Korte.[7] That said, diasporic movement, decolonisation and postcolonialism have undermined in a more concentrated way the claims to universal authority of a white, metropolitan standpoint. In addition, postcolonial studies of travel writing have grown more nuanced, going beyond crude models of domination to take into account local resistance and what Mary Louise Pratt calls transculturation. Pratt explains:

> Ethnographers have used this term to describe how subordinated or marginal groups select and invent from materials transmitted to them

> by a dominant or metropolitan culture.... While subjugated peoples cannot readily control what emanates from the dominant culture, they do determine to varying extents what they absorb into their own, and what they use it for. Transculturation is a phenomenon of the contact zone.[8]

The critical emphasis is increasingly on agency rather than oppression; on indigenous peoples' ability to adapt to the culture of the colonisers rather than being supine before it or crushed by it. Introducing a collection of essays on travel writing and empire, Steve Clark explains that 'Empire is the common preoccupation of the essays in this volume, but their analyses seek to resist the reduction of cross-cultural encounter to simple relations of domination and subordination'.[9] In a survey of travel writing theory, Mary Baine Campbell has proclaimed it 'an important advance to realise that ... the power of colonial masters was not as absolute or deracinating as the masters themselves, or even some of their colonial descendants, believed'.[10] Going further, the editors of a recent collection of essays on postcolonial travel writing announce their intention to extend Holland and Huggan's "countertravelers" paradigm 'by arguing that postcolonial travel writing is not just oppositional or a "writing back"; it offers frames of reference that exist outside the boundaries of European knowledge production'.[11] A striking example of this is Vikram Seth's opening to the brief, nine-line introduction to his travel book *From Heaven Lake*: 'I am an Indian, and lived in China as a student at Nanjing University from 1980–82. In the summer of 1981 I returned home to Delhi via Tibet and Nepal'.[12] Both the declaration of identity and the information on his itinerary seem to bypass the West completely. Yet the first two lines of his Acknowledgements express his gratitude to Stanford University and the Ford Foundation, 'who supported me in China for two years'.[13] The potential contradiction between Seth's narrative distance from the West and his indebtedness to U.S. institutions (as well as, of course, to the original publisher of the book, Chatto and Windus) symbolises one of the main dilemmas facing postcolonial travel writers: how far can they free themselves from, or modify for their own purposes, the structures (both socio-economic and literary) that they are seeking to reject, challenge or circumvent?

This chapter will focus on narratives of reverse travel from the descendants of colonised subjects. There are earlier accounts of journeys to Europe from beyond its borders, and of travel by non-whites outside Europe, but the discussion in the present chapter will be on postcolonial travel texts rather than their precursors, and it will concentrate in the main on two examples. A principal investigation will be into whether travel narratives that 'write back' to the so-called metropolitan centre change the literary conventions of the models with which they are in dialogue, as well as their perspectives, or whether they continue to operate within the same parameters as them. In this inquiry we shall be mindful of Korte's warning that:

> Proclaiming a *tradition* of inflected or inverted travelogues seems to be wishful thinking. To date, no postcolonial travel writer has established an entirely new line of the travel account. Nevertheless, postcolonial travellers – like women travellers – have certainly developed "other" *perspectives* which turn their texts, in the words of Mary Louise Pratt ... into vehicles for "transculturation" from the colonies to the metropolis. In a few instances, writers have also consciously reversed canonized patterns of travel.[14]

Before we move on to consider our examples, we ought to note the customary caution about the use of the label postcolonial. There have been many arguments over the problems and pitfalls of the term. Edwards and Graulund even 'ask if "the postcolonial" has become too embedded in European and North American institutions (particularly universities) for it to be an effective political and analytical frame of reference'.[15] They justify their own use of it on the grounds that it 'has always been – and will continue to be – an unstable and contested critical term'; that it contributes to 'lively and productive scholarly debate' and 'imparts potential for dislocation, disjuncture and even rupture when it is combined with a genre – travel writing – that has been harshly critiqued within postcolonial circles'. They aim to 'shake the reader's complacency'.[16] Korte warns that: 'As an umbrella term, "postcolonialism" blurs important distinctions between former colonies ... or between postcolonial cultures now located in the so-called Third and those in the First World. [It] also disguises the problematic relationship between dominant and subaltern groups within postcolonial societies themselves'.[17] Korte observes that these issues of terminology 'pose considerable problems for a definition of postcolonial travel writing'; indeed, she herself excludes the United States. Her observation that 'the borderline between the colonial and the postcolonial condition is fluid' may be extended to complement the fluidity of travel writing itself.[18] We should also take care not to bracket all postcolonial travel together. In Korte's words, 'The different cultures from which postcolonial travellers emerge all have their own special outlooks and traditions of travel. The conditions of postcolonial travel change significantly even within a single country'. Furthermore, individual postcolonial travellers will have different attitudes, ranging 'from allegiance to the old mother country to open critique of imperialism and its consequences, or, most recently, even to a globalized perspective'.[19] Thus, although the discussion that follows inevitably proceeds from observations on individual texts to general remarks, these are meant to be neither prescriptive nor universal.

An uneasy member of the western world

Richard Wright's *Black Power: A Record of Reactions in a Land of Pathos* (1954), described by the editor of a reprint issued half a century later as 'one of the richest texts in the tradition of travel literature',[20] is a narrative produced on the cusp of independence. One of the most prominent of African-American authors, best known for his collection of short stories, *Uncle Tom's Children* (1938), his autobiographical *Black Boy* (1945) and his novel *Native Son* (1940), Wright had been a member of the Communist Party from 1932–44, and since 1946 had lived in France. *Black Power* records his two-and-a-half month trip to the British colony of the Gold Coast in 1953 at the time of Prime Minister Kwame Nkrumah's campaign for self-government. The colony would be granted independence as Ghana four years later. Wright observes that during his own lifetime, 'some nations have disappeared and new ones have risen to take their places' (p.xxxv).

Wright's text, the narrative of his first visit to Africa, illustrates the complexity of colonialism. Its author-narrator cannot identify fully with the Africans or with his American compatriots. *Black Power* is neither a celebratory narrative of a return to one's roots nor an exercise in Western superiority. Instead, Wright employs the structures of travel writing to create a space in which he reinforces his individuality by distinguishing himself from Africans, from Americans and, above all, from the British. Whereas travel writing, as we have seen, has long been a means by which the self has been defined or reaffirmed against the Other, Wright uses the genre for more complicated manoeuvres. Unable fully to identify himself with coloniser or colonised, he observes and comments from a position he attempts to make and hold for himself. As he does so, *Black Power* preserves the individualistic quality of twentieth-century travel writing. Wright describes himself as an 'uneasy member' of the Western world (p.xxxvi) and refers to 'Five hundred years of European barbarism' in Africa (p.71).

Contemplating the trip, which has been suggested by Dorothy Padmore (wife of Caribbean writer George Padmore), Wright muses: 'I am an African! I'm of African descent.... Yet I'd never seen Africa; I'd never really known any Africans; I'd hardly ever thought of Africa' (p.4). He wonders: 'Being of African descent, would I be able to feel and know something about Africa on the basis of a common "racial" heritage?' Considering whether the centuries that have passed since his ancestor(s) departed Africa have imposed an unbridgeable psychological distance between himself and black Africans, he asks himself: '*But, am I African?*' (p.4, emphasis in original). This is not a straightforward account of self-discovery.

Wright's text is remarkable for its refusal of either an easy identification with or a straightforward rejection of the people from the area where his forebear(s) may have originated. The form of the travel book – especially its twentieth-century focus on the character of the protagonist – lends itself to his individual predicament and complements the interest in existentialism that Wright had increasingly shown after his movement away from Marxism. Amritjit Singh notices this stance when he notes that 'Wright positions himself as an interested outsider, as an *American* of African descent, as an African American shaped by his early experiences in the deep South, but even more, as an independent intellectual committed to realizing basic freedoms and amenities for all, regardless of ideology and culture' (p.xii). Once in the Gold Coast, Wright 'knew that I'd never feel an identification with Africans on a "racial" basis' (p.242).

Statements such as 'I'm of African descent and I'm in the midst of Africans, yet I cannot tell what they are thinking and feeling' (p.151) serve two main purposes. First, they emphasise Wright's individuality; second, they depart from Westerners' confident pronouncements on Africa. By admitting to failures of interpretation – especially when there is sentimental and political pressure on him to recognise affinity and kinship with Black Africans – Wright is undermining the traditional authority of the travel book. (He replaces this with some confident generalisations of his own, but ones that signal his apartness.) He is disorientated and unsettled by his experiences: he tells Nkrumah's secretary, '"I feel strange; I see and hear so much that I don't understand..."' (p.51); he is uneasy about being addressed as 'Massa' by servants, whose pidgin English he resents and makes him shudder (pp.52–3); his own American English is not easily understood by the people who are more used to hearing British English (p.75); he finds that 'the African's time sense was not like our own' (p.192), the use of the plural pronoun placing himself here firmly in and of the West; and he is frustrated at being treated by some Africans as an outsider and yet at several points (e.g. pp.140, 144), he confesses his inability to understand them. In short, 'being obviously of African descent, I looked like the Africans, but I had only to walk upon a scene and my difference at once declared itself without a word being spoken. Over and above these liabilities, I had a background steeped in Communism, yet I was no Communist' (p.152).

Despite all this and the 'dense illiteracy and the astonishing oral tradition [that] ... has erected a psychological distance between the African and the Western world and has made it increasingly difficult for the African to be known' (p.129), Wright's sympathies are 'with the pagans' (p.148). He is critical of missionaries and their legacy, and he is outspoken against the impact on Africans of British conduct and policy: 'They [the Africans] were uncertain, uneasy, nervous, split deep within themselves. I wondered if the British were sensitive enough to know what they had done to these people? Crimes have been committed in this world of so vast a nature that they have never been recorded in any criminal code' (p.115).

Indeed, in the conclusion to his book, a letter to Prime Minister Kwame Nkrumah, Wright uses Britain as the Other that allows him to reconcile the African and American. The means by which he achieves this emphasise common political cause over racial identity: 'Your fight has been fought before. I am an American and my country too was once a colony of England' (p.393). Wright has adapted the form of the travel text for an exploration and renegotiation of his identity, and this is achieved at the moral and political expense of Britain.

Former slaves wander freely

One of the best-known modern examples of a postcolonial travelogue is Caryl Phillips's *The European Tribe* (1987). Phillips – already a prominent playwright and novelist when he published the book (and on whom Wright was an influence) – arrived in Britain with his family from St. Kitts when he was just a few weeks old. In his own words, he 'grew up riddled with the cultural confusions of being black and British'.[21] He describes his book – in which, Korte points out, he 'mimics the pattern of the Grand Tour'[22] – as:

> [A] narrative in the form of a notebook in which I have jotted various thoughts about a Europe I feel both of and not of. Its impetus was provided by nearly a year's wandering from Europe's closest neighbour, Morocco, to her furthest flung capital, Moscow.
>
> I am not the first writer of fiction to find that the tension between myself and my environment is so urgently felt that the fictional mould seems too delicate a vessel to hold it. (p.xiii)

Phillips's statement contains two very important ideas. First, the feeling both part of and excluded from Europe is a condition that is shared by many from former colonies. At the same time, this paradoxically forces an impression of individuality, of not fully belonging, that suits very well the individual ethos of contemporary travel writing.[23] Second, the comment on form suggests that travel writing is a more robust genre than the novel for the expression of the tension between identity and environment. It may even be that the individualism of contemporary travel writing offers the resolution to 'the contradiction of feeling British, while being constantly told in many subtle and unsubtle ways that I did not belong' (p.9). Phillips decides that, 'A large part of finding out who I was, and what I was doing here, would inevitably mean having to understand the Europeans' (p.9).

Phillips's travels in Europe not only mimic or revise the Grand Tour; they put the direction of the colonising gaze in reverse. In doing so, Phillips grants himself the moral authority to pass judgement on the culture and conduct of white Europe. Thus, he criticises British tourists in Spain and the Caribbean for their drunkenness, vandalism, lewdness and lack of respect for their hosts (though he also points out the complicity of Spaniards for 'displaying an alarming lack of taste in their frantic scramble for the English pound') (p.37). France he finds 'proud, modern, aloof and full of self-importance' (p.56). In the Netherlands, 'the lifestyles of Dutch black people ... made me immediately question the appropriateness of the label "liberal".... I began to think that "liberal" meant not tackling drugs and pornography; that being the case, it might also mean not tackling racism' (p.67). In Germany, he wants to escape Munich after just eighteen hours. Applying an adjective that shows that national stereotypes are not the sole preserve of colonial travellers, he tells us: 'The cold Germanic faces snapped round in the street to look at me. They gazed as though I had just committed an awful crime, or was about to cannibalize a small child' (p.83). But as will African American writer Colleen J. McElroy on her later travels to Eastern Europe, Phillips has to come to terms with the fact that his economic status prevents a shared identification with other black people.[24] In East Berlin he senses that his being from the West was as important, in locals' eyes, as his blackness. Unlike them, he has the means to escape. He sees few black people there. Most of those that he does are students but his nodded greetings are often rebuffed: 'It hurt, and after three days in East Berlin I was beginning to feel very detached from the West. That the stares of hostility were motivated as much by envy as by racial antagonism did little to ease my discomfort' (p.88).

After nearly a year, Phillips returns to a Britain in recession, its people fearful of the future. Britain appears even more 'exclusive in its attitude' towards him (p.119). The transition from empire to commonwealth to common market is causing the nation much anguish and provoking a painful questioning of its status. For some, high up in government, 'it is useful to imagine that Empire still exists, in order that they may occasionally fan nationalistic pride and galvanize the nation, in war if necessary' (p.120). Phillips goes on, having assumed the authority to be able to tell the former imperial power about itself: 'Britain ... can no longer afford to think of herself as an impenetrable island. Her colonial legacy has returned to haunt her' (p.120). He insists that for Britain and Western Europe the 'days of imperialistic glory' are over. The former slaves wander freely among the rubble of Europe's formerly all-powerful cities (p.120)'. The United States now has economic, political and cultural power over Europe, leaving the latter 'with only the role of a moral leader to play' (p.120).

In acting as commentator on the state of Europe, including Britain, Phillips's analysis of its politics in relation to its social and economic condition seems no less applicable now. Phillips finds a resurgence of right-wing extremism, economic conditions being ripe for it, and he observes that Britain in particular is 'playing a very dangerous game. Riots continue to happen, perpetrated by British people. The discontented are not immigrants, as 40 per cent of the black population in Britain was born here. The attempts of politicians and the media to ignore the violence of feeling, while discussing 'integration', 'racial harmony', and 'multiculturalism', only serves to aggravate the situation' (p.122).

Phillips's reference to back people as 'we' and white Europeans as 'you' (e.g., p.128), an address that breaks sharply from the traditions of travel writing in which there is usually an assumed commonality between author and audience, can be disorientating to white readers. The use of the second person adds to the sense of confrontation: the (white) European gaze is directed back at itself. White readers are often discomfited by this. Carl Thompson notes that Phillips's tone is 'frequently angry and denunciatory as [he] seeks to make European readers appreciate how they themselves exhibit the tribalism which is routinely attributed to supposedly more backward cultures'. Thompson also observes that Phillips makes European readers 'appreciate what it is like to be the object of the travel writer's gaze' and understand what it is like to be represented partially (in both senses of the word). In that sense, Phillips is moulding the form of the travelogue for his own revisionist purposes, reversing the traditional perspective, but it remains a vehicle for individual expression achieved against Others. Thompson's conclusion that '*The European Tribe* is arguably both a continuation yet also a subversion of the Western travel writing tradition'[25] matches my own judgement on Black British writer Gary Younge's *No Place Like Home* and on African American travel writing.[26] Phillips's and Younge's texts invert the familiar positions and power relationships of the travel narrative but both struggle to free themselves from its constraints.

A dog on wheels

Explaining how a 'tribal man' like himself got from a forest village in Central India to the city of London, the Gond artist Bhajju Shyam tells us that he made the journey from his home of Patangarh because he was invited to decorate the walls of an Indian restaurant in Islington.[27] Shyam spent two months painting murals at the restaurant at the invitation of designer Rajeev Sethi.[28] He says of his feelings at the prospect of the trip that although he was happy on the outside, he was scared in his soul, thinking he might never see his family and home again.

In his description and visualisation of his train journey to Delhi, which lasted a whole day and a night, Shyam reveals a mode of perception and representation quite different from what readers of western travelogues will be used to. He exclaims: 'Though my body was sitting there, my mind had jumped beyond the train, beyond Delhi ... I was flying, and bright birds from all over the world were carrying me through the air, saying "Come to my country!" No, come to mine!"'

In his accompanying painting, 'Journey of the Mind' (reproduced on the cover of the present volume), he shows himself, dominating the page, striding above a small train of six carriages on a winding track. He has a suitcase in his right hand and coloured birds above and behind him fly in his direction. He explains that the train was not important to him and so he has drawn it small:

> This is the Gond way of thinking and painting – what is important should get more space. We are not interested in reality – only in how things are imagined in the mind, and our paintings try to show what is in the mind's eye. So I am much bigger than the train, and I have drawn my thoughts like birds, that are carrying me higher and tugging me in all sorts of new directions. My suitcase is the only heavy thing I have.

Shyam finds the airport more menacing than he expected, like a jail or a police station. It is somewhere he has to say goodbye to family and friends and in which he is going to be swallowed up and spat out. Never having flown before, and this occasion being at night, he learns in response to the question that he asks the man sitting beside him in a row of seats in a 'sort of long waiting room', that he is actually inside the plane. This is a sinister, disorientating place:

> The airport stuck in my mind as a huge bird of prey. An eagle that swallows humans who line up to be let inside like insects outside a termite hill. The airport is also a place of documents, stamps and seals. So I have combined all my images and put my bird of prey inside like a stamp, like the ones in my passport. Meaning to say – you can only fly if the eagle gives you permission.

Shyam copes by familiarising and domesticating it. He paints the plane as a colourful elephant – what we might call his version of a jumbo jet (Figure 1). Because the elephant is the heaviest animal he has seen, it came to his mind

Figure 1. 'The Miracle of Flight', from Bhajju Shyam, *The London Jungle Book* (London: Tara Publishing in association with the Museum of London, 2004). Reproduced with kind permission of the artist and publisher.

when he painted the aircraft. To Shyam, 'a plane taking off is as much of a miracle as an elephant flying'. He paints the trees upside down in the sky, with clouds beneath, because 'flying turned my world upside-down'. In representing through the known that which is strange to him, he does as all travellers do, but more overtly because visually. He incorporates the unfamiliar into his world.

He does the same with England itself when he sees it from far above for the first time. It does not look like anything he has imagined. It 'was more like a design, a pattern in bright, glowing green. I was going to a country that looked like a sari!' One of his paintings, titled 'England is an Emerald Sari', shows this impression, with fish and turtles around the country, in keeping with the Gond method of indicating water, to show that Britain is an island. As the plane descends, the pattern disappears and Shyam distinguishes features on the ground. Once he has landed he is struck by how different it is from India: the officials are friendly; people stand in neat lines; and there is quiet. The most important sign of difference, he observes, is that he does not understand anything the people are saying. Everyone he sees is a foreigner. He has seen foreigners before, when they visited his village to look at paintings, but now he realises there has been a strange development. His colour is different and his language has been taken away from him: 'I myself had become a foreigner!' Shyam's reaction differs from that of many Western visitors to other countries, including his own: rather than regarding the locals as the foreigners and himself as the norm, he recognises that he is the stranger.

In London, one of the most wonderful things Shyam sees is the underground. It is something that he says he will never forget, 'this idea of snuggling your way through the earth'. With the plane having flown him above the clouds and trains carrying him deep under the earth, his world has been turned 'truly upside-down!' Shyam is stimulated and excited by his new surroundings. Again, his painting melds his own culture and the one he finds in England. Combining London's underground with Gond beliefs about 'another world below this one', he uses snakes to represent the routes of the trains, and spiders sitting on their webs to indicate the stations.

Shyam's anthropomorphism of mechanised transport extends to buses, too. The number 30 bus that for the two months of his stay takes him from his accommodation in King's Cross to the restaurant in Islington becomes a reliable friend. He paints it as a dog on wheels because, 'like a dog, it was ... faithful and loyal'. It will take care of him, just like the dogs that guide the Gond through the forests.

A common complaint by British travellers before the twentieth century is that so-called primitive societies have no concept of time. Shyam reverses this, noticing (rather than condemning) the English obsession with it and that everyone is always checking their watches. By contrast, although he has a watch too, his 'symbol of time is still the Gond one – a rooster'. His painting of Big Ben combines the London and Gond symbols of time. He makes Big Ben's dial the eye of the rooster, because Big Ben seems to him 'like a big eye, forever watching over London, reminding people of the time'.

After Shyam has finished painting the walls of the restaurant he has a few days spare in which to see some tourist sights before he returns home. Among the places he visits are the British Museum, where, he is told, 'the British store the treasures they took from all over the world'.

Figure 2. 'The Bard of Travel', from Bhajju Shyam, *The London Jungle Book* (London: Tara Publishing in association with the Museum of London, 2004). Reproduced with kind permission of the artist and publisher.

Back in India, on the way home to his village and for ten days afterwards, Shyam finds himself speaking of nothing but London. Friends and enemies alike come to hear his stories. His travel experience has given him a new role and everyone listens to him: 'Now I had become the bard'. In the accompanying picture, 'The Bard of Travel' (Figure 2), Shyam paints himself as 'the "Bhujrukh", the traditional bard of the Gonds who remembers and re-tells all our myths and songs'. He paints his suitcase beside him, 'because it is this that has made me the bard'. In the top left of the painting he represents the moon as an underground sign. Across the middle of it he has written 'London' in

Hindi. The image is a fascinating fusion of nature and culture and it has Shyam appropriating a symbol of and from the heart of the metropolis as he brings it back to his village home. There is a reversal here of the process that occurs so often in earlier texts in which artefacts are removed from colonial spaces to the imperial centre.

The publishers of Tara Books, Sirish Rao and Gita Wolf, provide an afterword (although not labelling it as such), headed 'How London became a Jungle'. In it they repeat the refrain from standard commentaries that as travel has become commonplace and 'The vast unknown has shrunk', so the elements of danger and wonder have diminished. They find an antidote in the existence of: 'some unlikely travellers who can bring a freshness to familiar sights. Because they have never had the privilege to travel, they still carry in them the ancient ability to marvel at the new'.

Rao and Wolf's ascription of that facility to Shyam unwittingly indicates the problem they face. On the one hand, Shyam is at risk of being presented as an exotic figure who inhabits a different (and past) time zone from his readers who may impose on him what Johannes Fabian describes as 'the denial of coevalness';[29] on the other hand, Rao and Wolf do draw attention to the material circumstances that make Shyam's an important trip: 'He belongs to one of the poorest and most marginalized sections of society'.

Not only is Shyam's travelogue an example of a postcolonial 'writing back'; the editors conceive of it as such. They note that his people had been the object of study by anthropologists, most notably Verrier Elwin (1902–64), who 'lived among the Gonds, married a Gond woman, and wrote several books about the tribe'. Shyam, whose grandfather was Elwin's manservant, grew up with stories of the anthropologist. 'And now, by a quirk of fate, here was an opportunity for Bhajju to form his impressions about Elwin's homeland.' The anthropological subject has turned the scrutiny around. Rao and Wolf inform readers that getting Shyam's words down presented little difficulty but that for him to paint his view of London in Gond style required a radical departure from the art he was used to producing. They point out that Gond art:

> is by no means a timeless, ageless quantity, and speaking to Gond artists themselves, there is a sense that things must have changed and evolved within the tradition as we know it now. The important thing is to resist the temptation to essentialise the Gond imagination as the romantic other of our modern consciousness.

This is an important refusal of the urge to locate in the 'primitive' the repository of values that critics of and those working within post-industrial society feel have been lost. It is also a corrective to the fallacy that so-called traditional societies never change. As an example of the 'very complex way in which change is accommodated into older ways of being', Rao and Wolf cite the case of a number of Gond artists who, over the past two decades, have, like Shyam himself, moved to Bhopal, the capital of their state of Madhya Pradesh, to pursue opportunities: 'They now sell their work commercially, painting on paper or canvas, using drawing pens and acrylic paints. Their palette has expanded from the four earth colours they produced in the village, to the entire range of commercial paints'.

Rao and Wolf explain to us that the *London Jungle Book* meant that Shyam needed to 'develop a new visual language, which neither broke with the past, nor stayed within the known'. They report his asking them to tell him what symbols are important to Londoners so that he can use them, and, because they are writers, he asks them to 'bring out what I want to say. I need to work with you'. In addition, 'my story doesn't go in a straight line, saying I did this first, then that, then that happened'. They decide that Shyam should stay with them so that they could work on the project together, which they do, constructing the narrative over several months and reassuring him that it did not have to be a linear tale. Instead: 'He could tell his story in the manner of Gond paintings, using just the main incidents and the symbols that stuck in his mind'. They write down the story that he tells them in Hindi, 'and helped him isolate and conceptualise those parts of it that he could translate into images. Together, we tried to make connections between Gond mythology and what Bhajju was saying about London. Bhajju enjoyed the process of working together, of collective brainstorming and examining things that were almost subconscious for him'.

Non-linearity and collaboration or joint-authorship are two elements that contribute to the postcolonial nature of the text. The break from linearity is often associated with postmodernism and postcolonialism. It precedes both, of course, but is characteristic of postcolonial writing. Collaboration, too, has been used as a way of countering the perceived monologism of colonial travel writing.[30] Rao and Wolf are well aware of the models and conventions they are overturning:

> As the project came to a close, we realized that it had surpassed its original intent and was in fact doing something quite historical. In a modest and gentle manner, it had actually managed to reverse the anthropological gaze. We decided to call it *The London Jungle Book* for the resonance it has, not only with Bhajju's own view of London as a bestiary, but also for its ironical connection with Kipling's classic account of life in the Indian jungle.

The editors suggest that Shyam's story 'touches on many profound aspects of the act of travel itself'. They see his genial and easy-going character as making an important contribution. Part of his personality is his reluctance to criticise England. This reticence, they explain, comes from 'a culture of courtesy and decorum … that refrains from making negative comments, especially as a guest'. They view this as a welcome departure from the dominant voice of travel accounts: 'Too much travel writing converts the difference and newness of another place into a source of mirth or irritation. Bhajju, on the other hand, is a humble and open voyager, willing to show his vulnerability. He does not want to offend, or impress his taste on the world he is going to'.

Rao and Wolf inform us that the text of *The London Jungle Book* is edited from the 'various versions' Shyam has told them of his story. They 'have tried to keep his narrative in the form of the pithy vignettes and sharp one-liners that are characteristic of his storytelling style'. They acknowledge that they have not found it easy to retain Shyam's voice in translation, 'as is the case with any translation, especially from the oral', but they hope that they have preserved his 'special flavour' and that his comments on his paintings will acquaint interested readers with Gond aesthetics. Against this is the risk that all such editors face: of appearing to frame their subject. They must aim to ensure that the subject's voice is heard without being overly compromised or distorted.

I have dwelt on *The London Jungle Book* rather than on some of the better-known travel texts by more familiar authors from the postcolonial canon for a number of reasons. First, it is a little-discussed text that deserves greater attention. Second, it literally makes visible many of the themes central to this chapter and to the present volume. These include reverse travel, transculturation, translation and representation of the Other – complicated in this case by the negotiation between centre and margin within India; that is, by Shyam and his editors and publisher. There is also the dilemma facing many postcolonial works: that their force may be weakened through being consumed as exotic.

In its discussion of postcolonial travel writing, this chapter has concentrated on three examples of what Thompson has described as the 'surge' in recent decades of 'travelogues written by individuals from formerly colonised cultures, or alternatively, by Western travellers who are the descendants of formerly subject, "subaltern" peoples'.[31] That proliferation is vital and to be welcomed, but Holland and Huggan caution against an unthinking response to it: 'In a postcolonial era, "otherness" is a profitable business, even if the exotica it throws up might look very different in kind from those of earlier times and places'. The profit to be made from meeting the market for the voice of the Other means that 'Postcolonial travel writers, in this context, are necessarily embattled: they must struggle to match their political views with a genre that is in many ways antithetical to them – a genre that manufactures "otherness" even as it claims to demystify it'.[32]

Chapter 8 has discussed three different examples of Britain being Othered. Chapter 9 turns to women's and gay travel writing, which face similar problems of appropriation, complicated, as we shall see, by arguments over the degree to which women travellers are complicit with or free from the dominant ideology of the society from which they journey.

Chapter 9

Gender and sexuality

We've had a surfeit of willies in the jungle.
Dea Birkett and Sara Wheeler[1]

Being gay in a straight world, even in a hypothetically permissive straight world, is so alienating that the only way to avoid depression is through the assertion of one's own gay identity.
Edmund White[2]

Women's travel writing: Critical debates

Chapter 8 showed how postcolonial studies have changed our understanding of travel writing. Gender studies, incorporating theories of feminism, masculinity and sexuality have similarly affected our reading of travel narratives: not only the ways in which we read texts, but the range of texts that we read. In the last quarter of the twentieth century in particular, the growing interest in women's writing was accompanied by the initiatives of feminist publishing houses such as Virago that led to the recuperation of neglected narratives by women travellers, making them more accessible to general readers and scholars alike.[3] The recovery of women's travel writing helped give modern-day readers a more accurate sense of women's participation in travel. Virago's reprints, especially, have reached a cross-over audience and are also largely responsible for the subsequent wave of scholarly commentary on Mary Kingsley, who travelled in West Africa and the Congo in the late nineteenth century.[4] Nevertheless, the sense of the field being dominated by men continues, and, as we saw is the case with Black writers, has resulted in women having to chart their own path. 'We've had a surfeit of willies in the jungle', protest Dea Birkett and Sara Wheeler, introducing their collection of new women's travel writing in the late 1990s.[5] There were, Birkett and Wheeler remember, few role models when they began travel writing a decade previously, but now 'we're there – and each year a few more join the band of what we call the Amazonians'.[6] Their proud adoption of a name long associated with a legendary threat to civilisation (and that features, too, in Ralegh's *Discoverie*) is typical of the overturning of conventional values that characterises feminist and postcolonial thought.

The new attention to women's travel accounts has not resulted in a consensus on how best to read them; especially on whether and how they differ from men's. Some travel writers and critics are certain that women observe details inaccessible to or overlooked by men. Many proponents of this view also contend that women are more likely than men to exhibit empathy with colonised peoples. By way of illustration, consider African American writer Colleen J. McElroy's remark: 'When I have joined women in such places as Japan, Greece, Vietnam and Jordan, I have understood the tone, the social ramifications, without having understood every word. And when I presented my poems, I felt part of a larger, universal group'.[7]

McElroy's poetry and prose attest to the impossibility of an easy identification with other members of the African diaspora on essentialist grounds of 'race' or origin. Her awareness of her economically privileged position as a U.S. citizen prevents any naive celebration of a common identity with other Black people in, for example, Eastern Europe, Madagascar and Australia. Her physical resemblance to some of the Blacks whom she meets overseas is strong enough to suggest direct kinship but does not, in her view, erode the economic and cultural differences between them. McElroy's comments on feeling herself part of a group with Black people of other nations and on having an understanding that goes beyond language do not amount to a romanticised assertion of a full, shared identity with the women she encounters elsewhere.[8] She insists that '[a] male traveller will not have the same kind of experience that a female will have'. She points to the consequences for women of men's generalising on the basis of their own perspective: 'There is a certain series of travel books in which the writer makes assumptions about the people who are going to travel and those assumptions do not fit me. Male writers in particular don't understand this'.[9] The implication is that men present their travels and writings in ways that exclude women and yet purport to speak for them. As is the case with postcolonial travellers, women travel writers face the challenge both of making their voice heard and of developing literary models for that purpose.

Despite the importance of this question of adapting or breaking from available forms, many of the commentaries on women's travel writing are straightforwardly biographical. Indira Ghose complains of such approaches:

> While women travellers have become the focus of a tremendous upsurge in interest … work on [them] tends to wallow in the anecdotal and to concentrate on constructing a myth of the intrepid, autonomous heroine braving all odds in the wilds. … [I]n the case of female writers all critical faculties, so acutely deployed in the analysis of men's texts,

> are, it seems, suspended. . . . The historical context and the relations of power that the traveller is bound up in, are conveniently elided.[10]

Instead, a number of feminist critics, of whom Ghose is one, argue for a more sophisticated analysis of women's travel writing. They reject the biographical focus for two main reasons: first, for being overly celebratory and perpetuating what Ghose describes as 'the myth of [white] women's non-involvement in colonialism';[11] second, because by concentrating on individual actions, it ignores the reproduction of cultural forces and neglects the workings of discourse in white women's texts. Ghose insists that 'what needs to be looked at in more depth is how notions of gender were bound up with hegemonic ideologies, and how women were both made an instrument of, and were complicitous with, the politics of imperialism'. She hails as an exception the 'path-breaking work of Sara Mills on women travellers'.[12] Mills's book, *Discourses of Difference: An Analysis of Women's Travel Writing and Colonialism* (1991), was probably the first and certainly one of the most influential of the new wave of studies to move beyond biography and to undertake a serious examination of women's travel writing for textual features that distinguish it from men's writing. Mills lists a number of questions and issues that must be addressed in feminist analyses of travel writing. These include: 'how we are going to write about these women travel writers and for what purpose[?]'; 'whether these texts share more features with other female-authored texts than they share with male-authored texts'; that women's travel texts are often read as 'proto-feminist'; and 'the relation of these texts to the colonial system'.[13]

In a study of nineteenth- and early twentieth-century Bengali women's travel writing, Simonti Sen deduces from the narratives she consulted that 'in all essentials of representation and choice of themes it is very difficult to distinguish a woman's account from that of a man'.[14] On the other hand, Mary Morris, referring to women such as Isak Dinesen, Beryl Markham and pioneer Mary McLane, who travelled and wrote about their experiences because of circumstances, not because they sought excitement intending to write about it, states that they did so very differently from men.[15] And of herself, Morris declares, 'As a woman, I travel differently than a man. I believe most women do'.[16]

Differences in focus between men and women's travel texts are not, according to Ghose, 'a result of naturally or socially produced spheres of interest (domestic life for women travellers, for example), but are constrained by the web of conditions of production and reception for these texts'.[17] Ghose warns against seeing all women as more alike one another than they are different from men. Rather, she emphasises differences between women. She aims to present 'a plurality of [women's] gazes. There was not *the* woman traveller in India, but a variety of different women – there is no overarching story to be told'.[18] Nevertheless, the urge to generalise is strong. Cautions such as Ghose's often go unheeded. There are exceptions, however. Two male critics, Patrick Holland and Graham Huggan, declare that 'women travel differently . . . [and] their journeys can be used to install "difference" into the modern culture of travel',[19] yet, similar to Ghose's recognition of the diversity of women travellers, the same critics point to 'the enormous differences *within* the field of women's travel writing'. They also warn against the 'temptation [that] exists to conscript women's travel writing into the service of an emancipatory politics, most often through a combination of women's liberation and anticolonialism' (p.114). They advise that, 'The view of women's travel writing as necessarily liberating clearly needs adjusting just as much as the patriarchal models of imperial travel it often claims to disavow' (p.132). Holland and Huggan look beyond the writing itself to the contexts of its circulation. They make the interesting, if provocative, claim that 'the tendency to look for connections between different women's travel narratives . . . is a function, at least in part, of contemporary market forces: of the commodification of women writers, women's writing, women's literature, and the institutionalization of women's studies at Western universities' (p.113).

For all Holland and Huggan's admonitions against essentialising women's travel writing (p.113) and seeing it as inherently subversive or oppositional, many critics combine their caveats with an insistence that, in general, it does exhibit those qualities. Ghose, for example, advises that 'Feminist literary critics should . . . scrutinize the strategies of subversion of dominant discourses that women writers have employed'.[20] For Bernard Schweizer, 'What gives a woman's travel account a disruptive, radical edge is not so much the gendered nature of her writing as the actual politics that motivate it, a politics based on specific views about social class, nationalism, and comparative anthropology'.[21] Holland and Huggan themselves pronounce:

> Women's travel writing is not insulated from the criticisms levelled at its male counterpart: more specifically, it is not immune from imperialist and ethnocentric nostalgia. However, its interrogation of the identity of the traveling subject – a subject recognized as being constituted by the complex interactions of gender, race, and class – marks contemporary women's travel writing as a vehicle for the displacement of patriarchal and imperial identitary norms. (p.20)

In relation to the argument that women travellers are more empathetic towards colonial subjects, Ghose holds that 'Women, albeit marginalized, are nevertheless participants in the dominant culture'.[22] She maintains that 'women's perception of the other as constructed (not reflected) in their writings is certainly different from that of men' but that this difference is due not to 'an instinctive empathy with the other' but to social reality and gender ideology: 'what it was possible to *see* as a woman was determined by the discourses of femininity in circulation at a specific moment in history'.[23] Ghose is one of many scholars to focus on cultural rather than biological, essential differences; indeed, she reminds us that 'the category of woman is itself a social and cultural construction'.[24] Similarly, like Mills and several theorists of women's travel, Elizabeth Bohls acknowledges the difficulty of making firm distinctions: 'Of course, feminists cannot simply read culture as polarized along the axis of gender, but must account for multiple, interconnecting categories of difference'.[25] In her discussion of women travel writers and the language of aesthetics in the eighteenth and early nineteenth centuries, Bohls is careful not to posit a female essentialism: 'Women's appropriations of aesthetics ... are governed not by some feminine essence, but by specific historical pressures and rhetorical exigencies that give each text its distinctive texture'.[26]

An extension of the view that women are likely to be more empathetic than men is found in Birkett and Wheeler's statement that, 'For women, the possibility of becoming something other is particularly attractive'.[27] They suggest that nowadays, 'The long red line drawn across continents – the Cape-to-Cairo kick – has been replaced by an emotional journey. And women have a head start here: the emotional terrain is traditionally seen as the territory of women writers'.[28] Birkett and Wheeler link this with what many writers celebrate as the transforming power of travel, a feature they believe is often central to what they call 'New Travel Writing'. In the view of some, even the very fact of movement for women is transformative. A number of critics have pointed to a long-maintained cultural identification of travel with masculinity, and of stasis and domesticity with the feminine. Debbie Lisle argues that as a consequence, 'The public persona of the travel writer is empowered by a masculine, rational and aggressive organising scheme that succeeds to the extent that it writes over feminine characteristics in the self and in others'.[29] Leaving aside the fact that the designation of characteristics as masculine or feminine might uphold gender stereotypes, the significant point here is Lisle's contention that for women travel writers, 'The challenge ... is how to manage the discourse of masculinity that is so prevalent in travel writing as a whole' (p.97). One result of the masculine dominance is that, 'In effect, women travel writers must become "honorary men" in order to be recognised within a genre that is shaped so powerfully by a discourse of masculinity' (p.98). In other words, women are forced to adopt a manner of self-presentation associated with men, compromising and distorting their self-expression. A negative aspect to this is its reflection of gender inequalities in society and the consequent lack of social and literary models. This is reflected in Bohls's statement that 'Women did not fit the traveler's image as heroic explorer, scientist, or authoritative cultural interpreter'. A more positive view is that the figurative or literal adoption of a male guise may be liberating and allow for self-realisation, if expressed obliquely. This is hinted at in Bohls's observation that 'for women, travel may be 'destabilizing in ways that generate both anxiety and, at times, exhilaration'.[30]

Those more productive possibilities notwithstanding, the subordination of women in travel and its study cannot be overstated. Describing her own travels with her children, Sara Wheeler has pointed out that there are few mothers in the history of travel writing. She notices that the famous fathers of the genre usually had a wife who remained at home, looking after the children. Alluding to Paul Theroux's *The Great Railway Bazaar* (1975), she remarks: 'The Great Railway Bazaar: And the Kids Came Too. I don't think so'.[31] Wheeler's comment is as incisive as it is acerbic. Most travel writers do not travel (or write about travelling) with their children. Apart from practical obstacles, to do so would risk being seen by some readers as dulling with domesticity the author's adventures abroad. Yet the importance of acknowledging male privilege when it comes to travel should certainly not make us overlook the part played by women – including as scientists.[32] Sidonie Smith reminds us that for all the association of mobility with masculinity, 'women have always been and continue to be on the move'.[33] Smith sees women's mobility increasing in the late nineteenth and early twentieth centuries as a result of modernity ('democratization, literacy, education, increasing wealth, urbanization and industrialization'), and new technologies.[34] Whatever the extent of women's travel, many would agree with Ghose's statement that 'the very act of travel constituted a form of gender power for women'.[35] As for their travel accounts, Lisle asserts that: 'The very presence of women in the genre destabilises the masculine gaze of the travel writer' (p.99). A compelling example of this is Wheeler's own *Terra Incognita* (1996), in which she directly confronts the public-school boyish humour of the male scientists in whose Antarctic base she is resident ('British men doing what they did best – reverting to childhood and behaving like gits'[36]). At the start of the book, Wheeler refers to the 'male territory' in which she finds herself, 'like a gentleman's club, an extension of boarding school and the army'. She wittily remarks, deploying an image that transfers power from them to herself, that: 'Men had been quarrelling over Antarctica since it emerged from the southern mists, perceiving it as another trophy, a particularly meaty beast to be clubbed to death outside the cave'.[37] She also labels the men 'Frozen Beards'. Nevertheless, she arrives at a grudging respect for the achievements of Captain Scott in particular, and she later published a biography of Apsley Cherry-Garrard, the assistant biologist on and chronicler of Scott's last expedition.[38] *Terra Incognita* is a complex work, by turns lyrical, strongly argued, spiritual and contemplative. It is a powerful renegotiation of a space synonymous with an ascetic brand of British male myth-making.

Before moving on, we ought to note that the pressures on women to conform are not exerted only by men. The aviator Anne Morrow Lindbergh records women journalists asking her about her clothes and lunch boxes as she prepares to set off with her husband Charles to fly from the United States to the Orient: 'I felt depressed, as I generally do when women reporters ask me conventionally feminine questions. I feel as they must feel when they are given those questions to ask. I feel slightly insulted'.[39] The questions that provoke Lindbergh's irritation are testament to the reinforcement of ideology through internalisation. That is, dominant (in this case male) values are assimilated and further transmitted by those who are subject to it. The same process occurs with ideologies of class and 'race', especially in colonial situations. Lindbergh (herself an English graduate and a pioneer of aviation) appears more annoyed to be asked these questions by women than by men.

It is also important to note that women's journeys, books and actions can have material and directly political effects; we are not dealing only with textual detail. Annie Caulfield reminds us that Gertrude Bell was, after the First World War, 'a member of the Arab Intelligence Bureau in Cairo and played an influential part in the post-war carve-up of the Middle East by the British and the French authorities'. Caulfield suggests that the rise of Iraqi president Saddam Hussein, 'along with many current Middle Eastern troubles, can be traced clearly to the post-war, artificial creation of states in which [Bell's] writings and expertise were so important'.[40]

Gay travels

Whereas differences between women's and men's travel writing have been the subject of much critical discussion, gay travel writing has received considerably less attention. Homosexual travel has a long tradition, predating classical times, and was often important in social and literary movements that are usually examined for their other aspects. Ian Littlewood points out, for instance, that 'the erotic opportunities of the [Grand] Tour were homosexual as well as heterosexual'.[41] Scrutiny of gay travel writing is important for, among other reasons, its complication of narrative strategies and perspectives and of questions of gender and 'race'. Here, for example, is Christopher Isherwood looking back from the 1970s at his travels half a century before. He relates his memoir in the third person, creating a sense of detachment from his earlier self and demonstrating the difference between author and narrator.

> Christopher was suffering from an inhibition, then not unusual among upper-class homosexuals; he couldn't relax sexually with a member of his own class or nation. He needed a working-class foreigner. He had become clearly aware of this when he went to Germany in May 1928, to stay with an elderly cousin who was the British consul at Bremen. He had no love adventures while there but he looked around him and saw what he was missing.[42]

The admission of such desires adds another dimension to the function of the 'Other' in travel texts, and to the quest to make good a lack or want. Isherwood remembers how on a visit to New York in 1938, on his way back with Auden from the visit to China that would be written up in their *Journey to a War* (1939), he was introduced by George Davis, their 'host, guide and fulfiller of all their desires', to a young, intelligent youth of around eighteen whom in his book, *Christopher and His Kind*, he calls Vernon.[43] Isherwood grows infatuated with him and falls under the spell of New York: 'However, its spell was now largely Vernon's, The American Boy's. The American Boy is also the Walt Whitman Boy. And the Walt Whitman Boy is, by definition, a wanderer. So Christopher found it natural to indulge in daydreams of a future wander-comradeship with Vernon in the Whitman tradition'.[44]

Perhaps the best-known example of overtly gay literary travel writing is Edmund White's *States of Desire: Travels in Gay America* (1980).[45] 'The nature of gay life is that it is philosophical', White informs his audience: 'Once one discovers one is gay, one must choose everything, from how to walk, dress and talk to where to live, with whom and on what terms'.[46] The sense of an alternative or parallel nation is introduced as early as its Acknowledgements section, in which White reports that: 'I quickly learned how hospitable gays everywhere are to each other; the warmth and candor with which I was received bear witness to that kindness' (p.vi). White's journey exposes to the sight of those not already familiar with it a culture that does not get noticed in heterosexual travel texts. The process is apparent throughout the text. Two examples will suffice here, both relating to Los Angeles, where White notes that there are no 'afternoon bars in the manner of San Francisco. The cruising that does get done is executed en route – which leads to the erotics of automobiles, the semiology of makes. The coupe, suggesting the intimacy of the couple, is naturally favored over the family nightmare implied by four doors' (p.9).

He also guides his readers into bath-houses, as Lady Mary Wortley Montagu did her readers into women's Turkish baths. Introducing the 8709 Club Baths, the 'great baths' in Los Angeles (p.14), White suggests that 'In each city we might say there is one body type, the Platonic form for that locality' (p.15). In LA, which 'has the most beautiful men in the world' (p.14), 'the body is slender, the buttocks pneumatic with youth, a trail of gold dust shading the hollow just above the coccyx and between the pecs. Something fragile about the clavicle and tender about the nape causes the figure to oscillate between boyhood and maturity. The eyes are blue' (p.15).

White's sense of occupying a different, parallel country is shared by other gays. Rebecca Brown writes of lesbians:

> We have one country, one set of behaviours, one tradition in which we are raised and to which, for a time, we belong. …
>
> But we as lesbians have another country, too, the one in which we 'live really.' This is the country we discover on our own, or with the guidance of another woman who teaches us the customs. This is the country we explore to discover an important part of ourselves, where we learn how to speak a language new to us, but that we understand immediately. It is a country where what our parents regard as strange and dangerous is familiar, welcoming, desirous to us. It is a country where we recognize our kind.[47]

Brown's comments suggest that there is a different process of travel for homosexuals than for heterosexuals and her invocation of 'another country' echoes the title of gay African American novelist James Baldwin's famous novel (1962). Rather than constructing their identity against foreign Others, Brown implies, gays find themselves abroad through encountering and connecting with people who are similar because of their sexuality. In the previous quotation, Brown uses the concept of another country metaphorically but she means it literally also. For example, she writes: 'Like … other women who have traveled away from home, it took leaving my native land to realize I was a lesbian. I had to leave the country that made me to begin to make myself'.[48] For many gays, home is where identity is compromised and restricted rather than achieved. The writers collected in the volume to which Brown has supplied the foreword 'are fully aware that though they are sexual outsiders, they are also members of an international clan of self-made women'.[49]

Lucy Bledsoe, the editor of the volume in which Brown's foreword appears, exclaims that: 'As a traveler, what I want most is to get out of my cultural and geographical cage, or at least to get a view of it from a different angle'. She finds that:

> Being a lesbian, a sexual border-crosser, allows me this outsider's perspective within my own country, which, in turn, opens me up to unique insights when I travel across other borders. As a devoted fan of travel literature, I have long wanted to read stories from my own lesbian

> perspective, writing that addresses the intersection of sexual identity and geographical exploration.[50]

Bledsoe, then, draws an analogy between homosexuality and travel. Like White, she and Brown suggest that in their own country, gay people lead an existence that is invisible to straight people who may be their compatriots but who mainly inhabit a world outside homosexuals' one. In a reversal of the process we have seen up to now, gay travellers find themselves more at home when they are abroad, able to recognise and establish an affinity with homosexuals there. The excitement and reassurance provided by this gives Bledsoe a more positive outlook than we have found in other travellers. To her, 'Literature, like travel is about crossing borders'. By stepping over them, these are changed from barriers into gateways: 'Therefore, each new book read, each new geographical territory explored, expands the reader's and traveler's horizons'.[51]

Gay travel writing complicates the construction of otherness. Heterosexual companions may seem as different as the foreigners in whose country one is travelling; gay foreigners may seem closer. African Caribbean American Donna Allegra's tale of a dance study trip to Guinea describes tensions between the lesbian narrator and her five heterosexual companions. The uneasy atmosphere between them is intensified by her cynicism towards an easy, celebratory identification with Africans. Despite this, the narrator feels exhilaration and a stronger sense of belonging when dancing in front of villagers to a drum orchestra: 'It's a rare gift to be drawn into such ecstasy and emerge feeling entitled to a place in [the] community'. She writes that she will miss Guinea and that while 'I haven't come looking for a long-lost home, nor would I consider remaining in Africa, still ... [sic]'.[52] She explains that although she found the communal life difficult, 'I garnered some valuable lessons'. She will 'take back to the United States many Guinea ways – the frown, an even greater love for the dance and music, more acceptance of my African face and physique'.[53] In an expression of a movement towards wholeness or unity that seems to be a feature of much gay travel writing, she remarks: 'Travel always bestows pieces of myself I can't find in mirrors at home. I hold up for scrutiny my fears, strengths, accomplishments, judgments, and values'.[54]

Although Edmund White's book is on his own nation, it is as much a book of travel through gay existence as it is through a side of the United States hidden from, or not recognised by, straight people. (Similarly, the women in Bledsoe's anthology 'have access to secret and glorious lesbian subcultures invisible to other travelers'.[55]) In Utah, White focuses on an aspect of Mormon life that is usually overlooked by travel writers and reporters: the effect on gays, who 'are literally crying for succor'. Feminists and 'political gays', he observes, pose a disturbing challenge to the 'Mormon supremacy of the family' (p.113).

White's gayness might lead us to expect a radically different narrative identity from those in whatever we mean by conventional travel narratives. After all, he comments that: 'Whether becoming gay is a political act or not, homosexuality always carries some political impact. The *intention* may be personal, but the *function* of homosexuality is social' (p.114). He offers readers a quite different perspective and priorities: 'At the risk of oversimplifying, I would contend that Boston represents a center for gay radicalism and that Washington, D.C., is a stronghold for more conventional lesbian and homosexual politics. I would like to consider the two cities in that light' (p.297).

White's observations make us aware of the limits of the generalising view in traditional travel writing. He gives us the sense, lacking in many travel narratives, of a life and culture away from the surface existence that is normally the one reported by travel writers. His vision makes readers aware of one culture within another, scraping against it, leading us to question the depth and accuracy of other travel texts. White distinguishes territories by different criteria from those that govern mainstream travel narratives. Thus, for example, in Kansas City he 'met more rejections and incomprehension than anywhere else on my travels' (p.156). There, gay life is restricted to gay bars. Apart from in a bar or in bed, where 'a man may be gay', he is 'straight – a person just like anyone else'. There is no notion that one's gayness 'might color all of one's experience'. The visit to Kansas City reminds him of his adolescence; it is 'the Fifties in deep freeze' (p.156). The idea that after pairing off one 'returns to the "real" world of heterosexuality' promotes an attitude of self-hatred that is poisonous' (pp.157–8).

As we saw was the case with some modernist travel writers, White acknowledges the difficulties, even the impossibility, of making generalisations. Such an admission invites critical scrutiny of the processes by which travellers arrive at judgements about those among whom they travel. He shows an awareness of differences between how things look to outsiders and how they are to those whom one is observing; and he knows that the latter are not uniform: 'I have not, of course, described Ft. Lauderdale as it must seem to those gay men who live there; they, like people everywhere, lead varied lives not subject to generalization. But I have tried to single out the one feature that most strikes the tourist – that, indeed, exists *for* the tourist' (p.212).

Similarly, perhaps, he observes that there 'are so many different gay New Yorks that any project to enumerate them would be a pathetic failure' (p.261). Although this may testify to a multiplicity and variety that do exist, it also serves as a reminder that travellers' claims to speak for the whole depend upon a superficial, homogenous view. White is also aware that collective descriptions are often unavoidable, and so he invites readers to question and find dissatisfaction with what they are told: 'One of the crudest ways of describing the city is by neighborhood, a method that at least has the virtue of fixing the stereotypes so that they may be criticized and corrected' (pp.261–2).

A remarkable feature of White's narrative and certainly one that contrasts with conventional travel writing is its Epilogue, headed 'Self-Criticism'. Because travel narratives traditionally depend for their purpose and effectiveness upon the writer's authority, this explicit self-questioning is significant, inviting scrutiny of the author and, by extension, of his observations. White attributes his self-reflection not only to his gayness but to his politics: 'At the end of gay consciousness-raising sessions (and Maoist meetings), each participant briefly criticizes himself or herself, and so shall I at the end of my book' (p.334). White identifies as the 'most maddening fault' in his book 'a peculiar alternation between socialism and snobbism'. He detects a lessening of the snobbism and an increase in the socialism as the book goes on: 'Writing the book radicalized me'. He suggests that the two elements are contradictory and that there seems to be no way of reconciling them. 'Snobbism', he writes, 'was partly a prophylactic against the unfamiliar' (p.334). This sentiment does not sit easily with his earlier claim about the greater ease with which gays cross boundaries. He observes – and here we witness another instance of the assertion of individuality in modern travel writing – that 'My tastes and values were far from those of most Americans, even most gay Americans' (pp.334–5), and he thinks he is not suggesting that there is such a thing as a gay sensibility (pp.258–9). He has found travelling 'arduous and alienating' (p.335). Among his complaints are the frustration of listening to others and rarely talking, of eating alone and sleeping in rented rooms, and of his insecurity about his looks as he approached his fortieth birthday.

In a later work, *The Flaneur*, White refers to *The Spartacus International Gay Guide*, which, updated annually, 'directs the gay and lesbian tourist to the bars, saunas and cruisy spots in every city throughout the world and comments on them with an elaborate code of capital and lower-case letters. *AYOR*, for instance, stands for "At your own risk" and is a warning that danger (queer-bashing, police arrests, pickpockets) may be in the offing'.[56]

White recalls his own cruising days at the beginning of his time in Paris, where he arrived at the age of forty-three (leaving when he was nearly sixty). He acknowledges that most straight and gay people regard cruising as 'pathetic or sordid – but for me, at least, some of my happiest moments have been spent making love to a stranger below a glowing city'.[57]

White insists, despite not wanting 'to make too much of the democracy of gay life', that 'gay men undeniably are more likely than straights to reach across social and age barriers in search of sex'. He has 'friends of every age and ethnic background' and feels 'less insulated than my straight counterpart (I sometimes try to picture that poor hypothetical devil)' (p.288). He also suggests that straight women in New York, especially feminists, 'seem to be dealing with the same sort of questions gay men face' (pp.288–9). The idea of gays' movement across boundaries is elaborated by Bledsoe, who comments: 'Because border-crossings are about change, new territory, and anticipation, they make great stories. And because gay people have special expertise in crossing borders, we have access to a special kind of travel story'.[58]

Bledsoe remarks that all gay men and lesbians who 'come out' have crossed 'a border of sexuality', which for many contributes to the sense of being outsiders. The outsider status, she observes, can have a profound effect on their experiences of travel. In an argument that has been made for (heterosexual) women travellers also, Bledsoe suggests that 'It is possible, though certainly not always the case, that our experience of difference increases our sensitivity to difference abroad, allowing us to look more deeply into the place we are visiting, to see beyond cultural constructs – particularly our own'.[59] According to Bledsoe, 'Our strategies for negotiating as queer people in a straight world, strategies that work in some parts of the United States, may not work abroad or in other parts of this country' but 'for the lover of travel, these are exactly the reasons we do it: to place ourselves in contexts that challenge our assumptions, help us to see more clearly our individual and cultural characteristics. For the gay traveler, this opportunity is multidimensional'.[60] Interestingly, while Bledsoe makes a fascinating comparison between travelling and reading – 'Opening a book is much like entering a new country. I read for the same reasons that I travel: to pry open my limited world view'[61] – she seems, if inadvertently, to preserve the distinction between cultured traveller and mere tourist by disfavouring the reading only of books that reflect one's own ideas and lifestyle and of travelling 'in a manner that bolsters one's concept of oneself and one's place in the world'. Rather, 'a true traveler, like a true reader, enjoys stretching his or her limits, crossing borders, even scary ones'.[62]

Attempts to overturn dominant gender stereotypes are apparent in even more mainstream writers. Geoffrey Moorhouse explains that he undertook the arduous desert journey recounted in *The Fearful Void* (1974) 'partly to undermine the myth of the Superman who never behaves feebly or badly in trying circumstances. … I wanted to point out that there are no Supermen; only quite ordinary people who sometimes do things that are out of the ordinary'.[63] It may seem ironic to some readers that Moorhouse later confesses to being too embarrassed by the book to look at it again, as if the admission of vulnerability should not win out over an unemotional masculinity, but of greater note is his book's record of a journey that is too much for his strength and stamina. There is a deliberate undercutting of myths of male heroism here. Interestingly, Moorhouse's purpose in *The Fearful Void* seems not so different from Robyn Davidson's insistence in *Tracks* (1980), her narrative of her desert journey, that she is not an extraordinary person; that any woman can accomplish what she has achieved.

Another unpredictable critique of masculinity comes from Paul Theroux, whose confession that 'I have always disliked being a man' leads into an attack on U.S. masculinity: 'The whole idea of manhood in America is pitiful in my opinion. ... It is a hideous and crippling lie; it not only insists on difference and connives at superiority, it is also by its very nature destructive – emotionally damaging and socially harmful'. Theroux finds masculinity 'grotesque' because it 'celebrates the exclusive company of men' and 'denies men the natural friendship of women'.[64] From someone who prefers to travel alone, as we saw in Chapter 5, these remarks are surprising. He even goes so far as to claim: 'It is very hard to imagine any concept of manliness that does not belittle women'.[65] His assault on ideas of maleness culminates in the assertion that 'Any objective study would find the quest for manliness essentially right-wing, puritanical, cowardly, neurotic and fueled largely by a fear of women. It is also certainly philistine'.[66] The examples of Moorhouse and Theroux serve to show that gender roles may be questioned even where one might not expect them to be.

For a more radical destabilising of dominant gender and sex norms, we may apply to gay travel writers Littlewood's remark that homosexual tourists, more than others, have 'promoted the interplay of sex, travel and subversion'.[67] The homosexual and the traveller are transgressive identities, and 'the homosexual traveller compounds the potential for sedition',[68] though 'Often the travellers who raged against society's moral hypocrisy remained in other ways firmly committed to the values and material life-style of their class and country'.[69]

Sexual experimentation and liberation have long been sought, and often obtained, through tourism. Indeed, 'far from being marginal to what tourism is about, the sexual element is vital to it'.[70] As a result, sexual freedom has become associated with particular regions, perhaps chief among them the Mediterranean. The same is true of sexual orientation and practices.[71]

Recent discussions of sex tourism focus on issues of 'race', with young Thais, in particular, the subject of Westerners' desire to 'purchase a temporary sexual freedom that can be enjoyed without loss of social or moral status',[72] and to gain in self-esteem. This is achieved at the expense of those who service them, though arguments have been made that women are empowered in some such situations. We shall not dwell on these issues here, for this is a study of travel writing rather than of tourism. The former often arises from the latter, however, and just as they overlap, so do the politics of the exotic and the erotic.

Part III

Writing and reading travel

Chapter 10

Writing travel

Travel is a creative act.
Paul Theroux[1]

Travel writing creates worlds, it does not simply discover them.
Peter Bishop[2]

It will be evident by now that the contexts of and motivation for travel vary enormously, across and within periods. The same is true of travel *writing*. Authors of travel accounts may write primarily for themselves or for others (e.g., governments, sponsors, societies, expedition leaders, family and friends). The advice given to travellers differs accordingly, depending on the historical age, the type of travel, the medium employed for the travel narratives and the target audience. Francis Bacon, writing in 1615, advises young men to 'have some entrance into the language' before they travel and to be accompanied by 'a servant, or tutor, as knoweth the country'. The gentleman traveller should keep a diary, should not stay long in any one town or city, should change his accommodation from one end of town to another so as to get better acquainted with it, and should see and visit eminent persons. Bacon instructs his readers:

> The things to be seen and observed are: the courts of princes, especially when they give audience to ambassadors; the courts of justice, while they sit and hear causes; and so of consistories ecclesiastic; the churches and monasteries, with the monuments which are therein extant; the walls and fortifications of cities, and towns, and so the heavens and harbors; antiquities and ruins; libraries; colleges, disputations, and lectures, where any are; shipping and navies; houses and gardens of state and pleasure, near great cities; armories; arsenals; magazines; exchanges; burses; warehouses; exercises of horsemanship, fencing, training of soldiers, and the like; comedies, such whereunto the better sort of persons do resort; treasuries of jewels and robes; cabinets and rarities; and, to conclude, whatsoever is memorable, in the places where they go. After all which, the tutors, or servants, ought to make diligent inquiry. As for triumphs, masks, feasts, weddings, funerals, capital executions,

> and such shows, men need not to be put in mind of them; yet are they not to be neglected.[3]

This is travel report as inventory, supplying information with no interest in ambiguity, uncertainty or imagination.

Instructions are by no means limited to European travellers. Nabil Matar notes that in Ibn al-Sarraj's account of his journey to Mecca between 1630 and 1633 he:

> advises the prospective traveler in "the lands of God" to "observe and reflect on the differences in landscape, between mountains and valleys and wilderness, the sources of rivers and their courses, the ruins of ancient peoples and what happened to them and how they have become news of past history, after they had been seen and admired. He should also observe the differences in peoples, skin colors, languages, foods, drinks, clothes, customs and wonders".[4]

Matar explains that:

> The purpose of writing an account of a journey was to describe the lands, customs, religion, and social organization the traveler had seen – and which another wanted to confirm. Authors therefore invested themselves with an exemplary self in which their "I" was collective of all their coreligionists, thereby telling them more about the outer world they visited and the discussions and exposures they had than the inner world they experienced. (pp.xxxi–xxxii)

Nearly four hundred years later, Cynthia Dial, the author of a handbook guide for aspiring travel writers (mainly of travel journalism), tells her readers, 'you must absorb surroundings, note details, contrast and compare – whether it be a resort, an airline, a village, even a country. You're inherently observant and must put these observations into texts – honestly, interestingly and accurately'.[5] Although her advice is aimed at writers, instructing them on how to look at places differently from when they are mere tourists – 'As a travel writer, you're no longer a tourist' – it reinforces the discrimination we have already seen: travellers are thought to immerse themselves in foreign cultures deeper than do tourists and to appreciate them more fully. Dial's counsel also returns us to the question of the relationship between fact and fiction. Confiding that 'Reading fiction is one of my favourite forms of research',[6] she advises: 'Non-fiction can be as creative as fiction.... Note how to use fiction techniques in your non-fiction to draw the reader into the action'.[7] Travel writers, she reminds us, 'have the licence to distort time for effect, to develop or expand an on-location event for intrigue and to skip over the dullness'.[8] Dial avoids the fact–fiction separation by declaring that: 'A travel writer is both a journalist – bound by facts, opinions, observations, and other collected information – and an author dedicated to telling a persuasive story in a creative way'.[9] The primary criterion for a travel article should be '[r]eadability'.[10] For Dial, however, creativity does not mean falsehood. Under the heading 'Be objective but fair', she stipulates that travel articles must always be truthful. It is, she insists, a 'duty of the travel writer to be honest, bluntly honest at times, but always fair in your opinions'. She emphasises that 'honesty is especially important when free travel is involved', and tells her readers: 'It's your journalistic responsibility to compare your experiences with those of other hotel guests and airline passengers'.[11] Dial's call for objectivity, fairness, honesty, duty and responsibility is for journalistic values that we are not likely to associate with literary travel narratives. We may expect the latter to exhibit prejudice and exude superiority; to display unequal power relationships; have questionable veracity and to be – sometimes knowingly and ostentatiously – *ir*responsible.

The present chapter will consider some modern travel writers' statements on their craft and on the advice they have received and passed on. Contemporary criticism devotes much of its energy to the exposure of ideologies in accounts that previously might have been seen as objective and incontestable. Some of the most compelling work on travel writing demonstrates that even seemingly straightforward descriptions reinforce patriarchal, capitalist and racial ideologies. The tenor of these studies is that the politics of travel texts (as of literature and other cultural forms more generally) are so strong that writers operate unaware of how deeply they are affected by them and of their own roles in transmitting them. Such scholarship is valuable and necessary but rarely shows much regard for the conscious craft of the travel writer. This chapter aims to identify some of the deliberate techniques and strategies of travel writers while not losing sight of the politics of their texts. An appreciation of the art of the text may help restore a sense of authorial agency without abandoning a critique of its ideology.

Jonathan Raban has talked of how 'Fiction' comes not from an imaginary Latin verb fictio, meaning 'I make it up as I go along', but from the actual Latin verb fingo (from fingere) meaning, 'I shape'.[12] This is relevant to our concerns because Raban views his books as:

> variants of memoir. They're not travel books. They are books about journeys to some extent. And I think the thing about the journey is it's a very nice scale model of a life. But it's a life that has a beginning, a middle, and an end. And the person who makes the journey metaphorically survives his own death to write about a life posthumously. (p.58)

For Raban, 'The modern memoir seems to me to be a straight outgrowth of the novel. It requires the teller of the tale to both imagine and invent the past. Which doesn't mean make it up' (p.56). Raban explains that, with the exception of *Hunting Mister Heartbreak*, 'During a trip, I usually think I'm never going to write anything about this. I don't have a sense of an emerging book as I'm traveling' (p.60). Identifying himself with such writers of travel books as Redmond O'Hanlon, Paul Theroux and Bruce Chatwin, and distinguishing himself and them from Jan Morris and 'most of the travelling, see-the-world journalists', he remarks: 'Our books all come out of the same essential impulse: the drift of the novel as the major prose narrative form as it began to move out from being about just imaginary characters. I mean the emergence particularly of the total-recall memoir' (p.56). Similarly, and on the relationship between fiction and fact in travel writing, it is worth noting Paul Theroux's comment:

> The nearest thing to writing a novel is travelling in a strange country. Travel is a creative act – not simply loafing and inviting your soul, but feeding the imagination, accounting for each fresh wonder, memorizing and moving on. The discoveries the traveler makes in broad daylight – the curious problems of the eye he solves – resemble those that thrill and sustain a novelist in his solitude. It is fatal to know too much at the outset: boredom comes as quickly to the traveler who knows his route as to the novelist who is overcertain of his plot.[13]

Many critics suggest that travellers follow, literally and figuratively, in paths laid down by their prior exposure to cultural representations of a place. Carl Thompson puts it this way: 'some sort of script, born of an array of prior expectations and associations pertaining to the type of travel we are engaged in, will always be at work in our travelling, shaping our experiences … and forming an important part of how we perceive ourselves and portray ourselves to others'.[14] This applies to the stories we tell about our travel, too, though the situation described by Thompson may not work in the same way for travellers from postcolonial societies, for example, or for other groups whose perspectives are not accommodated by conventional models and who have to adapt these or formulate their own.

A common strategy employed by travel writers who are visiting areas that have already been written about is to distinguish their accounts from previous ones. This is often managed through humour and irony, qualities that help construct their narrative personae and that create a warm relationship between author-narrator and reader. One among countless examples is the description by U.S. writer and adventurer Richard Harding Davis of his visit to Panama during the construction of the Panama Canal, where he is given an inspection of the machine shops. He writes: 'We had read of the pathetic spectacle presented by thousands of dollars' worth of locomotive engines and machinery lying rotting and rusting in the swamps, and as it had interested us when we had read of it, we were naturally even more anxious to see it with our own eyes'.[15] What Davis and his companions find instead are locomotives and machinery protected, oiled and cared for.

> This was not as interesting as it would have been had we seen what the other writers who have visited the isthmus saw. And it would have given me a better chance for descriptive writing had I found the ruins of gigantic dredging-machines buried in the morasses, and millions of dollars' worth of delicate machinery blistering and rusting under the palm-trees; but, as a rule, it is better to describe things just as you saw them, and not as it is the fashion to see them, even though your way be not so picturesque.[16]

In fact, Davis declares, the care the company was taking of its machinery and equipment 'struck me as being much more pathetic than the sight of the same instruments would have been had we found them abandoned to the elements and the mud'. Davis compares it to 'a general pipe-claying his cross-belt and polishing his buttons after his army had been routed and killed, and he had lost everything, including honor'.[17] In a complicated manoeuvre, Davis leads us to expect a description in line with others' reports, confounds that expectation, suggests that previous visitors have styled their accounts to fit fashion rather than to present what they have seen, and then (further to underline his individuality in telling the truth of what he sees) claims that his truthful picture evokes more pathos than the false ones that have been styled for that effect. Such ploys cajole readers into trusting the narrator more than other travellers whose versions he contests, and, with that trust, to like him.

The more familiar the destination, the more the narrator relies on humour, personality and idiosyncrasy to distinguish him or herself from previous travellers. A century after Davis, Bill Bryson similarly parades his own credentials by finding former accounts to be at odds with what he finds. Thus, 'Such was the picture of appalling squalor [George] Orwell painted that even now I was startled to find how neat and well maintained Wigan appeared to be'. Progressing from the presentation of different perspectives to questioning Orwell's reliability, Bryson continues:

> Wigan Pier is an arresting landmark, yet – and here's another reason to be a bit cautious with regard to old George's reporting skills – after spending some days in the town, he concluded that the pier had been demolished. (So, too, for that matter, did Paul Theroux in *Kingdom by the Sea*.) Now correct me if I'm wrong, but don't you think it a bit odd to write a book called *The Road to Wigan Pier* and to spend some days in

> the town and never once think to ask anybody whether the pier was still there or not?[18]

Bryson does admit that the pier is much easier to find now as it has become a tourist attraction, but he has already expressed doubts about Orwell and poked fun at him. Reminding us that Orwell was 'an Eton boy from a fairly privileged background', he remarks that Orwell 'regarded the labouring classes the way we might regard Yap Islanders, as a strange but interesting anthropological phenomenon' (p.231). Such disparagement is a much-practised strategy for establishing one's own credentials. A traveller from whom Bryson seems particularly keen to distinguish himself is Paul Theroux, a stepping away that nicely parallels the latter's own determination to mark the distance between himself and others. For example, of the twelve-mile distance from Lulworth to Weymouth, Bryson writes that 'Paul Theroux gives the impression that you can walk it in an easy lope and still have time for a cream tea and to slag off the locals, but I trust he had better weather than I. It took me most of the day' (p.128).

In a more complicated set of manoeuvres, Bryson reports that on a journey from Chester to Llandudno he consults his copy of *Kingdom by the Sea* to check if 'Paul Theroux had said anything about the vicinity that I might steal or modify to my own purposes'. Bryson expresses his usual amazement that, 'along these very tracks', Theroux was typically 'immersed in a lively conversation with his fellow passengers'. Bryson wonders how Theroux does it: 'Quite apart from the consideration that my carriage was nearly empty, I don't know how you strike up conversations with strangers in Britain.... [I]t's so hard, or at least it is for me. I've never had a train conversation that wasn't disastrous or at least regretted' (p.244).

Bryson finds himself trapped by 'the world's most boring man' (p.245); 'not just a train-spotter, but a train-talker, a far more dangerous condition' (p.246), who sees the book he is reading and complains that 'Thoreau', as he calls him, 'Doesn't know his trains at all. Or if he does he keeps it to himself' (p.245). The passage marks Bryson off from Theroux but also, through the train enthusiast's knowledge, undermines Theroux's authority.

Moving around

The Black British writer, Gary Younge, a reporter on the *Guardian* newspaper, has said of his memoir-cum-travel book, *No Place Like Home* (1999), that while all the encounters and dialogue in it are true and that 'the stuff you make up is never as good as the stuff that happens', he did move one woman he met in a bar in New Orleans to a bus somewhere else, having been told by his agent that it was all right to move people around and that he may have included in the book things that happened to him on other trips to the same places in the South. Younge says that he does not have an ethical problem with this but can see that it might be 'the beginning of a very slippery slope where you get composite characters and then you just start making stuff up',[19] and that he would never do it in a piece for the *Guardian*. Similarly, the travel writer, journalist and historian, William Dalrymple, concedes that in his first book, *In Xanadu*, 'There's nothing in there which didn't take place, though one or two of the scenes did take place in other journeys and I've moved them into that one'.[20] He also describes how he 'devised quite a complicated structure for *City of Djinns*, which is a narrative of a notional year my wife and I spent in Delhi, but by the time it was written we had been there about four years, so it contained the best of the gleanings of my diaries'.[21] Just as Younge has moved at least one person around, Dalrymple has moved time around, while, he implies, remaining faithful to the pattern of events. Quite how this affects the classification of the texts is difficult to determine. The information is not available within the book itself, although once one has it the opening lines of the Acknowledgements hint at more than they suggest on the surface: 'This book, the story of one year in Delhi, has taken nearly four times that long to complete'.[22] *City of Djinns* is not fiction but neither is it what it presents itself – even in its subtitle – as being. It involves acts of compression and selection, but only on a greater scale than other travel books that are more faithful to the chronology of the experiences they record. It would thus seem to match Hulme's criterion, quoted in Chapter 1: 'All travel writing – because it is writing – is *made* in the sense of being constructed, but travel writing cannot be *made up* without losing its designation'.[23]

Dalrymple suggests that there are no fixed rules for travel books and that the important thing is that authors should signal clearly to the reader what they are trying to do: 'I don't think you can in one part of a book invent a whole section and then expect to be taken seriously when you uncover a massacre in another part of the book. You've got to decide what you're doing, but I think there's no problem in different books having different sets of rules'.[24] On the other hand, his comment that 'You cannot be prescriptive about travel books any more than you can about the novel or poetry' makes it clear again that, at least in the eyes of some practitioners, these genres are distinguishable from one another, whatever internal flexibility each employs.[25] Even taking this into account, it is still easy to distinguish most travel writing from other, if related, types of text. To point out the mutual borrowings and influences, however, is to show that there are similarities between genres and that they share some of the same elements. This is important because it is tempting to read travel writing as though it were autobiography. Yet, just as recent theories of autobiographies have emphasised the constructedness of that genre, so travel writers often adopt personae. Peter Hulme remarks, for example, that '[Paul] Theroux's innovation was the invention of an American persona which combined the rough edges of the hard-bitten traveller with the learning and literariness of his European counterparts'.[26] An assumption of a straightforward correspondence between narrator and author is an easy one to make, and many writers encourage that belief, creating the impression of a more direct reading experience and endowing themselves with a public identity linked firmly to their books, thus increasing their marketability also. Some writers deny inventing a distinct narrator; Dalrymple has stated that 'while I consciously changed the form I've written the different books in to suit whatever I'm trying to do, I never consciously created a persona around the "I"'.[27] Australian writer Robyn Davidson, on the other hand, has stated of her two travel books: 'If you're a writer, you're a writer, you're a writer. Both of the characters, it seems to me, the narrator in *Tracks* and the narrator in *Desert Places*, are created people, they're created characters, and I recognise both of them, but they're not quite me. They're bits of me, but they're not *me*'.[28]

Part of this, as Davidson describes, has to do with the various stages of the experience of an event, the memory of it and the reconstructed account of it.[29] It is the distinction between actor (involved in the travel), reviewer (remembering it), and author of it (some time after the event). Between these differences falls the narrator, a composite, in-between figure that is the result of experience, imagination and art. Davidson's statement that in both the novel and travel writing, 'the devices you use to make a good book are the same [although] ... it may manifest itself in the most extraordinary, different ways ... you're constructing something',[30] reminds us that travel writing is as much art or artefact as it is documentary. Understanding that will help us appreciate the literariness of travel writing. Apposite here is Borm's reminder that 'the *literary* is at work in travel writing'.[31]

Other voices and times

One of the most interesting of experimental travel writers is the Australian academic Stephen Muecke, whose books include *Reading the Country* (1984/1996) and *No Road* (1997). Muecke draws on poststructuralist and postmodern theory to produce work that has been marketed as 'A radically new way of writing about Australia',[32] and in which 'Irony and humour invert the usual expectations of a travel book; nobody seems to be going anywhere'.[33] Employing postmodern techniques of fragmentation, self-consciousness, bricolage and multiple perspectives, Muecke is concerned to rewrite Australia; to take note of the hidden Aboriginal history and place it alongside white settler history. Muecke is also a practitioner of ficto-criticism, a hybrid genre that blends the techniques of fiction with the critical essay. In one example of this, a short piece called 'Gulaga Story', first published in 2007, he presents a multi-layered travel account of Mount Gulaga (called Mount Dromedary by Captain Cook, who sighted it in 1770) on the coast of New South Wales. 'Gulaga Story' mixes a trip there by the author and his family, the visitation of Cook, fieldwork by anthropologist Deborah Bird Rose (whom Muecke knows) in the late 1990s and the tours of local Aboriginal guide, Yuin Kelly. Muecke combines the perspectives of European 'discoverer', indigenous peoples and white Australians, declining to discriminate between the different accounts. Rather, he shows them as all forming a part of the human history of the area, over which the mountain will continue to rise, long after humans have passed. Fittingly for a country making efforts at reconciliation between Aborigines and the whites who hold power, 'Gulaga Story' sets the stories side by side. Muecke announces in the abstract to his essay that, 'The fictocritical style tries to avoid the tendency to monologism of conventional scholarship and historical accounts'. That is, he aims to do away with the telling of a story in which just one, commanding, voice is heard. Instead, 'The article performs the idea of multiple travels and stories/histories; this particular site sees Cook's account intersect with and contradict that of the local Aboriginal people, the Yuin'. Muecke is explicit about the combination of his political and textual aim, stating of Cook's narrative and the Aboriginal version: 'Neither is given more authority, nor are the Aborigines confined to ancient or timeless tradition'.[34] He describes, matter-of-factly, Yuin driving a four-wheel-drive vehicle and talking about George Bush's New World order.[35] He also recounts her information that Jesus left 'Camel Rock' (Mount Dromedary) on the beach when he passed through two thousand years before Cook and walked on Lake Wallaga. Yuin's grafting of Christianity onto Aboriginal creation myths is a sign, no doubt, of her having received a Christian education, as so many Aborigines forcibly had.

Muecke's story is infused with a postcolonial sensibility which he expresses through his experiments with form. It is a remarkably rich story, interweaving many histories and perspectives on the land, and it refuses to choose between scientific, religious, mythological and personal accounts. Each has its own validity to the believer and helps constitute the meaning of the place. Muecke's is an intellectual project. That accounts both for its success and limitation.

'Gulaga Story' experiments with time and structure in exciting ways that complement and communicate the themes, but even students on literature degree courses can find it inaccessible. It is difficult to see such works reaching a wide audience – reaching, in fact, many of the readers whom one might wish exposed to its ideas.[36]

Travel writers have to make decisions on how to deal with several matters intrinsic to their genre. Most of these involve the figure of the narrator. The choice of whether to acknowledge the temporal difference between the narrator and author is fundamental. Ignoring the separation between them can make for more a direct reading experience, as though we are experiencing the journey with the traveller. Drawing attention to the time that has elapsed between the performance of travel and the writing of it invites reflection. The narrator may thus be treated as another character about whom the author may comment, rather like an autobiographer's view of his or her younger self. The presence of that temporal distance, therefore, coincides with a critical space, too, which can lead to a more tangible sense of the writing as a construction. That is to say, if a text directly makes us aware that there are at least two different versions of the 'I' – the one who travels and the one who later writes up the travel – we are more likely to be conscious of the means by which the story is put together. When, on the other hand, the author encourages us in the pretence that the journey takes place as we read about it, we are less likely to ask questions as we are swept along by the narrative. Different readers and writers will have different preferences; there is no right or wrong way to approach it.

To illustrate the significance and overt treatment of distance, we can turn to V. S. Naipaul's 1990 book, *India: A Million Mutinies Now*, in which he recalls having returned from his 1962 visit to the subcontinent and beginning, the following year, 'in an oppressive furnished flat in south London … to write my book about India'. He tells us that he had intended to write one but had begun to give up the idea after a few weeks:

> Travel writing was new to me, and I didn't see how I could find a narrative for a book about India: I was too overwhelmed by the distress I saw. I had kept no journal, made few connected notes. But money had been spent, and a book had to be written. A full two to three months after my return, I began to write.[37]

Naipaul's statement reminds us that the travel writing we read may be produced far away from the site of travel itself. In addition, it is a way of organising and making sense of one's experience. Naipaul comments on how after the book was written, 'order [had been] given to memories' and 'a narrative found'. It is a means of working things through; almost a catharsis: 'Indian emotions

[were] faced and written out' and 'the details began to fade' (p.493). Naipaul refers to 'writing, the ordering of events and emotion', as having 'made things manageable for me, helped me as it were to clear the decks' (p.498). In the book from which these quotations are taken, Naipaul largely removes himself from the narrative, taking up much of the space instead with the stories of people whom he has met and interviewed, though of course he is present as an orchestrator of them.

Travel writers who expose the workings of their craft often do so because they want to provoke thought about narrative processes and relationships that we normally take for granted. Even for those who have this as their aim, there are certain elements that it is difficult to change. For example, there is no travel without an encounter with landscape or people – even solitary inner journeys posit the psyche as a kind of terrain inhabited by characters or facets of them – and inevitably these serve a function. Usually they contribute to the narrator's enlightenment and sense of identity. If a writer wants to make the relationship between traveller, landscape and indigene less exploitative, the symbolic function still remains. Authors who suggest they learn from, rather than have superior knowledge to, indigenous peoples, or who portray the results of their journeys as indecisive, are still using the Other – at least in textual terms – in order to make a point for their own purposes. One should not overstate this: there can be no definition of the Self without an Other, and metaphorical is not the same as material exploitation, but it does mean that in travel writing it is impossible to disinvest the Other of symbolic significance. Consequently, the writer who genuinely aspires to include individual portraits will struggle to do so because those will either draw upon a reservoir of stereotypes or distinguish those individuals from the generality of others of their group.

Another problem facing the travel writer is how to represent dialogue. This has two aspects. First, the question of how to record one's exchanges. Some travel writers use digital voice recorders; others employ shorthand or detailed notes; others believe that any paper or electronic recording will erect a barrier between the parties and distort rather than accurately convey discussion. Travellers in that last group tend instead to write up conversations as soon after their occurrence as possible, while they can recall details, tone and nuance. Dial recommends making contemporaneous observations: 'Remember, time muddles memory. So whether you call it a diary, travel log, notebook or journal, its contents are your record of first impressions. These written notes, scribbled along the way, are invaluable in evoking atmosphere'.[38]

On the other hand, Jonathan Raban believes that: 'very often memory is more accurate in certain ways than a tape recorder can be. What the tape recorder picks up is dreck, junk'. Raban explains that after returning from a trip, he goes through a process of forgetting the irrelevant details. This is necessary because 'otherwise you're just landed up with the shapelessness of the journey instead of that imagined shape the journey begins to take on once you're far enough away from it for the irrelevancies to have leaped out of it, and you're left with various essential bits which you can then draw on when you write'.[39] Raban's comments are about the contexts and contents of conversations and incidents. The second aspect of recording exchanges has to do more specifically with how best to present the speech of the Other; of whether, even, it is feasible to co-produce the narrative with members of those whose culture is the subject of the work.

Methods employed to communicate cultural difference and local character can make members of host communities sound archaic and primitive (in the pejorative sense of the word). Sometimes words are left untranslated in the main text so that an impression of their foreignness remains. Authors then have to consider when and where to place the translations: in footnotes or endnotes or in a glossary at the beginning or end of the book, or even whether to dispense with translation altogether. The last of those options may preserve something of the quality of the meeting with the foreign, conveying a lack of understanding. Whatever option the author selects, there is a further question: should the existence of the interpreter be admitted or concealed in order to ensure a smoother flow to the narrative? The irony in doing so is obvious, but rarely addressed: translators and interpreters are the very people who facilitate cross-linguistic, cross-cultural dialogue but their presence is thought by some to be an awkward obstacle to the literary record of it. African American Colleen J. McElroy's book on her research trip to Madagascar not only includes mention of her assistant and translator but presents their relationship as mutually beneficial:

> Tiana Flora Tsizaza was a fourth-year student of English Literature at the University of Madagascar. She was particularly interested in American literature ... For her, the bonus was that I was an African American writer and a professor of literature. For me, the bonus was in having found an assistant who was not only interested in literature but was also able to translate from Malagasy and French into English.[40]

It is not only interpreters whose presence travel writers have to decide whether and how to admit. Explorers of Africa, for example, were reliant on porters and on local people and their knowledge. For the most part they are left anonymous and without voices. When they are noticed, it is often for what the explorers regard as disloyalty, theft, insubordination, desertion and other negative acts for which they are severely punished. Stanley does offer a number of individual portraits, especially of men who accompanied him on more than one of his expeditions, and there is evidence outside his books that he cared about their welfare, but they are clearly subordinate to him and his purpose and they provide a foil for him, enabling his self-presentation as a master who is by turns benevolent and stern, as the occasion demands.

Sometimes, and more frequently from the 1900s, it is not employees and servants but one's 'equal' companions, even members of one's family, that are the subject of such choices around inclusion or exclusion. Probably the most famous example of this is Graham Greene's near silence in *Journey Without Maps* on his cousin Barbara who accompanied him on his West African journey. Barbara later wrote up her own description of the trip in *Land Benighted* (1938), and while a comparison of the two has obvious interest for anyone wishing to evaluate the differences gender makes to travel and its record, it is not an easy or in many ways a fair comparison to make, for Barbara was not a professional author and her account lacks the metaphorical richness and multi-layered quality of her cousin's writing.

Travel writers have also to judge how best to structure their accounts. Few depart from a straightforward chronology. This predictability and lack of narrative adventurousness is no doubt a factor in the genre's reputation having suffered beside that of the novel, in which temporal jumps and switches are much more commonplace. Travel narrators do recall their younger selves or look forward to points beyond those being described but very rarely do they narrate journeys out of sequence. Where to begin the story is a question confronting all travel writers, regardless of how they handle the order of events. Some, like Jonathan Raban's *Coasting* (1986), which starts on board a vessel off the coast of England, begin *in medias res*, making for a more dramatic and engaging opening; others commence with preparations for their journey or, further back, with the suggestions and ideas that led to it, although these are usually dealt with briskly for fear of losing readers' attention. Paul Theroux points out that travel writing is often about the destination. Its 'convention is to telescope ... to start – as so many novels do – in the middle of things, to beach the reader in a bizarre place without having first guided him there'.[41] In *The Old Patagonian Express*, Theroux shifts the focus, choosing instead to write about the journey, 'since the going is often as fascinating as the arrival' (pp.11–12). That journey, he reminds us, begins at the starting point: 'From the second you wake up you are headed for the foreign place, and each step ... brings you closer' (p.12). Preferring the travel experience and narrative value of trains over aeroplanes, Theroux declares:

> What interests me is the waking in the morning, the progress from the familiar to the slightly odd, to the rather strange, to the totally foreign, and finally to the outlandish. The journey, not the arrival, matters;

> the voyage, not the landing. Feeling cheated that way by other travel books, and wondering exactly what it is I have been denied, I decided to experiment by making my way to travel-book country, as far south as the trains run from Medford, Massachusetts; to end my book where travel books begin. (pp.13–14)

Theroux does indeed delay his arrival until the end of his book, and when he gets to his destination, Patagonia, it is a place that he describes as being empty and nowhere.

> I had known all along that I had no intention of writing about being in a place – that took the skill of a miniaturist. I was more interested in the going and the getting there, in the poetry of departures. And I had got here by boarding a railway train filled with Boston commuters, who had left me and the train and had gone to work. I had stayed on and now I was in San Antonio Oeste in the Patagonian province of Rio Negro. The travel had been a satisfaction; being in this station was a bore. (p.408)

In fact, that suggestion of staying on the train is a conceit. He has changed trains several times, stayed in several places and revised some of his plans. Nonetheless, his indication of how his book differs from conventional travel books is meant to distinguish himself from other travellers also. Paradoxically, modern travel writers are characterised by their attempts to appear exceptional. In an age when few geographical or anthropological discoveries remain to be made, the character of the individual traveller assumes greater importance; it becomes in itself a subject of the narrative and a reason for buying and reading the book. Largely for that reason, contemporary travel writers cultivate a persona that foregrounds their difference from those they encounter, whether fellow travellers or inhabitants of the places they visit. Recognising the constructedness of that persona is important to critical readings of travel writing, as we shall see in Chapter 11.

Chapter 11

Reading travel writing

What the travel book needs is not an elegiac history but the ground rules of an intelligent criticism.

Jonathan Raban[1]

Crisis

Up to now, this volume has provided an historical overview of travel writing, offered a focus on enduring themes, and discussed travel writers' views and comments on their craft. The present chapter concentrates on what has been largely implicit in previous chapters: ways of reading travel writing. As we have noted, the modern criticism of the genre has developed rapidly since the last quarter of the twentieth century, impelled in the first instance by Edward Said's *Orientalism* (1978), which stimulated new attention to travel texts, and then gathered momentum with Peter Hulme's, Mary Louise Pratt's and Sara Mills's studies of travel and cultural encounter, especially in colonial contexts.[2] In the wake of these foundational works, scholars began to focus more critically on representations of the Other and to see in them self-serving motives and unequal power relationships. In the eyes of Said, and many of those writing under his influence, travel writing not only reflected and accompanied, but also helped facilitate the exercise of colonial power. Said's contention that 'ideas, cultures, and histories cannot seriously be understood or studied without their force, or more precisely their configurations of power, also being studied', and his assertion that 'The relationship between Occident and Orient is a relationship of power, of domination, of varying degrees of a complex hegemony', implicate travel writing as part of the process.[3] Propelled by new directions in critical theory at large, many scholarly readings make it their mission to uncover the presence and functions of ideology. Critiques of the constructions of 'race' and gender in travel narratives challenge stereotypes and dominant assumptions. They seek to expose, confront and overthrow what Said identifies as the idea that was 'the major component in European culture' and that was 'precisely what made that culture hegemonic both in and outside Europe: the idea of European identity as a superior one in comparison with all the non-European peoples and cultures'.[4] In a well-known passage, Said suggests that the things to look for in representations of the Other are 'style, figures of speech, setting, narrative devices, historical and social circumstances, not the correctness of the representation nor its fidelity to some great original'.[5] We might compare anthropologist Johannes Fabian's statement:

> Figures of speech – the use of possessive pronouns, first person singular or plural, in reports on informants, groups, or tribes – are the signs in anthropological discourse of relations that ultimately belong to political economy, not to psychology or ethics ... Temporalizations expressed as passage from savagery to civilization, from peasant to industrial society, have long served an ideology whose ultimate purpose has been to justify the procurement of commodities for our markets.[6]

That closing reference to 'our markets' unwittingly proves Fabian's point. Perhaps the simplest and yet single most important tip for reading travel writing (and news articles) is to examine that plural pronoun: who is meant by 'our'; what is meant by 'ours'? What kinds of distancing or exclusion are involved in the implied or stated 'you' and 'yours'? Do they signify a moral gap?

Much criticism takes Said's lead and devotes itself mainly to close analyses of passages that seem explicitly or unconsciously to communicate colonial and racial ideologies. Such approaches have been attacked by, among others, historians who believe this approach ignores specific historical conditions. Often, such complaints come from what sound like conservative voices, but they have also been made by those on the left. Marxist Aijaz Ahmed, for example, has countered that it is 'unimaginably difficult, if not altogether pointless' to refer to the setting and circumstances of a representation without 'raising, in some fundamental way', those issues of fidelity and correctness, for 'it is usually with reference to "historical and social circumstances" that worthwhile distinctions between a representation and misrepresentation are customarily made'.[7] Ahmad's anger is directed at those who attend to the textual rather than the material; at those who are more interested in '"fictions" of representation and cultural artefact' than in 'the "facts" of imperialist wars and political economies of exploitation', and in past colonialism rather than present imperialism.[8] More recent criticism has tended to question the earlier models of imposition and domination and to stress instead processes of negotiation, transculturation and even exploitation by 'native' peoples. Such studies tend to view the space of encounter and subsequent colonial rule as involving exchange and contestation rather than compliance, submission and imposition.

Interestingly, several critics make a point of espousing the virtues of their own approaches over the deficiencies of those they aim to displace, much as travellers distinguish themselves from their predecessors and from the Other. In fact, just as travel narratives reflect the conditions and attitudes that exist in the traveller's home culture, so scholarly readings of travel writing reflect their own context, including not only developments in literary studies but institutional expectations, too. Often missing from the declarations of advances in the field is an acknowledgement of their own situation and an admission that these advances will, in turn, be supplanted. Dennis Porter is a rare exception. Porter asks that we recognise the achievements of earlier travellers and avoid judging them by the standards of later ages: 'We do not stand in the place of truth any more than they did. We, too, will have to wait for future generations to tell us what it was that we mistook for our equivalent of mermaids in the ocean or sheep-trees on land'.[9] The same surely applies to scholarship. Caren Kaplan has cast critical light on the position of critics, declaring: 'the "travel" of theories and theorists' has not 'been fully considered as part of the legacy of imperialism [or] as part of the politics of cultural production in transnational modernities and postmodernities'.[10]

Many of the approaches to travel writing mentioned in this volume, and to literature in general, follow what is often termed the 'crisis in humanities', which was produced by the culmination of many factors in the 1960s and 1970s, including the rise of the new feminism, the Civil Rights and anti-Vietnam War movements, and decolonisation and liberation struggles. These contributed to, and coincided with, a general – and generational – questioning of authority and purpose. One result was what anthropologists George Marcus and Michael Fischer have written of as a 'crisis in representation' that 'arises from uncertainty about adequate means of describing social reality'.[11] That uncertainty, it has to be said, seems to be exhibited more frequently and intensely by critics of travel writing than by practitioners, but it has changed the way that travel writing is read, at least by those in universities, and it has affected the output of the more experimental and politically engaged travel writers.

My own readings of travel writing share the recognition by Marxist theorist Fredric Jameson that 'there is nothing that is not social and historical – indeed, ... everything is "in the last analysis" political'.[12] Travels that are presented to us as the experiences of a private individual are still socially significant acts. Alasdair Pettinger has noted that travel writing tends to promote the illusion of individualism by rarely describing scenes of actual travel, especially by public transport: 'One reason for this is the way that "travel" (at least since the end of the Eighteenth Century) has been conceived in terms of unique individual experiences – in contrast to the group experiences of "tourism"'.[13] Viewing individuals in the context from which they detach themselves is illuminating and instructive. Moreover, as Holland and Huggan assert, 'travel writing, however entertaining, is hardly harmless, and ... behind its apparent innocuousness and its charmingly anecdotal observations lies a series of powerfully distorting myths about other (often, "non-Western") cultures'.[14]

Of all literary genres, travel writing, which deals with encounter and observation, is best placed to transmit cultural values under the guise of straightforward report or individual impression. These often unacknowledged values need to be exposed and examined. At the same time, an exclusive concentration on textual politics risks ignoring the aesthetics of the text. This is not to say that aesthetics are not political. They are. However, it is to suggest that one should not overlook authors' handling of style and technique.

Ground rules

Jonathan Raban wrote in 1981 that 'What the travel book needs is not an elegiac history but the ground rules of an intelligent criticism'.[15] Those ground rules are still being established. Aspects of all the main literary theories – structuralism, poststructuralism, deconstruction, reception theory, psychoanalytic, Marxism, new historicism, postcolonialism, ecocriticism and theories of gender and sexuality – may be applied to travel texts.[16] In practice, these various elements often combine in critical approaches; many scholars find it impossible to separate them, opting instead to emphasise one or more. Behind all of them lies the premise that, in Barbara Korte's words, 'accounts of travel are never objective; they inevitably reveal the culture-specific and individual patterns of perception and knowledge which every traveller brings to the travelled world'.[17] That pronouncement is itself a product of the modes of reading generated by the new literary theories.

There have, however, been very few sustained applications of theory to travel texts, and no general travel theory as such has emerged. The influence of postcolonial and gender theories has been noted in earlier chapters. Theorists from other traditions whose ideas have rich promise for travel studies and are being increasingly utilised include, in particular, Roland Barthes (semiotics), Mikhail Bakhtin (dialogism) and Gilles Deleuze and Félix Guattari (nomadism).[18] Yet theoretical readings of travel writing attract hostility from some in disciplines outside English (as well as within it).

Although Said and other postcolonial theorists had a significant impact on the study of travel narratives, making it harder for historians, for example, to take accounts of encounters at face value, there are those who decry theory's frequent neglect of historical context and of textual editing. As D. B. and Alison Quinn put it, 'in an historical study of a text the context is all-important, whereas in literature many tell us the text, without its context, is the vital thing'.[19] On the other hand, in welcoming recent attention by literary critics to Columbian (and by extension to other exploration) texts, David Henige suggests that they 'bring perspectives and attitudes that have largely eluded mainline historians' and that both views can combine. In a blunt assessment of literary and historical approaches to narratives, Henige judges that 'historians need literary critics far more than literary critics need them'.[20] However, both are important and at their best complementary.

Archive research may uncover different manuscript (and printed) versions of a published narrative or reveal travel accounts that have not been published at all. These can change our view of a writer or even of a period, destination or the genre itself. Editorial interventions and interpretations can mediate in significant ways texts that do get published. Indeed, with many travel texts, especially older ones, there is the problem of whose text we are actually reading. We often tend to think of editors performing censorious roles, cleaning up narratives for polite public consumption. Yet editors – even (or especially) scholarly ones – can construct texts in ways that are quite different from the original and from one another's versions. Taking at random a passage of around 800 words from three modern editions of Las Casas's *Historia*, David Henige has shown:

> none of the editors was able successfully to duplicate the capitalization, paragraphing, and punctuation of the manuscript itself and … they each failed in ways different from the others. … As a result of the conscious and unconscious manipulation of the text, there are probably 40 to 50 discrepancies between and among modern editions for just this relatively short passage, sometimes with material consequences.[21]

Other elements to consider in the reading of travel writing include: aesthetics, audience, gender, genre, ideology, journey, landscape, language, motive, narrator, Otherness, period, place, plot, sexuality, textual status and translation, all of which have been discussed elsewhere in this book. We now turn to some of those that have received less attention in the previous pages. First, the importance of regional and textual specificity has been addressed by Susan Morgan, who states, in her book on Victorian women's travel writing about Southeast Asia:

> I have tried with the partial success attendant on any efforts of self-consciousness to abandon my well-taught and well-learned urge to 'unify' through an underlying critical emphasis on an underlying pattern or structure "in" the material. Instead, I have made an effort to

> attend as much as possible to the details, the particular and the peculiar as I see them, the representation of self and locale in a few Victorian travel books, considering each as an imperialist text. The "underlying pattern" to the argument is that there is no bare-bones British Victorian imperialist, no bare-bones British Victorian imperialism. Late twentieth-century critics approaching these travel books need to resist not only traditional truisms about Victorian culture but also more recent critiques which generalize about the nineteenth-century imperialist project. If one of the continuing villainies of imperialism has been located in an inherited European rhetoric which racially essentializes and reduced the colonized ("the Malay"), I cannot fight it or partly distance myself from it, in myself and others, through a rhetoric which essentializes and reduces the would-be colonizers ("British imperialism" or "the British colonial/imperial perspective").[22]

Morgan's sensitivity to particular circumstances and to the individual is admirable, though one must be wary of some critics' and biographers' attempts to remove individual travellers from the group they represent and whose values they transmit, even where that transmission is accompanied by a complex ambivalence or personal suffering. Recent attempts to rehabilitate Stanley and other agents of empire are a case in point. Morgan's remarks point to the truth that one of the weakest spots of travel studies has been its often blanket coverage of imperialism – stereotyping and generalising as much as some of its subjects. However, it is possible to individualise too much. Commonalities need to be observed and political as well as historical and literary inferences ought to be drawn. Morgan's is one of the less cited works in the wider field, a fact that illustrates the unfortunate and damaging truth that works on regions that are not thought marketable will either not get published – even by university presses – or not be widely read (or both). Academic colleagues in smaller, more specialised disciplines (as well as some in larger ones) struggle to get their work circulated. That is to the detriment of us all, for it means the perpetuation of dominant paradigms.

There is also the related matter of limited opportunities for travel writers and scholars working in languages other than English, or other than the major European ones, to get their voices heard. Apart from finding a willing publisher, the costs of translation can be prohibitive. Yet, as Holland and Huggan point out, 'Reading travel narratives from the perspective of the zone, rather than from that of the traveler as experiencing subject, necessarily inhibits perception of the modern traveler as pioneer/discoverer or cultural discloser'.[23]

On more mainstream questions of translation, Michael Cronin, writing in 2000, objected that, 'Indifference to the question of language in many of the key texts on writing and travel that have been published over the last two decades has led to a serious misrepresentation of both the experience of travel and the construction of narrative accounts of these experiences'.[24] In particular, he remarks with quiet amazement that the prominent historian and cultural critic James Clifford managed in his book *Routes: Travel and Translation in the Late Twentieth Century* (1997) to 'completely ignore the entire body of scholarly work on translation in a work allegedly discussing the question of translation and travel'.[25]

On a related topic, Charles Forsdick is one of a number of scholars to have complained about the dominance of the Anglophone in travel writing studies. The researches of Forsdick, Claire Lindsay and Thea Pitman who have written on Latin American travel writing, and Wendy Bracewell, who works on East European travel, are among those that complicate or question commonplace assumptions about travel writing that have developed through a lack of attentiveness to non-Anglophone examples. Forsdick suggests: 'Travel writing, as a result of its subject matter, is an inherently transcultural, transnational, even translingual phenomenon. Travel accounts travel, through time, through space, through different cultures and between languages, often ... being transformed by such processes', but 'the extent to which this essential characteristic of travel writing is reflected in the ways in which the form is studied remains unclear'. Forsdick argues that 'much criticism still appears to evolve along exclusively national or monolingual lines', although he notes 'a number of recent collections' that he believes suggests 'a genuine internationalisation of research in the field is well under way'.[26] Those recent collections are in European languages. More attention to travel accounts in non-European languages would not only expand and confront dominant assumptions but would alert us to different conceptions and metaphors of travel, shaking the general framework of analyses. For example, Nabil Matar argues that 'The Arabic travel accounts cannot ... be approached through the theoretical models with which European accounts have been studied by writers as different as Stephen Greenblatt, Edward Said, and Gayatri Spivak'. According to Matar, Arab travellers did not possess the attitudes and preconceptions shown by Europeans towards, say, the Orient; they 'were not harbingers of an Islamic imperialism':

> Rather, they wrote empirical accounts about Europe with the same precision that many of their coreligionists used to describe their journeys within the world of Islam, and in the case of the Christian travelers, within the world at large. Furthermore and unlike the European travelers who used classical or biblical sources as their guides, the Arabs did not have previous models with which to compare or

> contrast Europe and America. They went with an open mind and a clean slate....
>
> ... the writers viewed travel as a means of experiencing rather than denouncing that which was culturally and socially different.

Matar emphasises that in the matter of religion, the 'one area in which Muslim travelers were constantly vociferous and condemnatory ... the hostility to the Euro-Christians remained doctrinal and historical (based on their own and their predecessors' experiences), not racial or cultural'.[27] Whatever the truth of this, the important point is his claim that it would be inappropriate to apply to these texts the theoretical models that are employed in readings of European ones.

Cronin's case is distinct from this. He points out that communication between or even within languages is not as transparent or straightforward as it is usually depicted in travel accounts, and he compares the translator 'ceaselessly moving between languages and cultures' with the nomad, in what we might call a liminal space.[28]

Loredana Polezzi delineates some of the elements of 'the connected nature of travel and translation', which include: 'the way in which travellers have always relied upon interpreters, as well as acting as intermediaries in their own right; the need experienced by both translators and travellers to relay the new through the known, the unfamiliar in terms of the familiar; the ultimate unreliability of those who travel and those who translate; their potential to deceive, confound and betray, as well as to act as reliable guides, mediators and witnesses'.[29] Translation studies have been affected by the ideas we have outlined from travel and postcolonial studies. Pointing to the complications caused by 'the presence of multilingual, multicultural audiences', Polezzi notes: 'Both the traveller/writer and the translator are finding it increasingly difficult to avoid the question posed by postcolonial scholars ... : who speaks, and also who translates, for whom? There is no single, absolute answer to this interrogation'.[30] The circumstances that have led to an increased market for literary translation 'gives rise to both production and reception scenarios which do not easily fit with well-worn binary models of "here" and "there", "home" and "abroad"'. Increasingly, authors are addressing 'multiple, complex audiences'.[31] Polezzi offers another explanation for the phenomenon we noted earlier in the book: 'the rise in the number of self-deprecating, ironic travel texts and the increasingly popular choice of irreverent but also unprepossessing personae on the part of their authors/narrators'.[32] According to Polezzi, this increase is probably due, at least in part, to travel writers' growing awareness that their narratives may circulate among their subjects. The assumption of a single truthful position will no longer do. Indigenous people look at and write back to those under whose gaze they were formerly fixed.

Drawing on the work of Robert Young and James Clifford, Polezzi points out that 'both travellers and translators, as well as their products, are deeply enmeshed in relationships of power and in their constant renegotiation.... both travel and translation practices are involved in the making and unmaking of representations which have a central role to play in creating and maintaining (or destabilizing) cultural as well as political and economic hierarchies'.[33] They, 'far from being neutral or academic, have both practical and moral consequences'.[34]

In short, translation furnishes another example of layers of mediation between the act of travel and its relation. There are many other external and internal factors to consider if we are to appreciate the layers that are interposed between the experience of travel and its narrative. As mentioned earlier, the type of transport taken influences how people travel and how they write up their travels. Journeys by foot, horseback, ship, stagecoach, train, bicycle, motorbike, car and plane each result in accounts that owe something of their structure and perspective to the mode and pace of motion. Yet the writing itself is not straightforward. Roy Bridges, an historian of East African exploration, has identified three categories of production in explorers' documents: 'There is the first-stage or "raw" record made as [the explorer] went along, the more considered and organised journal or perhaps letter written during intervals of greater leisure and finally the definitive account of the expedition, usually composed after his return to Europe with a view to publication'.[35] Whether one views the initial, 'raw' record or the polished, published account as the most accurate, neither is unmediated truth. We may think of the former as undertaken on the spot, immediately or very soon after the event that is described. But how travellers approach events that are noted in the 'raw' record is already influenced, if not determined, by their socialisation; by their cultural contexts and ideology.[36] Nonetheless, to make this qualification is to introduce another layer between the traveller and his or her account. Bridges is just one of a number of scholars to have delineated different stages between the initial writing and the public consumption of it. Leila Koivunen quotes from Ian MacLaren, who has shown that explorers' texts were 'often considerably changed during four stages of composition ... and were thus not reliable records of what a traveller had experienced'.[37] These four stages are: 'the field note or log book entry which is written en route, the journal where the field notes are built into sentences and paragraphs, the draft manuscript for a book and the publication'.[38] Koivunen herself examines the factors affecting the visual representation of Africa in nineteenth-century travel accounts.

In a further distinction, Jeremy Black advises that 'published travel literature should be sharply differentiated from letters and journals never intended for publication'.[39] This is because travellers will address private and public audiences differently and because the conventions expected by publishers, reviewers and general readers of the genre will further intervene between the traveller's experience and his or her relation of it. Black recognises that this does not mean that the more intimate record is necessarily the more truthful: artifice could still play a role and activities might be disguised, but, he maintains, 'even if the written record was somewhat contrived, there was a major difference between writing for an intimate circle, and producing a work for a large anonymous market'.[40] Moreover, what Black has stated of the eighteenth century generally, that travel literature is 'at a remove from the experiences of ordinary tourists', applies in other periods, too.[41] Black has mainly on his mind the overlapping conventions of eighteenth-century fiction, especially the picaresque. Similar processes are at play with the literature of other centuries, but – besides differences in social class that may distinguish the traveller from the tourist – it is also likely that the traveller who intends to write (at least for publication) will see and travel differently from the one who does not.

Nor are travel texts only about reading. They are about looking, too. Many are illustrated. Art historian Leila Koivunen reminds us:

> Pictures had been utilized in disseminating information for Europeans since at least the Middle Ages, but during the nineteenth century this reached new dimensions. New methods for printing pictures were introduced which in combination with other technological innovations meant that the mass production of illustrated newspapers, books and pamphlets could now be carried out at a reasonable price. . . . Consequently, more images were printed and circulated than ever before. . . . The general visualization of Western culture and the growing emphasis on vision has often been estimated to have had an immense, even a revolutionary, effect on people's conceptions of the world.[42]

Although hers is far from being the only study of visual images and travel, Koivunen's observation that 'the practices of visual documentation during the journeys of exploration in Africa have yet to be thoroughly examined' is true of illustrations in travel accounts more generally, and her surprise at the 'almost complete absence of studies on the effects the publishing and illustrating processes had on new illustrations' is justified.[43] Her study is also a caution against attributing to a single author responsibility for the entire content of illustrated travel books: 'In the late nineteenth century, every picture still had to go through a complex, multistage process to be included in printed matter whereby several persons – publishers, artists, engravers, lithographers, printers and many others – were involved and influenced the results'.[44]

Where we enter

As Barbara Korte rightly observes, 'More acutely than any other genre ... travel writing is defined by the interaction of the human subject with the world'.[45] That interaction and the ways in which it is described ensure that the main elements of travel writing all lend themselves to theoretically informed readings. The world with which the subject interacts is made of landscape, people and cultures. Increasingly, scholarship has shown how landscape is not a natural given but is an ideological construct, reflecting the values of the beholder and his or her society. What we are presented with is not a view of nature but a reflection of culture; of social factors. Additionally, readings of travel texts may be influenced not only by the geographical region that is travelled to but by the kind of terrain encountered. Descriptions of travel in mountains, seas, deserts, forests, cities and the countryside all have their own characteristics and there have been some specialist studies of each of these, examining the similarities and differences between texts. There is plenty of scope for these investigations to be furthered.

Holland and Huggan state that 'travel writing enjoys an intermediary status between subjective inquiry and objective documentation'.[46] This immediately entails two things: the construction of the self and of the other and the relationship between fact and fiction. Both may be suggested in Holland and Huggan's observation that 'The roving "I"s of travel narratives ... are often drawn to surfaces – more particularly, to bodies – onto which they project their fears and fantasies of the ethnicized cultural "other."'[47] The travelling first-person narrator not only looks at those who inhabit the places through which he or she passes, but views them in ways that throw light on his or her own anxieties and desires and (some critics would say) of the home culture. The subjectivity revealed in this process compromises the objective quality and it is carried through some of the techniques and strategies of fiction. Travel texts display a combination of both facets, with each often in tension with the other. We should not expect to find consistency in most texts.

Besides, or rather because of, what is now commonly referred to as the hybridity of travel writing, there is what seems to be a hybridity of approaches to the reading of it. Not only are these informed by a selection of ideas from many schools of literary and cultural theory, but different scholarly disciplines have different interests, points of focus, principles and conventions. Part of the difficulty is identified by Steve Clark: 'the genre [travel writing] presents a problem for academic studies. It seems too dependent on an empirical rendition of contingent events, what happened to happen, for entry into the literary canon, yet too overtly rhetorical for disciplines such as anthropology, sociology, geography or history'.[48]

Travel writing, probably even more than other forms of literature, is capable of being read differently by a range of disciplines. It is, of course, open to diverse interpretations by scholars within any one of those fields of study. Some travel authors strive for this openness; others write more closed texts but these are nevertheless subject to readings that open them up. Either way, a sense of fluidity, of movement, is generated that complements their subject. That impression extends from the micro-level to the macro; from the individual text (or passage from it) to the body of travel writing in general. The field itself is dynamic. Broadly speaking, readings of travel texts have veered between the literal and (using the term very loosely) the deconstructive. The former take travel narratives as uncomplicated, straightforward renderings of truth. They see texts as recording what the traveller saw and they accept the observations as accurate. The critical readings are more suspicious of them. They aim to expose the ideological workings of texts and they maintain that, far from showing the truth, texts are value-laden, reflecting the perspective and attitudes of the author and his or her audience. Common to both approaches – or at least not identified exclusively with either – is the formalist approach, in which the literary techniques and devices of the travel narrative are examined. A result of these different approaches is that texts are liable to different readings. This is true of any literary work that is subject to the gaze of critical theory, but applied to travel writing it has the effect of keeping texts on the move. They cannot be pinned down or fixed.

Holland and Huggan have observed that 'Travel narratives strive to express the unfamiliar, but also to contain it',[49] by which they mean 'contain' in the sense of include but also in the sense of enclose. That is, the process of describing other landscapes, cultures and so on necessarily entails incorporation and enclosure; the things that travellers witness and the people that they encounter are brought into the frame. Critical emphasis on hybridity and transgression may be taken as a way of avoiding or overcoming this exercise of power. Travel texts are not fixed or stable: their meanings are determined by readers as much as by authors, and those meanings may vary according to readers' social, geographical and historical contexts and according to the critical approach consciously adopted.

The readings covered in this volume are produced from within the academy, albeit in response to broader social and intellectual developments. They differ, at least in emphasis, from those of the general public, for whom the pleasure of the narrative and the interest of the information may take priority over the politics of the text. That is not to say that readings for critical analysis afford no pleasure, nor that people outside universities read unthinkingly or uncritically. In general terms, though, the gap between scholarly criticism of travel books and the wider public's appreciation of them is similar to that concerning other kinds of literature, but it seems more striking in the case of travel writing because of the popularity of the form. It is, however, fitting that travel narratives should be the subject of varied, competing and sometimes contradictory readings, for these approaches and responses reinvest the texts with movement, thus refusing attempts to fix the world. The desirability of this lies in their exposure of the ways in which views are shaped, constructed and recycled.

Whether academic or non-academic, the audience helps determine the form and content of travel texts. The market decides what gets published. Experimental texts reach a small, probably academic readership, whereas publishers wanting to maximise sales rely on established and popular formulae. Holland and Huggan's claim – in their valuable book, one of the very best examinations of modern travel writing – that 'Travel writing, for all its sensationalism, is inherently conservative, its narratives serving to repeat and consolidate tropological myths', should implicate readers as much as authors.[50] There are many travel books that are radical in their politics and adventurous in their treatment of form, but they tend not to sell well, or to be disparaged, even by their authors, and they soon fall from sight, their presence too fleeting and their visibility too low to prevent such assumptions from being made, repeated and consolidated. Be that as it may, the point on which we should end this chapter is the determinant that we often ignore: ourselves.

In her 1935 book, *North to the Orient*, aviator Anne Morrow Lindbergh describes coverage of her and her husband's 1931 take-off from Long Island on 27 July 1931:

> I had a moment to wait and watch the crowd. A radio announcer was speaking into his microphone. 'Mrs. Lindbergh,' he started smoothly, with a glance at me, 'is wearing a leather flying helmet and leather coat, and high leather flying boots'.
>
> 'Why!' I thought blankly, looking down at a costume which did not correspond at all to his description. What nonsense! It was much too hot to wear leather. The sun beat down on my bare head and sticky cotton blouse; the hot planks of the pier burned through my thin

> rubber sneakers. What made him say that, I wondered. Oh, of course, it isn't the conventional flying costume. They have to say that I am dressed in leather. I see, you needn't bother to tell me again, I thought, looking at the announcer. I know, 'The Great Radio Public must not be disappointed!'[51]

It is not so much the radio announcer who is responsible for re-dressing Anne Lindbergh in leather (assuming she is telling us the truth about the episode); rather it is the readers whose expectations are being met. We are the ones who clothe the aviator.

Chapter 12

The way ahead: Travel writing in the twenty-first century

All the time, the horizons shift for travel writers. There are still stories to tell.
Annie Caulfield[1]

There is a widespread perception that travel and writing about it have lost their value in our global age as they become more accessible to and practised by more people. Jan Morris, for example, has complained that 'Few of us want to be called travel writers nowadays, the genre having been cheapened and weakened in these times of universal travel and almost universal literary ambition'.[2] Such grumbles are far from new. In 1891, W. Fraser Rae observed: 'The complaint now is that too many persons think the trips which they make under the auspices of Messrs. Thomas Cook and Son deserving of commemoration in a volume'. Simply leaving globetrotters' books alone will, Rae advises, 'ensure a cessation of an old tale being retold'.[3] It was unlikely that their books would be left alone in Rae's time and it is impossible for their modern avatars to be ignored now; the proliferation of blogs and the increasing ease of self-publishing means that the production of travellers' accounts will not be halted by any decline in readership. That should be no cause for alarm or despondency; universal travel and literary ambition should be cheered. Volume does not impede quality. We ought to celebrate what Jonathan Raban has hailed as 'the resilience of the form [of travel writing], its omnivorous appetite for writing of all kinds – fact, fiction, drama, note, testament'.[4]

Travel writing has historically been associated with discovery, expansion and settlement. Yet we are accustomed to thinking of the twenty-first century as one in which the world has grown smaller, thanks to globalisation and new media technologies. Having reviewed the history and some of the characteristics of travel writing, it is now time to wonder how it might develop. Some of the following remarks will inevitably apply to twentieth-century texts (and to earlier ones also). There is no reason why literature published early in a new century should differ significantly from that published in the late years of the old one: the urge to classify art by century is as powerful as it is arbitrary, but it remains a common and psychologically appealing way of defining literary and other works. So, travel writing of the twenty-first century, the subject of some thoughts in this final chapter, will be indistinguishable in some respects from its predecessors. Nonetheless, the time at which I write this, early in the second decade of the century, affords an opportunity both to notice some continuities and developments and to make some predictions about the path ahead.

Cybertravel

Travel writing, like all literature, responds to new technologies. The means and speed of motion affect the way people experience their travel as well as how they write about it. The Internet presents a special case. Sidonie Smith, writing in 2001, anticipates that 'undoubtedly, new kinds of travel narratives will emerge with this new technology of postmodernity', and sees signs of them already doing so.[5] She does not see the Internet as a complete departure: she compares travel in cyberspace to modern business travel, in which people are transported 'from one geographical location to another at high speeds' and are insulated by airport terminals, shuttles and international hotels from everyday local life.[6] For Smith, 'Airplane travel with its network of routes, hubs, terminals, and homes away from home, maps global space in ways analogous to the geography of the communications networks that take people from their computer terminals into cyberspace'.[7] The Internet enables actual travel but the experience of using it creates the feeling of travel taking place. Sue Thomas describes how her discovery of the Internet in 1995 led her to 'spend my days constantly travelling without leaving my desk'.[8] Her paradoxical claim to have travelled without travelling illustrates what Michael Cronin, among others, has noted: 'the Internet is saturated with the rhetoric of travel'.[9] That language includes: home, site, surfing, landing, navigating, portal, visiting, entering, exiting and the hyperlink (a 'piece of code which makes it possible for us to travel smoothly through cyberspace as easily as we walk around our own cities and homes'[10]). For many users, the practice goes beyond metaphor; for them, it really is a method of travel. Thomas proclaims that the Internet allows her to manufacture new and multiple identities: 'Overnight, it seemed, I went from being one person with a single name to existing as a number of identities created by me but not always recognisable as me, even by myself. And these bodies inhabited new and varied landscapes' (p.9). The Internet means that, 'We have an alternative mental geography now' (p.39). Thomas quotes 'cybergeographer' Martin Dodge as observing that we now exist in 'an experiential continuum, running from the materiality of geographic space through to the virtuality of cyberspace'.[11] Quite how far this continuum extends in the perceptions of some is evidenced by Thomas's sudden thought that 'The landscape is itself a hypertext'. In the countryside around her home, 'Moving from one field to the next, making choices at each gateway, is just like browsing web-pages' (p.263). Thus, if we accept this premise, not only does the Internet provide a new mental geography; it alters one's reading of the external world. Just as the traveller sees the destination through the lens of the familiar, the Internet traveller reconfigures the landscape outside.

In some media discourse, the Internet is a scary and dangerous place, but for Thomas it seems a more welcome home than the physical world outside, or 'RL' as she calls Real Life to distinguish it from 'VL' or Virtual Life (p.27). She tells us that she has never been sure where she belongs, 'but cyberspace is much more comfortable than any other place I know' (p.64). That idea of not knowing where one belongs is another expression of the contemporary urge, articulated most persistently and powerfully by Bruce Chatwin, to posit oneself as rootless and on the move. For Thomas, the increased interconnectedness, miniaturisation and portability of the computer world means that 'We are learning to be nomads again' (p.39). Nomadism, as we have seen, has become a popular trope in travel writing and theory.

It is not only a matter of image and metaphor, however; there are structural considerations, too. Critics have pointed to the effect of the Internet on narrative. Thomas's proclamation that 'an increasing number of artists are discovering that time and terrain have very different qualities in cyberspace' (p.69) is even truer now than it was when she made it in 2004. Yet while there have been academic studies on the composition of computer games, the same attention has not been given to how the Internet has affected narratives of travel. The Internet is widely seen as democratic, bringing about greater collaboration and more open access. Thomas points to the collective nature of cyberspace: 'It is rarely the product of an individual creative act produced by a lone genius novelist. Instead, net life is the outcome of a complex sequencing of the collective imagination. Indeed, its very topography depends on the makings of all those engaged with it' (p.11).

There are two important implications here. First, the collaborative quality has the potential to alter radically the way travel stories are told. Travel narratives are traditionally told by individuals and, despite some attempts inspired by ethnographic theory to be dialogic (i.e., to introduce the voice of the Other), they largely remain monologic.[12] Second, of real significance for travel writing is the greater democratisation that Internet access is often said to bring. Users have information available to them in previously unimaginable quantities, but are also able to make their own narratives look professional and to circulate them on an unprecedented scale. The travel reflections of non-professional writers are distributed globally.

Travel experiences that in earlier times would have remained private, seen only by family and friends, are now available for all to read online. In addition to being posted on social network sites such as Facebook, these are often in the form of blogs, which are commonly assumed to be a sign of greater opportunity and empowerment, allowing anyone who can get online to publish their thoughts and experiences. Some sites let users map their travels. While one may assume that these opportunities will result in greater individuality and diversity, many sites offer proforma blogs. Such sites include: http://www.travellerspoint.com/blog.cfm which, at the time of writing, is a free travel blog that offers those who register with it a number of features.[13] Among these is the facility to plot one's journey on a map prior to departure. The user's blog entries will automatically be tied to their map, and their map can be embedded in their blogs. The map can also be added to their Facebook profile. Travel photos can be added to their blogs and videos can also be uploaded. Furthermore, the journeys of others on the web can be tracked. The use of Google Analytics means that one can see what visitors to one's site have viewed immediately before landing on it, and what articles they have read. Friends and families can comment on one's site and multiple authors can be added to one's blog, which can also be password protected. The site boasts: 'We're a global site, blog in **any language** and it just works'.

Although they may offer a variety of templates or allow customisation, the very fact of a template implies standardisation. The availability of these forms and formats raises the question of whether users' freedom is as great as generally believed. One might argue that these constraints simply make visible the kinds of generic limits with which travel writers have always operated, working with existing conventions and physical forms, but it is more likely that the use of prescribed formats constrains presentation and expression. Blogs may not represent the increased independence and creativity that many take for granted is the case. How far the individual ethos of literary travel narratives is challenged by the collective voice of travellers' discussions on the Internet is far from certain.

Among the many other blog sites are travelblog and travelpod.[14] Some of these, too, offer the facility to plot one's course on a map. Also important to the recording and sharing of travel experiences are Tumblr and Flickr, while Twitter offers more brevity than the postcard. There is no doubting the opportunities that such sites have given travellers for the recording of their journeys. In that sense, there has certainly been an empowerment of the ordinary traveller. Yet the sheer number of blogs means that, whether one looks for them through the host site or independently, only a handful of people who are not already friends or family with the authors are likely even to find them, let alone read them. There are also a growing number of sites that provide a forum for travel writers to publish online.

An obvious difference between the blogs and literary travels is that the former are, on the whole, simply a record of the traveller's journey, however attractively packaged. Most lack the quality of the narrative persona that raises the recounting of experience above the mundane and banal. It is not right to conclude from this that the Internet has been detrimental to travel literature. Computer technology has allowed for cheaper reprints and free scans of older travel books (both well-known and obscure), as well as newly edited versions, making many of them available widely and instantaneously, on demand. Even as the new is formed, the old enjoys freer and greater circulation.[15] In addition, there are now more interactive and multi-layered editorial possibilities, and E-readers mean portability also.

The swift pace of change in the Internet era makes it difficult to predict further innovations. Recent and current trends include electronic guides, providing tourist and travel information about the area through which one is moving. It is likely that these will give an increased semblance of being personally tailored to the individual user based on knowledge of his or her preferences. How far they will differ from printed guidebooks in their positioning of the tourist remains to be seen.

These largely positive developments are compromised by the inequalities that restrict use of the Internet as much as they do physical travel. What Smith observed at the start of the twenty-first century still holds: 'Access to the Net and to cyberspace is still the prerogative of a relatively privileged group of people ... There is little to no access to computer technologies, let alone networks and cyberspace, for millions of women and men across the globe'.[16] Furthermore:

> Cyberspace travel not only reproduces unequal relations of class and caste, it also reproduces the gendered social relations of (post) modernity. For the terrain of entry is not an alternative terrain, an elsewhere to the cultural relations of "real" space. The objects that are made for this kind of mobility and the environment surrounding those objects are fully inflected with codes and spectacles of masculinity and femininity that permeate the real world.[17]

Although the Internet enables physical and figurative travel, it also reflects the gender constructions of the world outside the computer. As Smith puts it, 'Like the air of early aviation, virtual air is saturated with the values of the larger society'.[18] Indeed, one of the Internet's most prolific uses, pornography, may be seen as a kind of sex tourism, the more so when non-white women (and men) are presented as exotic objects for the gratification of white males. Arguments that some women actively engage with and profit from the activity may parallel those about the extent to which local peoples benefit from the exploitation of tourists' appetites.

Smith recognises that

> The cyberspace traveler can fabricate identities to defy, evade, or confuse the constitutive constraints of normative femininity in the world outside the Net. She can take a man's name, for instance, or a gender-neutral name, as she traverses the multiple itineraries available to her on the Net. Or she can assume the identity of someone from an entirely different culture.... Here is travel with radically undefining effects.[19]

These are opportunities not easily available to print authors unless they write under pseudonyms, in which case the marketing of the persona is impossible without the author breaking cover. On the other hand, Smith goes on, there is, at the heart of the Internet and of virtual travel, a disembodiment; a repression of the body. According to Smith, it is the 'suspicion and devaluing of embodiment that has kept the place of woman a place of sessility', and 'This unmarked body of the virtual world is the normative subject of travel, empowered, masculine and white. He is an Odysseus of the virtual'.[20] In Smith's view, 'The challenge cybertravelers face is how to negotiate virtual journeying so that women become resistors along the circuits'.[21] This complements Debbie Lisle's diagnosis of women travel writers having to work within male structures.

Prognosis

To return to the travel book itself, the prognosis may at first seem bleak. The grim outlook of practitioners such as Jan Morris, who want to disown the label, has been noted in Chapter 1 and above. And if several prominent critics are to be believed, there is little prospect of an escape from what many believe to be the ideological origins of the genre. Thus Lisle, for example, insists that 'embedded in the cosmopolitan vision of many travel writers is a reconstructed framework of colonialism and patriarchy'.[22] Patrick Holland and Graham Huggan argue that contemporary travel writing has survived and flourished 'by invoking a number of late-capitalist cultural possibilities. Three of these [are] ... commodification, specialization, and nostalgic parody'.[23] Holland and Huggan do admit that, 'Counter-travel, of one sort or another, has certainly energized travel writing and, increasingly, travel theory in the decades since the war' but they maintain that 'such oppositional narratives cannot escape being haunted by an array of hoary tropes and clichés (originary, primitivist, exotic, etc.), any more than they can hope to distill "authentic" encounters from their commodified sources'. Holland and Huggan concede that their own book may be complicit with the market, a rare acknowledgement from critics that their own practice is not immune from the faults they find in others.[24] Perhaps their example will yet encourage more self-critical scrutiny.

The tenor of much critical work on travel writing, and one shared increasingly by travel writing itself, is of ethical concerns. In the main, these revolve around the traveller's relationships with the community he or she is visiting, with an emphasis on less exploitative practices. Travel writer, photographer and 'responsible tourism expert' Jeff Greenwald advises would-be ethical travellers to 'Learn some of the local language. Most importantly, realize that the people in the place you visit are human beings like you. They're not objects in a museum display case. Treat people as you would wish to be treated'.[25]

Many more travellers now are keen to enjoy a harmonious relationship with the environment. Ecological interests foster a sense of a shared world. Fears of global warming reinforce the feeling of common cause. Greenwald addresses the paradox facing those who attempt to reconcile the principles of ethical travel with the mode of transportation that many take:

> One of the first things you can do to become a more ethical [traveller] is to offset the carbon emissions of your flight. Jets burn tons of fuel, and produce huge amounts of carbon dioxide. By the simple act of traveling, you are contributing to the problem. Why not be part of the solution? There are a number of non-profits that offer carbon buy-backs, and plant trees to offset your calculated carbon emissions.[26]

For the investigative journalist and environmental campaigner George Monbiot, that paradox cannot be resolved: 'it has become plain to me that long-distance travel, high speed and the curtailment of climate change are not compatible. If you fly, you destroy other people's lives'.[27]

Twenty-first century travel writing may see a proliferation of narratives born of these anxieties and new commitments. Ethical, 'green', sustainable and eco-tourism are all cognate, if not synonymous, terms for responsible, environmentally and politically concerned leisure travel. Slow travel, though it has a tradition going back at least to nineteenth-century pedestrianism, is another facet of this phenomenon. One anticipates a new generation of travel narratives that will either succumb to or break free from the older tropes of anti-modern primitivism.

Nature writing is enjoying a resurgence with the rising concern about the loss of habitats and species, global warming and the future of the planet. Readings of green travel are being deepened by the development of ecocriticism. Some of the narratives are redolent of salvage ethnography, with the air of preserving for us in the text lifeways that are about to disappear. Other texts exhibit the kind of remembrance for a now lost golden age that Raymond Williams, in his *The Country and the City*, traces back to classical times and sees as typically applying to a period half a century before the writer's own.

Although there may now be a greater general desire for a more empathetic, less exploitative approach to the Other, there remains the fact, inherent in the genre, that 'Difference in any form is domesticated by the travel writer's power to arrange events, others and objects into a coherent narrative'.[28] No matter how well-intentioned in its wish to break from past models that reinforced inequality, travel writing has its authors orchestrate and tame the foreign and unfamiliar. Difference will always be compromised and mediated, however serious the attempts to respect and represent it; even to facilitate its self-representation. Indeed, the preservation of difference is desired, for 'In effect the more difference displayed by locals, the more authentic the encounter is'.[29] Difference marks the sign and the evidence of travel and encounter. This is true of guidebooks, as well as of literary travel writing. David Callahan has noted, for example, that 'Lonely Planet texts of different types are inevitably caught up in an emphasis on difference and consequently the essentializing of difference'. He observes that travel guides are 'selling signposts to potential pleasure in the future for their readers'.[30]

As always with travel writing, we will continue to see tensions within the corpus and within individual examples. Holland and Huggan expound their thesis 'that travel writing frequently provides an effective alibi for the perpetuation or reinstallment of ethnocentrically superior attitudes to "other" cultures, peoples, and places'. They write that 'This thesis is complicated, though, by the defamiliarizing capacities of travel writing, and by its attempts, keeping pace with change, to adjust its sights to new perceptions – both of "other" cultures, peoples, and places'.[31] Thus, whatever attempts travel writers make to have their writings reflect the realities of twenty-first century life, they will be working within the constraints of the genre, stretching and teasing them but finding it hard to break them out of shape.

Probably the most common kind of travel writing at present is the 'footsteps' genre, or what Peter Hulme calls the 'ambulent gloss' and what Maria Lindgren Leavenworth calls the 'second journey', in which the author-protagonists journey in the steps of earlier travellers (ones to whom they might or might not be related).[32] Many of these are thin and dreary offerings, but there are some very honourable exceptions, including Jonathan Raban's *Old Glory*, in which the author-narrator pilots a boat on the Mississippi, partly in the wake of Huck Finn. While this popular motif provides the gimmick and the tag that appeal to publishers' marketing departments and to readers, it suggests, on another level, that foreignness exists in the past. Earlier travellers and their contexts offer other territories to be explored. This type of book, which dominates the shelves of travel writing sections of bookshops, is generally as predictable in content as it is unadventurous in form. Alongside it sit reprints of classic travel texts, another sign that earlier publications are used to fulfil the same function as distant lands once did: to serve up the exotic. Leavenworth, however, is more optimistic about the footsteps or 'second journey' (sub)genre that some find uninspired and stale. She writes that 'the recycling of itineraries indicates not exhaustion but a process of renewal'.[33] An attraction of the latter is that it can create a distance between ourselves and earlier values with which we are uncomfortable or suspect that we should be. This method can be a way of neutralising nostalgia for the days of empire and patriarchy.

Whatever the extent of revision and renewal or rebirth, travel writing remains (at least in its Anglophone and other European versions) predominantly written by white authors. It may at best be in dialogue with its forebears, and there are plenty of examples of postcolonial and countertravel texts; and neglected manuscript accounts are being newly published.[34] Yet the kinds of experiences and voices that would provide a real counter are found mostly outside travel writing; even outside *writing*. Indigenous and migrant voices are more widely disseminated now, via the Internet.[35] Many of these are told in visual or oral form but some are transcribed and can be classed as travel writing according to our strict definition of the term. Such initiatives will only increase.

Experiments in form, technique and style have attracted more academic than popular attention (and sometimes not even much academic notice). Others have won a wide readership. W. G. Sebald's *The Rings of Saturn* (1995, translated 1998), with local, rural walks as a structural motif, laid the path for sophisticated, intricately woven layers of narrative, digression and the exploration of history and memory. Joseph Brodsky's *Watermark* (1992) uses the author's many visits to Venice as a point of reflection and meditation. More postcolonial travellers are travelling and writing back to the so-called centre, or journeying from within it. Although these experiments do exist, we should not be too celebratory of our own era. Experiments were conducted in earlier periods as well; they are not unique to our own. Nor is our own period marked by a more general liberal attitude. Stereotyping of other cultures still occurs, along with ethnocentrism, even xenophobia, and an arrogant reassertion of dominant Western values. Corinne Fowler has shown how nineteenth-century images of Afghanistan from travel writing and other literature and media were recycled during 'Operation Enduring Freedom'.[36] There is still also a preponderance of volumes that repeat many of the elements afflicting earlier examples: laughter at funny foreigners; a self-obsessive or self-aggrandising narrator; gimmicks; lack of interest in and knowledge of the place travelled to its culture, and so on.

Nevertheless, questions are still posed by the content and form of the genre, especially in the hands of poets and novelists who turn their hand to it. As its title suggests, Peter Carey's *Wrong about Japan* (2004) questions its own authority as a travel text. The author, an Australian resident in the United States, does not get Japan right. He understands it less than does his twelve-year old son Charley, who has gained prior and up-to-date knowledge of the country through *manga* and *anime* and through Takashi, a friend he has made on the Internet and whom they meet. Charley is more at ease in the country than is his father, whose experiences cause him to write at one point: 'It is the nature of tourism that one returns not only with trinkets and postcards but also with memories of misunderstandings, hurts ignorantly inflicted across the borderlines of language and custom'.[37] Carey's realisation, reached largely through the guidance of his son, that the 'real Japan' does not consist only of classical culture, is about the only thing he does come to understand.

Perhaps this turning to a pre-teen child for comprehension is a sign of a loss of certainty in the postcolonial world. Yet it might be, too, as the conclusion of the book suggests, that Carey ends up restoring a stereotype of Japan as mysterious. When Charley leaves with Takashi's grandmother a present for her grandson and she kisses him, her action surprises them. They wonder if they have seen in this unexpected gesture the real Japan, and Charley tells his father, 'Let's get out of here before we learn we're wrong' (p.121). Because Charley has been right more often than his father, the implication that staying longer will expose further misunderstandings can be taken to reinforce a sense of mystery. If it is misleading to take this undermining of authority as a dominant or even typical trend in contemporary travel writing, its self-questioning nevertheless invites doubt about the status of the genre – doubts that are only compounded by the subsequent revelation that Carey's account is not as factual as it seems. Self-referentiality, fragmentariness, decentering, deferral of meaning and unreliability are features of enough travel writing already this century to suggest that readers will find themselves more aware of its structural and other textual devices as these are directly commented upon. Once noticed in works where they are held up for attention, they will be observed and scrutinised in other books where they lie concealed. When we see that authors have deliberately made their handling of literary conventions and strategies visible, we will be more attuned to these and look for them when we turn to works by authors who prefer not to draw our attention to how they tell their story.

A fast-growing area is the production of comic books or graphic novels dealing with travel. Examples include Guy Delisle's *Pyongyang: A Journey in North Korea* (2006) and *Shenzhen: A Travelogue from China* (2006), and Joe Sacco's *Safe Area Goražde* (2000), *Palestine* (2003) and *Footnotes in Gaza* (2009). Some historical material has also been reworked into graphic novel form. For example, the translated text of the 1634 journal of Dutch trader Harmen Meyndertsz van den Bogaert's journey into what is now New York State has been given comic book treatment to show his adventure and his encounters with Native Americans. These utilise many of the same general features of conventional travel accounts: first-person narratives of journeys that have been undertaken by the author, usually told in chronological order, but with their framing more visible. The illustrations that accompany the text are indeed more an integral part of it than those in predominantly prose narratives, and they offer another level of mediation between the travel and the representation of it; between the author and his or her narrative figure. In this regard, there is an extra degree of exteriority or distance than is to be found in conventional travelogues.

Literary conventions and gendered discourses will continue to be challenged by gay travel writing, as we saw in Chapter 9. It remains too little discussed, although in recent years there have been more openly gay travel texts, prominent among them Duncan Fallowell's. This is an area of travel writing in which innovation will continue, raising further questions about both the writing and reading of travel, as well as about the practice of travel itself.

New technologies will continue to affect how travel is written about, represented visually and made available in multi-media formats. The century has also seen astronauts delivering messages from space via Twitter. The first of these was from Mike Massimino who tweeted to his quarter-of-a-million followers in May 2009: 'From orbit: Launch was awesome!! I am feeling great, working hard, & enjoying the magnificent views, the adventure of a lifetime has begun'.[38] Such messages may be read as electronic postcards. One might question whether tweets, emails, blogs and texts count as travel writing at all. The question would return us to the problem of definition with which this book began. That is not inappropriate, for discussions of travel writing as a genre are circular. As for literary travel writing, it is difficult to see the trend for ever greater individuation decreasing. At one end of the range, new gimmicks will be found; at the other, sophisticated narrative voices and personae will be developed.

So far as academic studies of travel writing are concerned, technology will continue to lead to new developments here as well. Some cannot be foreseen, but a significant pointer is the use, under the project leadership of Adrian Wisnicki, of spectral imaging to make readable a letter of Dr. Livingstone's that was previously illegible. Appropriately, the process and results are themselves detailed on the Internet.[39] Greater interactivity is likely to come into play as editorial and digital practices combine over the next few years. Publishers' finances and willingness permitting, we shall see more studies of travel to, from and within countries and regions that have so far been neglected, and one hopes to see more locally inflected theories of travel emerge from under the dominance of Anglo-American models. These may be built on and would complement the wealth of archive sources in many of the former colonies. Essays and monographs on, and editions of, travel writing in many more national and linguistic traditions in the Americas, Africa and Asia and in the former communist countries of Eastern Europe will (again, depending on committed publishers) appear in larger numbers. Under-studied subjects that have rich potential include age and travel writing. One expects also more studies of the relationship between transport innovations and travel writing and on indigenous perspectives. The effect will be to challenge further the view of travel writing as conservative or monolithic.[40] Perhaps a result of such work will be the need to re-emphasise the complicity of some travel writing with empire and capitalism. Historiographies of travel writing criticism are needed so that accounts of its trajectory in works like the present one can be challenged or confirmed.

Conclusion

The observations in this chapter imply that travel writing has become no easier to define or classify. If anything, its forms have become more diverse. However, the ethical function of travel remains strong, even if ideas of values and morality may have changed over the years. William Dalrymple takes the familiar notion that travel broadens the mind, but he extends it to suggest the benefits of being altered by one's travels. He states:

> Being changed by your travels is something that happens much more imperceptibly and slowly [than one's immediate impressions of a country], but if you engage with where you are change is inevitable, even if you don't realise it at the time. I certainly feel my travels have changed me, and for the better. When I look at my contemporaries who have remained rooted in their Englishness and have never seen

> the wider world I can't help but sometimes find their concerns and nationalism a little parochial. Serious travel should give you the birds [sic] eye view, and free you from the imprisonment of your own culture and upbringing.[41]

Similarly, Ian Littlewood observes: 'travel tends to undermine moral absolutes.... Tyrants never like their subjects to travel: as long as there are no grounds of comparison, there is no basis from which to challenge the existing order. Anything that provides images of a different way of life poses a potential threat'.[42]

The ethical importance of travel writing is stronger than ever. Nationalism and xenophobia are on the rise in many societies suffering economic recession, and the ability to travel is diminishing for large sectors of the population. Yet rather than being in decline, as several commentators and practitioners have claimed, the future of travel writing – this often exasperating, often exhilarating, 'fluid and adaptable genre'[43] – is assured. It is as open to new directions and stimuli as its study.

Notes

Chapter 1 Introduction: Defining the terms

1 'A Long Way from Home: Jonathan Raban', in Michael Shapiro, ed., *A Sense of Place: Great Travel Writers Talk about their Craft, Lives, and Inspiration* (Palo Alto, CA: Travelers' Tales, 2004), p.56 (pp.51–82).
2 Carl Thompson, *Travel Writing* (London: Routledge, 2011), pp.1–2.
3 Patrick Holland and Graham Huggan, *Tourists with Typewriters: Critical Reflections on Contemporary Travel Writing* (Ann Arbor: University of Michigan Press, 1998), pp.x–xi.
4 Michael Kowaleski, 'Introduction: The Modern Literature of Travel', in Michael Kowaleski, ed., *Temperamental Journeys: Essays on the Modern Literature of Travel* (Athens, GA: University of Georgia Press, 1992), p.7, my emphasis.
5 Charles Forsdick, 'French Representations of Niagara: From Hennepin to Butor', in Susan Castillo and David Seed, eds., *American Travel and Empire* (Liverpool: Liverpool University Press, 2009), p.58.
6 Barbara Korte, *English Travel Writing from Pilgrimages to Postcolonial Explorations*, Catherine Matthias, trans. (Basingstoke: Macmillan, 2000), p.1.
7 Korte, *English Travel Writing*, p.8.
8 Jonathan Raban, 'The Journey and the Book' [1982], in *For Love and Money: Writing, Reading, Travelling, 1969–1987* (London: Collins Harvill, 1987), p.253 (pp.253–60).
9 Raban, 'The Journey and the Book', p.254.
10 We have further discussed the problem of definition in the pamphlet *Talking about Travel Writing: A Conversation between Peter Hulme and Tim Youngs* (Leicester: The English Association, 2007).
11 John Frow, *Genre* (London: Routledge, 2006), p.2. That Frow's book neglects travel writing supports another of the arguments of the present volume.
12 Frow, *Genre*, p.2.
13 Frow, *Genre*, p.1.
14 Frow, *Genre*, p.25.
15 Frow, *Genre*, p.3.
16 Dinah Roma Sianturi, '"From Colonial to Cosmopolitan Visions": Detours in the Theory of Travel'. Unpublished paper presented at a workshop on *Travel Writing: Practice, Pedagogy and Theory*, Asia Research Institute, National University of

Singapore (February 2011). I am grateful to the author for permission to quote from her paper, which I heard delivered when much of this book was drafted.

17 Jan Borm makes a similar point. Jan Borm, 'Defining Travel: On the Travel Book, Travel Writing and Terminology', in Glenn Hooper and Tim Youngs, eds., *Perspectives on Travel Writing* (Aldershot: Ashgate, 2004), pp.13–26, see especially pp.15–16.
18 *Talking about Travel Writing*, p.3.
19 Casey Blanton, *Travel Writing: The Self and the World* (New York: Twayne, 1997), p.2.
20 *Talking about Travel Writing*, p.3.
21 *Talking about Travel Writing*, pp.4–6.
22 Kowaleski, 'Introduction', p.13.
23 Korte, *English Travel Writing*, p.1.
24 Korte, *English Travel Writing*, p.10, my emphases.
25 Korte, *English Travel Writing*, p.11, my emphasis.
26 Korte, *English Travel Writing*, p.10.
27 *Talking about Travel Writing*, p.3.
28 *Talking about Travel Writing*, p.4.
29 Chloe Chard, *Pleasure and Guilt on the Grand Tour: Travel Writing and Imaginative Geography 1600–1830* (Manchester: Manchester University Press, 1999), p.4.
30 Korte, *English Travel Writing*, p.8.
31 Korte, *English Travel Writing*, p.14.
32 Holland and Huggan, *Tourists with Typewriters*, p.xiii.
33 Holland and Huggan, *Tourists with Typewriters*, p.8.
34 Korte, *English Travel Writing*, p.9.
35 Borm, 'Defining Travel', p.13.
36 Jill Steward, '"How and Where to Go": The Role of Travel Journalism in Britain and the Evolution of Foreign Tourism, 1840–1914', in John K. Walton, ed., *Histories of Tourism: Representation, Identity and Conflict* (Clevedon: Channel View Publications, 2005), p.41.
37 Guillaume Thouroude, 'Towards generic autonomy: The *récit de voyage* as mode, genre and form', *Studies in Travel Writing* 13, 4 (December 2009), 383 (381–90).
38 Thouroude, 'Towards generic autonomy', 389.
39 Kowaleski, 'Introduction', p.9.
40 Korte, *English Travel Writing*, p.2.
41 Kowaleski, 'Introduction', p.2.
42 *The Guardian*, Review section, 25 September 2004.
43 Shapiro, ed., *A Sense of Place*, p.56.
44 Geoffrey Moorhouse, 'The Inward Journey, the Outward Passage: A Literary Balancing Act', *Studies in Travel Writing* 3 (1999), 19 (17–25).
45 Tim Youngs, 'Interview with William Dalrymple', *Studies in Travel Writing* 9, 1 March (2005), 37–63. See also Tim Youngs, 'Interview with Gary Younge', *Studies in Travel Writing* 6 (2002), 96–107.

46 Moorhouse, 'The Inward Journey, the Outward Passage', 20.
47 Moorhouse, 'The Inward Journey, the Outward Passage', 21.
48 Dea Birkett and Sara Wheeler, 'Introduction', in Dea Birkett and Sara Wheeler, eds., *Amazonian: The Penguin Book of Women's New Travel Writing* (London: Penguin, 1998), p.ix.
49 Birkett and Wheeler, 'Introduction', p.x.
50 Blanton, *Travel Writing*, p.xi.
51 Debbie Lisle, *The Global Politics of Contemporary Travel Writing* (Cambridge: Cambridge University Press, 2006), p.58.
52 See for example Christopher Herbert, *Culture and Anomie: Ethnographic Imagination in the Nineteenth Century* (Chicago: University of Chicago Press, 1991), Ch. 4 'Mayhew's Cockney Polynesia'.
53 Among many examples, in politics: Agnes Smedley, *China Fights Back: An American Woman with the Eighth Route Army* (London: Victor Gollancz, 1938); in aesthetics, the work of Stephen Muecke, discussed later in the present volume.
54 Raphael Kadushin, 'Introduction' in Raphael Kadushin, ed., *Wonderlands: Good Gay Travel Writing* (Madison, WI: University of Wisconsin Press, 2004), p. 5 (pp. 3–7). Germane to this is Richard White's comment that 'Throughout its white history, there have been countless attempts to get Australia down on paper and to catch its essence. Their aim is not merely to describe the continent, but to give it an individuality, a personality. This they call Australian, but it is more likely to reflect the hopes, fears or needs of its inventor.' Richard White, *Inventing Australia: Images and Identity 1688–1980* (Crows Nest: Allen & Unwin, 1981), p.ix.
55 Roy C. Bridges, 'Nineteenth-Century East African Travel Records', *Paideuma* 33 (1987), 179–96; I. S. MacLaren, 'In Consideration of the Evolution of Explorers and Travellers into Authors: One Model', *Studies in Travel Writing* 15, 3 (September 2011), 221–41; Tim Youngs, 'Interview with Robyn Davidson', *Studies in Travel Writing* 9, 1 (March 2005), 21–36.
56 Michael Cronin, *Across the Lines: Travel, Language, Translation* (Cork: Cork University Press, 2010); Loredana Polezzi, 'Translation, Travel, Migration'. Loredana Polezzi, ed., *Translation, Travel, Migration*. Special issue of *The Translator* 12, 2 (2006), 169–88.
57 Blanton, *Travel Writing*, p.xii.
58 See for example, 'Catherine Helen Spence in England, 1865', in Ros Pesman, David Walker, and Richard White, eds., *The Oxford Book of Australian Travel Writing* (Melbourne: Oxford University Press, 1996), pp.7–13.
59 For such stories, see for example Janet Austin, *From Nothing to Zero: Letters from Refugees in Australia's Detention Centres* (Melbourne: Lonely Planet, 2003); Jennifer Langer, ed., *Crossing the Border: Voices of Refugee and Exiled Women* (Nottingham: Five Leaves Press, 2002).
60 Youngs, 'Interview with William Dalrymple', 45.
61 Caren Kaplan, *Questions of Travel: Postmodern Discourses of Displacement* (Durham, NC: Duke University Press, 1996), p.103.

62 Raban, 'The Journey and the Book', p.257.
63 Elizabeth A. Bohls, *Women Travel Writers and the Language of Aesthetics, 1716–1818* (Cambridge: Cambridge University Press, 1995), p.17.
64 Jaś Elsner and Joan Pau Rubiés, 'Introduction', in Elsner and Rubiés, eds., *Voyages and Visions: Towards a Cultural History of Travel* (London: Reaktion, 1999), p.2 (pp.1–56).
65 Bohls, *Women Travel Writers*, p.18.
66 Freya Stark, 'The Philosophy of Exploration' (1947), in *The Spoken Word: Travel Writers* (London: British Library, 2012), audio recording.
67 Holland and Huggan, *Tourists with Typewriters*, p.viii.
68 Indira Ghose, *Women Travellers in Colonial India: The Power of the Female Gaze* (Delhi: Oxford University Press, 1998), p.2.
69 For example, Blanton asserts that 'Genuine "travel literature," as opposed to what has been called "pretravel," depends upon a certain self-consciousness on the part of the narrator that was not seized upon until after the Renaissance and, in fact, not highly developed until the concern with "sensibility" in the eighteenth century'. Blanton, *Travel Writing*, p.4.
70 Elsner and Rubiés, 'Introduction', p.4. Elsner and Rubiés comment that a *cultural* history of travel (which their volume proposes) invites an examination of that relationship. So then, I suggest, may a study of the history of travel *writing* specifically.
71 See Chapter 8 of the present volume and Tim Youngs, 'Pushing against the black/white limits of maps: African American writings of travel', *English Studies in Africa* 53, 2 (2010), 71–85.
72 For example, in the week that I completed this Introduction, I took delivery of Satnam, Vishav Bharti, trans., *Jangalnama: Travels in a Maoist Guerilla Zone* (New Delhi: Penguin Books, 2010). The blurb reads: '*Jangalnama* is not merely a travelogue recording Satnam's days in the jungle. It is a compelling argument to recognize the humanity of those in conflict with the mainstream of Indian society and to acknowledge their dream of a world free of exploitation.' Its humanising of the guerrillas also challenges dominant ideas about the role of Othering in travel narratives.
73 Raymond Williams, 'Forms of English Fiction in 1848', in *Writing in Society* (London: Verso [n.d.]), p.150.
74 Elsner and Rubiés, 'Introduction', p.5.
75 Mary Baine Campbell, *The Witness and the Other World: Exotic European Travel Writing, 400–1600* (Ithaca, NY: Cornell University Press, 1988), p.166.

Chapter 2 Medieval and early modern travel writing

1 Richard Hakluyt, *The Principal Navigations, Voyages, Traffiques & Discoveries of the English Nation, Made by Sea or Overland to the Remote and Farthest Distant Quarters of the Earth at Any Time within the Compass of these 1600 Yeeres* 8 vols. (London: J. M. Dent and Co., [n.d.]), i, p.3.

2 Dehatkadons, an Onondaga Iroquois chief, quoted in Ronald Wright, *Stolen Continents: The Indian Story* [1992] (London: Pimlico, 1993), p.5.
3 Stephen S. Gosch and Peter N. Stearns, *Premodern Travel in World History* (New York: Routledge, 2008), p.14. Further page references will be given parenthetically as GS.
4 N. K. Sanders, 'Introduction', *The Epic of Gilgamesh: An English Version with an Introduction* (Harmondsworth: Penguin, 1972), pp.12, 7 (pp.7–58). Further page references to this work will be given parenthetically.
5 Maria Pretzler, *Pausanias: Travel Writing in Ancient Greece* (London: Duckworth, 2007), p.48. Further page references will be given parenthetically as MP.
6 Jaś Elsner and Joan Pau Rubiés, 'Introduction', in Elsner and Rubiés, eds., *Voyages and Visions: Towards a Cultural History of Travel* (London: Reaktion, 1999), p.8 (pp.1–56). Further references will be given parenthetically as ER.
7 Noreen Humble, 'Xenophon's *Anabasis*: Self and Other in Fourth-Century Greece', in Patrick Crowley, Noreen Humble and Silvia Ross, eds., *Mediterranean Travels: Writing Self and Other from the Ancient World to Contemporary Society* (London: Modern Humanities Research Association and Maney Publishing, 2011), p.14 (pp.14–31). Further page references will be given parenthetically as NH.
8 For the continuing cultural, political and military influence of Xenophon, see especially Tim Rood, *The Sea! The Sea! The Shout of the Ten Thousand in the Modern Imagination* (London: Duckworth Overlook, 2004) and *American Anabasis: Xenophon and the Idea of America from the Mexican War to Iraq* (London: Duckworth Overlook, 2010).
9 Marozzi's book has appeared as *The Man Who Invented History: Travels with Herodotus* (London: John Murray, 2008) and as *The Way of Herodotus: Travels with the Man Who Invented History* (Philadelphia, PA: De Capo Press, 2008).
10 Pretzler gives the likely dates of composition on p.8 and some information about manuscript versions on p.3. The text, she notes, never mentions title or author. The title by which it has become known, *Periegesis Hellados*, is translated as *Tour around Greece* (p.3) and the work 'consists of ten books in which the text follows a complex itinerary through different parts of central and southern Greece' (p.4).
11 David P. Moessner, *Lord of the Banquet: The Literary and Theological Significance of the Lukan Travel Narrative* (Minneapolis, MN: Augsburg Fortress Press, 1989).
12 M. H. Abrams, 'Introduction: Spiritual Travellers in Western Literature', in Bruno Magliocchetti and Anthony Verna, eds., *The Motif of the Journey in Nineteenth-Century Italian Literature* (Gainesville: University Press of Florida, 1994), p.1 (pp.1–20). The square brackets are in the original.
13 Mary Baine Campbell, *The Witness and the Other World: Exotic European Travel Writing, 400–1600* (Ithaca, NY: Cornell University Press, 1988), p.15.
14 Campbell, *The Witness and the Other World*, p.53.
15 An obvious example is the continued representation of the Congo as the heart of darkness. See Tim Youngs, 'Africa/Congo: The Politics of Darkness', in Peter Hulme and Tim Youngs, eds., *The Cambridge Companion to Travel Writing* (Cambridge: Cambridge University Press, 2002), pp.156–73.

16 Campbell, *The Witness and the Other World*, p.17.
17 For early pilgrimages see John Wilkinson, *Jerusalem Pilgrims before the Crusades* (Warminster: Aris and Phillips, 2002).
18 Donald R. Howard, *Writers and Pilgrims: Medieval Pilgrimage Narratives and their Posterity* (Berkeley: University of California Press, 1980), p.29. Further page references will be given parenthetically as H.
19 Diana Webb, *Medieval European Pilgrimage, c.700-c.1500* (Houndmills: Palgrave, 2002), p.159.
20 Abrams, 'Introduction', pp.7–8.
21 Abrams, 'Introduction', pp.7–8.
22 Paul Zumthor and Catherine Peebles, 'The Medieval Travel Narrative', *New Literary History*, 25, 4 (Autumn, 1994), 809–824 (quotation at 809).
23 John Masefield, 'Introduction', to Marco Polo, *The Travels of Marco Polo the Venetian* (London: J. M. Dent, 1908), p.xii (pp.vii-xiii).
24 Masefield, 'Introduction', p.xi. Just as influential, however, were Mandeville and Odoric of Pordenone.
25 Masefield, 'Introduction', p.x.
26 Zumthor and Peebles, 'The Medieval Travel Narrative', 813–15. Zumthor and Peebles note the existence of 143 manuscripts of the work (809).
27 Marco Polo, *The Travels of Marco Polo the Venetian* (London: J. M. Dent, 1908), p.9. Further page references will be given in the text.
28 For some of the debate on Polo's veracity, see Frances Wood, *Did Marco Polo Go to China?* (London: Secker and Warburg, 1995).
29 Campbell, *The Witness and the Other World*, p.91. The anonymous reader of this volume points out that Campbell's comment describes the work of John of Plano Carpini and William of Rubruck just as well as Polo's, and both were missionaries rather than merchants. Translations of both these mid-thirteenth-century Latin records of journeys into the Mongol Empire are included in Christopher Dawson, ed., *Mission to Asia* (Toronto: University of Toronto Press, 1980), itself a reprint of *The Mongol Mission: Narratives and Letters of The Franciscan Missionaries in Mongolia and China in the Thirteenth and Fourteenth Centuries* (New York: Sheed and Ward, 1955).
30 Casey Blanton, *Travel Writing: The Self and the World* (New York: Twayne, 1997), p.9.
31 Zumthor and Peebles, 'The Medieval Travel Narrative', 815.
32 Campbell, *The Witness and the Other World*, p.34.
33 Andrew Hadfield, *Literature, Travel, and Colonial Writing in the English Renaissance, 1545–1625* (Oxford: Oxford University Press, 1998), p.6.
34 Campbell, *The Witness and the Other World*, p.149. By contrast with this 'father', see *The Book of Margery Kempe*, a spiritual autobiography (the earliest autobiography in English) that includes accounts of the author's pilgrimages across England, Europe and the Holy Land. Kempe (c. 1373–1440) dictated her account later in her life.

35 C. W. R. D. Moseley, 'Introduction', *The Travels of Sir John Mandeville* trans. with an Introduction by C. W. R. D. Moseley (London: Penguin, 1983), p.9 (pp.9–39). Zumthor and Peebles note that 'it was translated into ten languages, including Latin; three hundred manuscripts and ninety editions remain, printed from 1475 to 1600!' Zumthor and Peebles, 'The Medieval Travel Narrative', 819.

36 Campbell, *The Witness and the Other World*, p.122.

37 Moseley, 'Introduction', p.9.

38 See Elsner and Rubiés, 'Introduction', pp. 38–9 for the sources.

39 Moseley, 'Introduction', p.10.

40 Moseley, 'Introduction', p.12. Zumthor and Peebles also claim that while '"Mandeville" shamelessly plunders his "predecessors," … in the material borrowed from others, much of the information can be trusted'. Zumthor and Peebles, 'The Medieval Travel Narrative', 819.

41 Campbell, *The Witness and the Other World*, pp.140–1.

42 Campbell, *The Witness and the Other World*, pp.10–11.

43 Campbell, *The Witness and the Other World*, p.127.

44 Campbell, *The Witness and the Other World*, pp.110–11.

45 Campbell, *The Witness and the Other World*, pp. 191, 209.

46 Blanton, *Travel Writing*, p.9.

47 Nabil Matar, ed. and trans., *In the Lands of the Christians: Arabic Travel Writing in the Seventeenth Century* (New York: Routledge, 2003), p.xiii. Further page references will be given in the text. See also Roxanne L. Euben, *Journeys to the Other Shore: Muslim and Western Travelers in Search of Knowledge* (Princeton, NJ: Princeton University Press, 2006) and Houari Touati, trans. Lydia G. Cochrane, *Islam and Travel in the Middle Ages* (Chicago: Chicago University Press, 2010).

48 Hadfield, *Literature, Travel, and Colonial Writing*, p.27.

49 Campbell, *The Witness and the Other World*, p.211.

50 Hadfield, *Literature, Travel, and Colonial Writing*, p.12.

51 Hadfield, *Literature, Travel, and Colonial Writing*, p.24.

52 Hadfield, *Literature, Travel, and Colonial Writing*, p.32.

53 Hadfield, *Literature, Travel, and Colonial Writing*, pp.32–3.

54 Hadfield, *Literature, Travel, and Colonial Writing*, p.59.

55 Hadfield, *Literature, Travel, and Colonial Writing*, p.58.

56 Hadfield, *Literature, Travel, and Colonial Writing*, p.64.

57 Hadfield, *Literature, Travel, and Colonial Writing*, p.66.

58 Hadfield, *Literature, Travel, and Colonial Writing*, p.67.

59 Anthony Payne, *Richard Hakluyt: A guide to his books and to those associated with him 1580–1625* (London: Bernard Quaritch, 2008), p.36. Further page references will be given parenthetically as AP.

60 The new edition dropped the extra 'l' from *Principall.*

61 Hakluyt, i, p.2.

62 Hakluyt, i, p.2.

63 Hakluyt, i, p.3.

64 Gesa Mackenthun, *Metaphors of Dispossession: American Beginnings and the Translation of Empire*, 1492–1637 (Norman: Oklahoma University Press, 1997), p.162.

65 Mackenthun, *Metaphors of Dispossession*, p.163.

66 Mary C. Fuller, *Voyages in Print: English Travel to America, 1576–1624* (Cambridge: Cambridge University Press, 1995), p.149.

67 The description is from the website of the National Maritime Museum in London, which hosted a conference in May 2008 to help establish a consortium to work and advise on the project, co-edited by Daniel Carey and Claire Jowitt. http://www.nmm.ac.uk/researchers/research-areas-and-projects/richard-hakluyt-conference accessed 24 January 2012.

68 Peter C. Mancall, ed., *Travel Narratives from the Age of Discovery: An Anthology* (Oxford: Oxford University Press, 2006), p.312.

69 Mancall, *Travel Narratives*, p.313.

70 Harriot in Mancall, p.317.

71 Harriot in Mancall, p.318.

72 Harriot in Mancall, p.319.

73 Harriot in Mancall, p.320.

74 Harriot in Mancall, pp.321–2.

75 Charles Nicholl, *The Creature in the Map: Sir Walter Ralegh's Quest for El Dorado* [1996] (London: Vintage, 1995), p.3. For two new editions of the *Discoverie* with thorough introductions and notes, see those by anthropologist Neil L. Whitehead (Manchester: Manchester University Press, 1997) and historian Joyce Lorimer (Hakluyt Society, 2006).

76 The information in this paragraph is taken from Nicholl, pp.3, 5, and Mackenthun, p.165.

77 Mackenthun, *Metaphors of Dispossession*, p.165.

78 Campbell, *The Witness and the Other World*, pp.5–6.

79 This paragraph draws on information from Nicholl, *The Creature in the Map*, p.23.

80 Nicholl, *The Creature in the Map*, p.301.

81 Nicholl, *The Creature in the Map*, p.304.

82 Hadfield, *Literature, Travel, and Colonial Writing*, pp.11, 7.

83 Mackenthun, *Metaphors of Dispossession*, p.173.

84 Nicholl, *The Creature in the Map*, p.304.

85 Mackenthun, *Metaphors of Dispossession*, p.174.

86 Nicholl, *The Creature in the Map*, p.313.

87 Nicholl, *The Creature in the Map*, p.318.

88 Mackenthun, p.162.

89 Sir Walter Ralegh, *The Discoverie of the Large, Rich and Bewtiful Empyre of Guiana*, transcribed, annotated and introduced by Neil L. Whitehead (Manchester: Manchester University Press, 1997), p.196.

90 Ralegh, *The Discoverie*, p.178.

91 In the mid-thirteenth century, William of Rubruck likewise commented on finding to be false things that had long been held true (for example, that the Caspian Sea gave into the Ocean Sea and that there were monstrous races in Asia). I am grateful to the anonymous reader of the present volume for this comparison.
92 Mackenthun, *Metaphors of Dispossession*, p.171.
93 Mackenthun, *Metaphors of Dispossession*, p.170.
94 Blanton, *Travel Writing*, p.10.
95 Nicholl, *The Creature in the Map*, p.231.
96 Nicholl, *The Creature in the Map*, p.201.
97 Mary C. Fuller, *Remembering the Early Modern Voyage. English Narratives in the Age of European Expansion* (New York: Palgrave Macmillan, 2008), p.5.
98 Hadfield, *Literature, Travel, and Colonial Writing*, p.1.
99 Ronald Wright, *Stolen Continents: The Indian Story* [1992] (London: Pimlico, 1993), p.5.

Chapter 3 Travel writing in the eighteenth century

1 Mary Wollstonecraft, *Letters Written During a Short Residence in Sweden, Norway and Denmark* [1796] (Fontwell: Centaur Press, 1970), p.xvii.
2 James Cook, *The Journals*. Prepared from the original manuscripts by J. C. Beaglehole for the Hakluyt Society, 1955–67. Selected and edited by Philip Edwards London: Penguin, 2003), p.386. Further page references will be given parenthetically.
3 Ian Watt, *The Rise of the Novel: Studies in Defoe, Richardson and Fielding* [1957] (London: The Hogarth Press, 1987).
4 Charles L. Batten, Jr., *Pleasurable Instruction: Form and Convention in Eighteenth-Century Travel Literature* (Berkeley: California University Press, 1978), p.1.
5 Batten, Jr., *Pleasurable Instruction*, p.26.
6 Coriat Junior [Samuel Paterson], *Another Traveller! Or Cursory Remarks and Critical Observations Made upon a Journey through Part of the Netherlands in the Latter End of the Year 1766*, 2 vols. (London: Joseph Johnson and J. Payne, 1767), i, 339.
7 Coriat Junior [Samuel Paterson], *Another Traveller!*, i, 340–1. One might compare this with Mandeville's statement near the end of his book that 'I do not want to say any more about marvels that there are there, so that other men who go there can find new things to speak of which I have not mentioned'. *The Travels of Sir John Mandeville* trans. with an Introduction by C. W. R. D. Moseley (London: Penguin, 1983), p.188. I am grateful to Cambridge University Press's anonymous reader for reminding me of this.
8 Carl Thompson, *The Suffering Traveller and the Romantic Imagination* (Oxford: Clarendon Press, 2007), p.4.
9 Thompson, *The Suffering Traveller*, p.5. Thompson rightly notes that 'In our own day, as in the 1820s, there is undoubtedly a romantic glamour, possibly even a

kudos or subtle cultural prestige, that attaches to the idea of taking risks and pains in one's travelling' (p.3). This is witnessed in pursuits such as extreme travel.

10 Thompson, *The Suffering Traveller*, pp.6–7.
11 Thompson, *The Suffering Traveller*, p.8.
12 Thompson, *The Suffering Traveller*, p.18.
13 Thompson, *The Suffering Traveller*, p.12. On pedestrianism, see Robin Jarvis, *Romantic Writing and Pedestrian Travel* (Basingstoke: Macmillan, 1997).
14 Quoted in Donald R. Howard, *Writers and Pilgrims: Medieval Pilgrimage Narratives and their Posterity* (Berkeley: University of California Press, 1980), pp.1–2.
15 Nigel Leask, *Curiosity and the Aesthetics of Travel Writing 1780–1840* (Oxford: Oxford University Press, 2002), p.15.
16 Roy Bridges, 'Exploration and Travel outside Europe', in Peter Hulme and Tim Youngs, eds., *The Cambridge Companion to Travel Writing* (Cambridge: Cambridge University Press, 2002), p.54 (pp.53–69).
17 See Thompson, *The Suffering Traveller*, pp.15–16 and Carl Thompson, ed., *Romantic-Era Shipwreck Narratives: An Anthology* (Nottingham: Trent Editions, 2007).
18 Thompson, *The Suffering Traveller*, p.13.
19 Percy G. Adams, *Travelers and Travel Liars, 1660–1800* (Berkeley: University of California Press, 1962), p.88.
20 Dennis Porter, *Haunted Journeys: Desire and Transgression in European Travel Writing* (Princeton, NJ: Princeton University Press, 1991), p.18.
21 See, for example, Pat Hohepa, 'My Musket, My Missionary, and My *Mana*' in Alex Calder, Jonathan Lamb and Bridget Orr, eds., *Voyages and Beaches: Pacific Encounters, 1769–1840* (Honolulu: University of Hawai'i Press, 1999), pp.180–201.
22 Leask, *Curiosity and the Aesthetics of Travel Writing*, p.15.
23 Leask, *Curiosity and the Aesthetics of Travel Writing*, p.16. In a not dissimilar vein, Jonathan Lamb has written on the debilitating effects of scurvy and has argued that 'the connection between the symptoms of scurvy and the South Seas voyage narratives is extensive and exact'. Jonathan Lamb, *Preserving the Self in the South Seas, 1680–1840* (Chicago: University of Chicago Press, 2001), p.127.
24 Leask, *Curiosity and the Aesthetics of Travel Writing*, p.17.
25 Leask, *Curiosity and the Aesthetics of Travel Writing*, p.18.
26 Leask, *Curiosity and the Aesthetics of Travel Writing*, p.18.
27 William Gilpin, *Three Essays: On Picturesque Beauty; on Picturesque Travel; and on Sketching Landscape: to which is added a Poem, on Landscape Painting* (London: R. Blamire, 1792), p.42.
28 William Gilpin, *Observations on the River Wye, and Several Parts of South Wales, &c. Relative Chiefly to Picturesque Beauty: Made in the Summer of the Year 1770* [1782] 4th ed. (London: T. Cadell Junior and W. Davies, 1800), pp.1–2. Further page references will be given parenthetically.
29 Ian Littlewood, *Sultry Climates: Travel and Sex since the Grand Tour* (London: John Murray, 2001), p.7.

30 Littlewood, *Sultry Climates*, p.14. Modern guidebooks have similarities with the structure and contents of medieval pilgrim guides also.

31 Bruce Redford, *Venice and the Grand Tour* (New Haven and London: Yale University Press, 1996), p.10. Further page references will be given parenthetically as R.

32 Giles Barber, 'The English-Language guide book to Europe up to 1870', in Robin Myers and Michael Harris, eds., *Journeys through the Market: Travel, Travellers and the Book Trade* (New Castle, DE: Oak Knoll Press, 1999), p.97 (pp.93–106).

33 Jeremy Black, 'The Grand Tour', in Robin Myers and Michael Harris, eds., *Journeys through the Market: Travel, Travellers and the Book Trade* (New Castle, DE: Oak Knoll Press, 1999), p.65 (pp. 65–91).

34 Littlewood, *Sultry Climates*, p.13. Littlewood suggests that the Tour was usually expected to last 'at least a couple of years' (p.13).

35 Black, 'The Grand Tour', p.76.

36 Black, *The British Abroad: The Grand Tour in the Eighteenth Century* (Stroud: Sutton, 1992), p.18.

37 Black, *The British Abroad*, p.56. The two states in the Low Countries were the United Provinces, which included Holland and were Protestant, and the Austrian Netherlands, which were Catholic.

38 Littlewood, *Sultry Climates*, p.13.

39 Black, *The British Abroad*, p.86.

40 Black, 'The Grand Tour', p.65.

41 Black, 'The Grand Tour', p.71.

42 Littlewood, *Sultry Climates*, p.5.

43 Littlewood, *Sultry Climates*, p.56.

44 Laurence Sterne, *A Sentimental Journey through France and Italy* [1768] (Harmondsworth: Penguin, 1967), p.35.

45 Lady Mary Wortley Montagu, *The Turkish Embassy Letters*, introduction by Anita Desai; Malcolm Jack, ed. (London: Virago, 1994), p.44. The letters were written between 1716 and 1718 but not published till 1763. It should be noted that although Montagu had what seems to be unprecedented access to Turkish women, her dismissal of other travel accounts extends to their misrepresentations and imaginings of many other matters also. She is also, of course, claiming authority over male writers.

46 Carl Thompson, *Travel Writing* (London: Routledge, 2011), pp.48–9.

47 Elizabeth Hagglund, 'Reviews of travel in the *Monthly Review*, 1749–1758: An introductory survey with an appendix on travel-related books reviewed by the *Monthly Review*', *Studies in Travel Writing* 2 (Spring 1998), 2, 6 (1–45).

48 Sylva Norman, 'Introduction' to Mary Wollstonecraft, *Letters Written During a Short Residence in Sweden, Norway and Denmark* [1796] (Fontwell: Centaur Press, 1970), pp.v, xii (pp.v-xv).

49 Mary Wollstonecraft, *Letters Written During a Short Residence in Sweden, Norway and Denmark* [1796] (Fontwell: Centaur Press, 1970), p.xvii. Further references will be given parenthetically.

50 Norman, 'Introduction', p.ix.
51 One might compare with Wollstonecraft's sentiments Freya Stark's statement a century and a half later that the mark of the true explorer is the exercise of toleration towards others. Freya Stark, 'The Philosophy of Exploration' (1947), in *The Spoken Word: Travel Writers* (London: British Library, 2012), audio recording.
52 Adams, *Travelers and Travel Liars*, p. 131.
53 Batten, Jr., *Pleasurable Instruction*, p. 79.
54 Richard White, 'Travel, Writing and Australia', *Studies in Travel Writing* 11, 1 (March 2007), 2–3 (1–14).
55 Bridges, 'Exploration and Travel', p.55.

Chapter 4 Travel writing in the nineteenth century

1 Henry David Thoreau, *Walden, or Life in the Woods* [1854] *and On the Duty of Civil Disobedience* [1866] (New York: The New American Library, 1960), p.72. Further page references will be given parenthetically.
2 Mark Twain, *The Innocents Abroad, or The New Pilgrim's Progress* [1869] (New York: Airmont, 1967), p.51. Further page references will be given parenthetically.
3 Ian Littlewood, *Sultry Climates: Travel and Sex since the Grand Tour* (London: John Murray, 2001), p.120. On the railway see Wolfgang Schivelbusch, *The Railway Journey: Trains and Travel in the Nineteenth Century* (Oxford: Wiley-Blackwell, 1980).
4 On readership, the classic study is Richard D. Altick, *The English Common Reader: A Social History of the Mass Reading Public 1800–1900* (Chicago: University of Chicago Press, 1957).
5 Littlewood, *Sultry Climates*, p.55.
6 James Buzard, *The Beaten Track: European Tourism, Literature, and the Ways to 'Culture' 1800–1918* (Oxford: Clarendon Press, 1993), p.19.
7 Littlewood, *Sultry Climates*, p.55.
8 Buzard, *The Beaten Track*, p.121.
9 Littlewood, *Sultry Climates*, p.111.
10 Littlewood, *Sultry Climates*, p.108.
11 Littlewood, *Sultry Climates*, p.106.
12 Littlewood, *Sultry Climates*, p.119.
13 Buzard, *The Beaten Track*, p.19.
14 Buzard, *The Beaten Track*, p.156.
15 Buzard, *The Beaten Track*, p.158.
16 Roy Bridges, 'Exploration and Travel outside Europe', in Peter Hulme and Tim Youngs, eds., *The Cambridge Companion to Travel Writing* (Cambridge: Cambridge University Press, 2002), p.55 (pp.53–69).
17 Bridges, 'Exploration and Travel', p.54.
18 The information in this paragraph is from Bridges, 'Exploration and Travel', p.55.

19 See Henry M. Stanley, *Through the Dark Continent* [1878] (London: Sampson Low, Marston, Searle and Rivington, 1890), p.571; Norman R. Bennett, ed., *Stanley's Despatches to the New York Herald 1871-1872, 1874–1877* (Boston: Boston University Press, 1970), p.387. I discuss this in my *Travellers in Africa: British Travelogues, 1850–1900* (Manchester: Manchester University Press, 1994), pp.73–4.

20 See Ian Anstruther, *I Presume: H. M. Stanley's Triumph and Disaster* [1956] (Gloucester: Alan Sutton, 1988).

21 Stanley, *Through the Dark Continent*, p.143.

22 R. Wardlaw Thompson, *My Trip in the 'John Williams'* (London: London Missionary Society, 1900), p.vii. On missionaries, and the LMS, see Anna Johnston, *Missionary Writing and Empire, 1800–1860* (Cambridge: Cambridge University Press, 2003).

23 See, for example, Stephen Donovan, 'Tourism in Extremis: Travel and Adventure in the Congo', in Tim Youngs, ed., *Travel Writing in the Nineteenth Century* (London: Anthem Press, 2006), pp.37–54.

24 Giles Barber, 'The English-Language guide book to Europe up to 1870', in Robin Myers and Michael Harris, eds., *Journeys through the Market: Travel, Travellers and the Book Trade* (New Castle, DE: Oak Knoll Press, 1999), p.102 (pp.93–106).

25 Buzard, *The Beaten Track*, p.18.

26 Buzard, *The Beaten Track*, p.47.

27 W. Fraser Rae, *The Business of Travel: A Fifty Years' Record of Progress* (London: Thos. Cook and Son, 1891), p.10.

28 Jeremy Black, 'The Grand Tour', in Robin Myers and Michael Harris, eds., *Journeys through the Market: Travel, Travellers and the Book Trade* (New Castle, DE: Oak Knoll Press, 1999), p.70 (pp.65–91).

29 On the heroic treatment of explorers of Africa, see, for example, N. D'Anvers, *Heroes of North African Discovery* (London: Marcus Ward and Co., 1880) and N. Bell [N. D'Anvers], *Heroes of Discovery in South Africa* (London: Walter Scott Limited [nd]).

30 Quoted in Anthony Payne, *Richard Hakluyt: A guide to his books and to those associated with him 1580–1625* (London: Bernard Quaritch, 2008), p.1.

31 See Stephen Fender, *Sea Changes: British Emigration and American Literature* (Cambridge: Cambridge University Press, 1992), esp. chapters 7–9, and Andrew Hassam, *Sailing to Australia: Shipboard Diaries by Nineteenth-Century British Emigrants* (Manchester: Manchester University Press, 1994). On booster literature, see Dominic Alessio, 'Tourism and Travel: Imagining New Zealand's Cities and Towns at the Turn of the 20th Century', *Studies in Travel Writing* 14, 4 (December 2010), 383–96.

32 Buzard, *The Beaten Track*, p.1.

33 Buzard, *The Beaten Track*, p.6.

34 Buzard, *The Beaten Track*, p.8.

35 See, for example, Buzard, *The Beaten Track*, p.28.

36 Chloe Chard, *Pleasure and Guilt on the Grand Tour: Travel Writing and Imaginative Geography 1600–1830* (Manchester: Manchester University Press, 1999), p.11.

37 Barber, 'The English-Language guide book', p.105.
38 Barber, 'The English-Language guide book', pp.101–2.
39 Barber, 'The English-Language guide book', p.103.
40 Buzard, *The Beaten Track*, p.65.
41 Buzard, *The Beaten Track*, p.67.
42 Buzard, *The Beaten Track*, p.67.
43 Buzard, *The Beaten Track*, p.72.
44 Buzard, *The Beaten Track*, p.75.
45 Buzard, *The Beaten Track*, p.222.
46 It is important to note that although Thoreau writes positively of his experiences, he does not recommend others follow him: 'I would not have any one adopt *my* mode of living on any account; for, beside that before he has fairly learned it I may have found out another for myself, I desire that there may be as many different persons in the world as possible; but I would have each one be very careful to find out and pursue *his own* way, and not his father's or his mother's or his neighbor's instead'. Thoreau, *Walden*, p.53.
47 Ralph Waldo Emerson, 'Self-Reliance' [1841], in *Selected Essays* (Harmondsworth: Penguin Books, 1982), p.197. Further page references will be given parenthetically.
48 For Americans in Europe, see chapters 6 and 7 of Alfred Bendixen and Judith Hamera, eds., *The Cambridge Companion to American Travel Writing* (Cambridge: Cambridge University Press, 2009).

Chapter 5 1900–present

1 D. H. Lawrence, *Sea and Sardinia* [1923] (Harmondsworth: Penguin, 1944), p.7.
2 Paul Theroux, *The Old Patagonian Express: By Train through the Americas* [1979] (London: Penguin Books, 1980), p.99.
3 Wyndham Lewis, *Filibusters in Barbary* (London: Grayson and Grayson, 1932), p.115.
4 Barbara Korte, *English Travel Writing from Pilgrimages to Postcolonial Explorations*, Catherine Matthias, trans. (Basingstoke: Macmillan, 2000), p.18.
5 J. E. Vincent, *Through East Anglia in a Motor Car* (London: Methuen & Co., 1907), p.xix.
6 Thomas D. Murphy, *British Highways And Byways From A Motor Car: Being A Record of A Five Thousand Mile Tour In England, Wales And Scotland* [1908] 2nd ed. (Boston: L. C. Page and Company, 1909), p.5.
7 Murphy, *British Highways*, p.4.
8 Anne Morrow Lindbergh, *North to the Orient* (London: Chatto & Windus, 1935), p.4. Subsequent page references will be given parenthetically in the text.
9 Paul Fussell, *Abroad: British Literary Traveling between the Wars* (New York: Oxford University Press, 1980), p.9.

10 Fussell, *Abroad*, pp.10–11.
11 Philip Dodd, 'The Views of Travellers: Travel Writing in the 1930s', *Prose Studies*, 5, 1 (1982), 128 (127–38).
12 Stan Smith, 'Burbank with a Baedeker: Modernism's Grand Tours', *Studies in Travel Writing*, 8, 1 (2004), 2 (1–18).
13 David G. Farley, *Modernist Travel Writing: Intellectuals Abroad* (Columbia: University of Missouri Press, 2010) is a recent and rare book-length exception.
14 For a recent discussion, see Alexandra Peat, *Travel and Modernist Literature: Sacred and Ethical Journeys* (New York: Routledge, 2011).
15 Smith, 'Burbank with a Baedeker', 6.
16 See, for example, Louise Bryant, *Six Months in Red Russia: An Observer's Account of Russia before and during the Proletarian Dictatorship* (New York: Gorge H. Doran, 1918); Emma Goldman, *My Disillusionment in Russia* (London: C. W. Daniel Company, 1925).
17 Glen MacLeod, 'The Visual Arts', in Michael Levenson, ed., *The Cambridge Companion to Modernism* (Cambridge: Cambridge University Press, 1999), p.194 (pp.194–216).
18 Lewis, *The Cambridge Introduction to Modernism*, p.3.
19 Fussell, *Abroad*, p.36.
20 W. H. Auden and Louis MacNeice, *Letters from Iceland* (London: Faber and Faber, 1937), p.21. For more on this, see Tim Youngs, 'Auden's travel writings', in Stan Smith, ed., *The Cambridge Companion to W. H. Auden* (Cambridge: Cambridge University Press, 2004), pp.68–81.
21 Smith, 'Burbank with a Baedeker', p.6.
22 E. E. Cummings, *Eimi* (New York: Covici, Friede, 1933), p.137.
23 Cummings, *Eimi*, pp.89, 289.
24 Greene, *Lawless Roads*, p.5.
25 Helen Carr, 'Modernism and Travel (1880–1940)', in Peter Hulme and Tim Youngs, eds., *The Cambridge Companion to Travel Writing* (Cambridge: Cambridge University Press, 2002), p.74 (pp.70–86).
26 D. H. Lawrence, *Mornings in Mexico* (London: Martin Secker, 1927), p.9.
27 Lewis, *Filibusters*, p.viii.
28 Lewis, *Filibusters*, pp.23, 24.
29 Fussell, *Abroad*, p.4.
30 Robert Byron, *The Road to Oxiana* [1937] (London: Penguin, 1992), p.47. Further page references will be given parenthetically as *RO*.
31 Lewis, *Filibusters*, pp.vii–viii.
32 Auden and MacNeice, *Letters*, p.51.
33 Tim Youngs, 'Interview with William Dalrymple', *Studies in Travel Writing* 9, 1 (March 2005), 40 (37–63).
34 Sara Wheeler, *Terra Incognita: Travels in Antarctica* [1996] (London: Vintage, 1997), p.152. In keeping with Byron's fondness of incongruity, Wheeler is shocked to see a copy of the book in the hands of her project leader on a fuel flight to Central West Antarctica (p.152).

35 Jonathan Raban, 'The Journey and the Book' [1982], in *For Love and Money: Writing, Reading, Travelling, 1969–1987* (London: Collins Harvill, 1987), p.255 (pp.253–60).
36 Raban, 'The Journey and the Book', p.256.
37 Raban, 'The Journey and the Book', p.255.
38 John Steinbeck, *A Russian Journal* with photographs by Robert Capa (New York: The Viking Press, 1948), p.7. Further references to this work will be given parenthetically.
39 Casey Blanton, *Travel Writing: The Self and the World* (New York: Twayne, 1997), p.95.
40 John Steinbeck, *Travels with Charley in Search of America* (New York: The Viking Press, 1962), p.3. Further page references to this work will be given parenthetically.
41 As critics have observed, Steinbeck is deliberately echoing Robert Louis Stevenson's *Travels with a Donkey in the Cévennes* (1879).
42 Jack Kerouac, *Lonesome Traveler* (New York: McGraw-Hill, 1960), p.1. Further page references will be given parenthetically.
43 Blanton, *Travel Writing*, p.xiv.
44 Pico Iyer, *The Global Soul: Jet Lag, Shopping Malls and the Search for Home* [2000] (London: Bloomsbury, 2001), p.5. Further page references will be to this edition and given parenthetically.
45 Theroux, *The Old Patagonian Express*, p.182. Further page references will be given parenthetically.
46 Patrick Leigh Fermor, *A Time of Gifts: On Foot to Constantinople: From the Hook of Holland to the Middle Danube* [1977] (London: John Murray, 2004), p.13.
47 Eric Newby, *A Traveller's Life* [1982] (London: Picador, 1983), p.302.
48 Hugh Brody, *Maps and Dreams: Indians and the British Columbia Frontier* [1981] (London: Faber and Faber, 1986). Further page references will be given parenthetically. For a different anthropological study of travel, travel writing and oral tradition in the North Pacific, see Julie Cruikshank, *Do Glaciers Listen? Local Knowledge, Colonial Encounters, and Social Imagination* (Vancouver: University of British Columbia Press, 2005).
49 Bill Bryson, *Notes from a Small Island* [1992] (London: Black Swan, 1998), p.110. Further page references will be given parenthetically.

Chapter 6 Quests

1 Raphael Kadushin, 'Introduction' in Raphael Kadushin, ed., *Wonderlands: Good Gay Travel Writing* (Madison: University of Wisconsin Press, 2004), p.7 (pp. 3–7).
2 Jaś Elsner and Joan Pau Rubiés, 'Introduction', in Elsner and Rubiés, eds., *Voyages and Visions: Towards a Cultural History of Travel* (London: Reaktion, 1999), p.47 (pp.1–56). Further references will be given parenthetically as ER.

3 For a discussion of this phenomenon and variants on it, see Peter Hulme, 'In the Wake of Columbus: Frederick Ober's Ambulant Gloss', *Literature & History* 3rd series 6, 2 (Autumn 1997), 18–36.
4 Freya Stark, *The Valley of the Assassins and other Persian Travels* [1934] (New York: The Modern Library, 2001), pp.86–7.
5 John Steinbeck, *Travels with Charley in Search of America* (New York: The Viking Press, 1962), p.125.
6 Steinbeck, *Travels with Charley*, p.126.
7 Mary Baine Campbell, *The Witness and the Other World: Exotic European Travel Writing, 400–1600* (Ithaca, NY: Cornell University Press, 1988), p.4.
8 Fanny Parkes, *Wanderings of a Pilgrim in Search of the Picturesque, during four and twenty years in the East; with revelations of Life in the Zenāna*, 2 vols. (London: Pelham Richardson, 1850) vol. 2, p.496.
9 Paul Genoni, 'The Pilgrim's Progress across Time: Medievalism and Modernity on the Road to Santiago', *Studies in Travel Writing* 15, 2 (June 2011), 157 (157–75). Further page references will be given parenthetically.
10 On this revival, Genoni deploys Nancy Frey's term, 'reanimation' from Nancy Louise Frey, *Pilgrim Stories: On and Off the Road to Santiago* (Berkeley: University of California Press, 1998).
11 Stark, *The Valley of the Assassins*, p.235.
12 I refer here to literary New Age travellers, not to the communal kinds of experience discussed in Kevin Hetherington, *New Age Travellers: Vanloads of Uproarious Humanity* (London: Cassell, 2000).
13 Robert Clarke, '"New Age trippers": Aboriginality and Australian New Age travel books', *Studies in Travel Writing* 13, 1 (February 2009), 27 (27–43).
14 Sidonie Smith, *Moving Lives: Twentieth-Century Women's Travel Writing* (Minneapolis: University of Minnesota Press, 2001), p.56.
15 Robyn Davidson, *Tracks* [1980] (London: Vintage, 1992), pp.49–50. Further page references will be given parenthetically.
16 Smith, *Moving Lives*, p.56.
17 See for example, Mary *Rowlandson, The Sovereignty and Goodness of God, Together, with the Faithfulness of his Promises Displayed Being a Narrative of the Captivity and Restauration of Mrs. Mary Rowlandson* (1681) and Daniel J. Vitkus, ed., *Piracy, Slavery and Redemption: Barbary Captivity Narratives from Early Modern England* (New York: Columbia University Press, 2001).
18 Syed Manzurul Islam, *The Ethics of Travel: From Marco Polo to Kafka* (Manchester: Manchester University Press, 1996).
19 Patrick Holland and Graham Huggan, *Tourists with Typewriters: Critical Reflections on Contemporary Travel Writing* (Ann Arbor: University of Michigan Press, 1998), p.123.
20 Chinua Achebe, 'An image of Africa: Racism in Conrad's *Heart of Darkness*', in *Hopes and Impediments: Selected Essays 1965–1987* (Oxford: Heinemann International, 1988), p.8 (pp.1–13).

21 Joseph Conrad, *Heart of Darkness* [1902] (Harmondsworth: Penguin, 1973), pp. 7, 33.
22 Peter Matthiessen, *The Snow Leopard* [1978] (London: Harvill, 1989), p.13. Further references will be given parenthetically.
23 On belatedness, see Ali Behdad, *Belated Travelers: Orientalism in the Age of Colonial Dissolution* (Durham, NC: Duke University Press, 1994).
24 Peter Bishop, 'The Geography of Hope and Despair: Peter Matthiessen's *The Snow Leopard*', *Critique* 26, 4 (1985), 206 (203–16).
25 Michael Shapiro, 'The Snow Leopard: Peter Matthiessen', in Michael Shapiro, ed., *A Sense of Place: Great Travel Writers Talk about their Craft, Lives, and Inspiration*' (Palo Alto, CA: Travelers' Tales, 2004), p.359 (pp.345–60).
26 Casey Blanton, *Travel Writing: The Self and the World* (New York: Twayne, 1997), p.81.
27 Blanton, *Travel Writing*, p.81.
28 Mitch Cullin, 'Crows in the Hair', in Raphael Kadushin, ed., *Wonderlands: Good Gay Travel Writing* (Madison: University of Wisconsin Press, 2004), p.270 (pp. 263–74).
29 Susan Fox Rogers, 'Traveling with Desire and Father', in Lucy Jane Bledsoe, ed., *Lesbian Travels: A Literary Companion* (San Francisco: Whereabouts Press, 1998), p.157 (pp.156–66).
30 Rogers, 'Traveling with Desire and Father', p.164.
31 Rogers, 'Traveling with Desire and Father', p.166.
32 Lawrence Ferlinghetti, *Seven Days in Nicaragua Libre* (San Francisco: City Lights Books, 1984), np.
33 Joan Didion, *Salvador* (London: Chatto and Windus, 1983), p.19. Further page references will be given parenthetically.
34 George Monbiot, *Poisoned Arrows: An investigative journey through Indonesia* (London: Michael Joseph, 1989), p.241.
35 Monbiot, *Poisoned Arrows*, p.242.
36 Bill Bryson, *Notes from a Small Island* [1992] (London: Black Swan, 1998), p.225. Further page references will be given parenthetically.
37 Nicola J. Watson, *The Literary Tourist: Readers and Places in Romantic and Victorian Britain* (Houndmills: Palgrave, 2006) and Nicola J. Watson, ed., *Literary Tourism and Nineteenth-Century Culture* (Houndmills: Palgrave Macmillan, 2009); Shapiro, ed., *A Sense of Place*, p.387, my emphasis.

Chapter 7 Inner journeys

1 Colin Thubron, *Among the Russians* [1983] (London: Penguin, 1985), p.1.
2 Sara Wheeler, *Terra Incognita: Travels in Antarctica* [1996] (London: Vintage, 1997), p.250. Further page references will be given parenthetically.
3 Noreen Branson and Margot Heinemann, *Britain in the Nineteen Thirties* (London: Weidenfeld and Nicolson, 1971), p.258.

4 Graham Greene, *Journey Without Maps* [1936] (London: Pan, 1957), p.7. Further page references will be given parenthetically. Although not usually regarded as a modernist, Greene was a contemporary of those who were, and *Journey without Maps* mirrors many modernists' employment of Freud.

5 For the background to this trip and more on Greene's notices, see Tim Butcher, 'Graham Greene: Our Man in Liberia', *History Today* 60, 10 (2010). Available at: historytoday.com/tim-butcher/graham-greene-our-man-liberia, last accessed 14 January 2012. Butcher is also the author of *Chasing the Devil: The Search for Africa's Fighting Spirit* (2010), in which he follows in the footsteps of Greene, as he had Stanley in *Blood River: A Journey To Africa's Broken Heart* (2007).

6 Paul Fussell, *Abroad: British Literary Traveling between the Wars* (New York: Oxford University Press, 1980), p.67.

7 Sigmund Freud, 'Civilization and Its Discontents' [1930], in Freud, *Civilization, Society and Religion,* The Penguin Freud Library, vol.12 (London: Penguin, 1985), pp.286–7 (pp.243–340).

8 Carl Thompson also makes this point. Thompson, *Travel Writing* (London: Routledge, 2011), pp.121–2. My reading of the text differs from Thompson's, however, in that I believe Greene does comment directly on the connections between his childhood, recent past and the images of Africa he presents and is explicit about the psychological benefit he hopes to gain (cf. Thompson, pp.114, 121).

9 Abdul R. JanMohamed, 'The Economy of Manichean Allegory: The Function of Racial Difference in Colonialist Literature', *Critical Inquiry* 12, 1 (Autumn 1985), 64 (59–87).

10 JanMohamed, 'The Economy of Manichean Allegory', 64.

11 Philip Dodd, 'The Views of Travellers: Travel Writing in the 1930s', *Prose Studies* 5, 1 (1982), 131 (127–38).

12 George W. Stocking, Jr. *Race, Culture, and Evolution: Essays in the History of Anthropology* [1968] (Chicago: Chicago University Press, 1982) p.126.

13 Bernard Schweizer also makes this connection. Schweizer, *Radicals on the Road: The Politics of English Travel Writing in the 1930s* (Charlottesville: University Press of Virginia, 2001), pp.146–51.

14 Another way of making this point about intertextuality is to say, in the words of the reader's report on the present volume, that 'travel writing grows out of itself as well as out of journeys'.

15 Butcher, 'Graham Greene'. Butcher claims that Greene was 'in effect, working as an agent for the Anti-Slavery and Aborigines' Protection Society' to investigate the authorities' selling of their own people as slaves.

16 Schweizer, *Radicals on the Road*, p.146.

17 Michael Kowaleski, 'Introduction: the Modern Literature of Travel', in Michael Kowaleski, ed., *Temperamental Journeys: Essays on the Modern Literature of Travel* (Athens, GA: University of Georgia Press, 1992), p.9. Further page references will be given parenthetically.

18 Dea Birkett and Sara Wheeler, 'Introduction', in Dea Birkett and Sara Wheeler, eds., *Amazonian: The Penguin Book of Women's New Travel Writing* (London: Penguin, 1998), p.viii.
19 Birkett and Wheeler, 'Introduction', p.ix.
20 Birkett and Wheeler, 'Introduction', p.ix.
21 Nigel Leask, *Curiosity and the Aesthetics of Travel Writing 1780–1840* (Oxford: Oxford University Press, 2002), p.23.
22 Dennis Porter, *Haunted Journeys: Desire and Transgression in European Travel Writing* (Princeton, NJ: Princeton University Press, 1991), p.5. Further page references will be given parenthetically.
23 Wayne Koestenbaum, 'Goodbye Vienna', in Raphael Kadushin, ed., *Wonderlands: Good Gay Travel Writing* (Madison: University of Wisconsin Press, 2004), p.193 (pp. 185–95).
24 Geoffrey Moorhouse, 'The Inward Journey, the Outward Passage: a Literary Balancing Act', *Studies in Travel Writing* 3 (1999), 21 (17–25).
25 Mary Morris, 'Women and Journeys: Inner and Outer', in Kowaleski, ed., *Temperamental Journeys*, p.25 (pp.25–32).
26 Morris, 'Women and Journeys: Inner and Outer', p.30.
27 Mitch Cullin, 'Crows in the Hair', in Raphael Kadushin, ed., *Wonderlands: Good Gay Travel Writing* (Madison: University of Wisconsin Press, 2004), p.269 (pp.263–74).
28 Cullin, 'Crows in the Hair', p.270.

Chapter 8 Travelling b(l)ack

1 Richard Wright, *Black Power: A Record of Reactions in a Land of Pathos* [1954] (New York: Harper Perennial, 1995), p.148.
2 Colleen J. McElroy, *A Long Way from St. Louie* (Minneapolis: Coffee House Press, 1997), p.iv.
3 Indira Ghose, *Women Travellers in Colonial India: The Power of the Female Gaze* (Delhi: Oxford University Press, 1998), p.9.
4 Barbara Korte, *English Travel Writing from Pilgrimages to Postcolonial Explorations*, Catherine Matthias, trans. (Basingstoke: Macmillan, 2000), p.153.
5 Patrick Holland and Graham Huggan, *Tourists with Typewriters: Critical Reflections on Contemporary Travel Writing* (Ann Arbor: University of Michigan Press, 1998), p.22.
6 Korte, *English Travel Writing*, p.159.
7 See, for example, Michael H. Fisher, *Counterflows to Colonialism: Indian Travellers and Settlers in Britain, 1600–1858* (Delhi: Permanent Black, 2004) and *The Travels of Dean Mahomet*, Michael H. Fisher, ed. (University of California Press, 1997), and Simonti Sen, *Travels to Europe: Self and Other in Bengali Travel Narratives, 1870–1910* (Hyderabad: Orient Longman, 2005).

8 Mary Louise Pratt, *Imperial Eyes: Travel Writing and Transculturation* (London: Routledge, 1992), p.6.

9 Steve Clark, ed., 'Introduction', *Travel Writing and Empire: Postcolonial Theory in Transit* (London: Zed Books, 1999), pp.1–28, quotation at p.3.

10 Mary Baine Campbell, 'Travel writing and its theory', in Peter Hulme and Tim Youngs, eds., *The Cambridge Companion to Travel Writing* (Cambridge: Cambridge University Press, 2002), p.264 (pp.261–78).

11 Justin Edwards and Rune Graulund, 'Introduction: Reading Postcolonial Travel Writing', in Justin Edwards and Rune Graulund, eds., *Postcolonial Travel Writing: Critical Explorations* (Houndmills: Palgrave Macmillan, 2011), p. 3 (pp.1–16).

12 Vikram Seth, *From Heaven Lake: Travels through Sinkiang and Tibet* [1983] (London: Phoenix, 2001), p.xi.

13 Seth, *From Heaven Lake*, p.vi.

14 Korte, *English Travel Writing*, p.159.

15 Edwards and Graulund, 'Introduction', p.5.

16 Edwards and Graulund, 'Introduction', pp.5–6.

17 Korte, *English Travel Writing*, pp.152–3.

18 Korte, *English Travel Writing*, p.154.

19 Korte, *English Travel Writing*, p.154.

20 Amritjit Singh, 'Introduction' to Richard Wright, *Black Power: A Record of Reactions in a Land of Pathos* [1954] (New York: Harper Perennial, 1995), p.xxi (pp.xi-xxxiv). Further page references to this work will be given parenthetically.

21 Caryl Phillips, *The European Tribe* [1987] (London: Faber and Faber, 1988), p.2. Further page references will be given parenthetically.

22 Korte, *English Travel Writing*, p.161.

23 For discussion of this question in relation to another Black British travel text, see Tim Youngs, '"A Personal Journey on a Historic Route": Gary Younge's *No Place Like Home*', in Hagen Schulz-Forberg, ed., *Unravelling Civilization: European Travel and Travel Writing* (Brussels: Peter Lang, 2005), pp.323–39.

24 On McElroy, see Tim Youngs, 'Pushing against the black/white limits of maps: African American writings of travel', *English Studies in Africa* 53, 2 (2010), 71–85.

25 Carl Thompson, *Travel Writing* (London: Routledge, 2011), p.164.

26 See Youngs, '"A Personal Journey"', and Youngs, 'Pushing against the black/white limits of maps'.

27 Bhajju Shyam, with Sirish Rao and Gita Wolf, *The London Jungle Book* [2004] (London: Tara Publishing in association with the Museum of London, 2005), [np]. Because the book is unpaginated, further quotations from it in this section will not be referenced.

28 Sirish Rao and Gita Wolf, 'How London became a Jungle', in *The London Jungle Book*. Rao and Wolf's essay at the end of the book explains its genesis and context. Shyam worked alongside another Gond artist, Ram Singh Urvethi, who is mentioned only in the afterword.

29 Johannes Fabian, *Time and the Other: How Anthropology Makes its Object* (New York: Columbia University Press, 1983), p.31.
30 See, for example, the work of Stephen Muecke, discussed in Tim Youngs, 'Making it Move: The Aboriginal in the Whitefella's Artifact', in Julia Kuehn and Paul Smethurst, eds., *Travel Writing, Form, and Empire: The Poetics and Politics of Mobility* (New York: Routledge, 2009), pp.148–66.
31 Thompson, *Travel Writing*, p.163.
32 Holland and Huggan, *Tourists with Typewriters*, p.65.

Chapter 9 Gender and sexuality

1 Dea Birkett and Sara Wheeler, 'Introduction', in Dea Birkett and Sara Wheeler, eds., *Amazonian: The Penguin Book of Women's New Travel Writing* (London: Penguin, 1998), p.viii.
2 Edmund White, *States of Desire: Travels in Gay America* [1980] (London: Picador, 1986), p.144.
3 The reprinted titles by Virago include Emily Eden, *Up the Country: Letters from India* [1866] (1997), Lady Mary Wortley Montagu's *The Turkish Embassy Letters* [1763] (1994), Isabella L. Bird, *A Lady's Life in the Rocky Mountains* [1879] (1982), Lucie Duff Gordon, *Letters from Egypt* [1865] (1983), and, most famously, Mary Kingsley, *Travels in West Africa* [1897] (1982).
4 See, for example, Alison Blunt, *Travel, Gender, and Imperialism: Mary Kingsley and West Africa* (New York: The Guilford Press, 1994).
5 Birkett and Wheeler, 'Introduction', p.viii.
6 Birkett and Wheeler, 'Introduction', p.xi.
7 Glen Winfield, 'Interview with Colleen J. McElroy', *Studies in Travel Writing* 16, 1 (2012), 73.
8 See Tim Youngs, 'Pushing against the black/white limits of maps: African American writings of travel', *English Studies in Africa* 53, 2 (2010), 71–85.
9 Winfield, 'Interview with Colleen J. McElroy', 74.
10 Indira Ghose, *Women Travellers in Colonial India: The Power of the Female Gaze* (Delhi: Oxford University Press, 1998), p.3.
11 Ghose, *Women Travellers*, p.9.
12 Ghose, *Women Travellers*, p.4.
13 Sara Mills, *Discourses of Difference: An Analysis of Women's Travel Writing and Colonialism* (London: Routledge, 1991), pp.27–30.
14 Simonti Sen, *Travels to Europe: Self and Other in Bengali Travel Narratives, 1870–1910* (Hyderabad: Orient Longman, 2005), p.23.
15 Mary Morris, 'Women and Journeys: Inner and Outer', in Michael Kowaleski, ed., *Temperamental Journeys: Essays on the Modern Literature of Travel* (Athens, Ga.: University of Georgia Press, 1992), p.30 (pp.25–32).
16 Morris, 'Women and Journeys: Inner and Outer', p.31.
17 Ghose, *Women Travellers*, p.10.

18 Ghose, *Women Travellers*, p.10.

19 Patrick Holland and Graham Huggan, *Tourists with Typewriters: Critical Reflections on Contemporary Travel Writing* (Ann Arbor: University of Michigan Press, 1998), p.131. Further page references will be given parenthetically.

20 Ghose, *Women Travellers*, p.6.

21 Bernard Schweizer, *Radicals on the Road: The Politics of English Travel Writing in the 1930s* (Charlottesville: University Press of Virginia, 2001), p.81.

22 Ghose, *Women Travellers in Colonial India*, p.6.

23 Ghose, *Women Travellers in Colonial India*, p.10.

24 Ghose, *Women Travellers in Colonial India*, p.5.

25 Elizabeth A. Bohls, *Women Travel Writers and the Language of Aesthetics, 1716–1818* (Cambridge: Cambridge University Press, 1995), p.6.

26 Bohls, *Women Travel Writers*, p.12.

27 Birkett and Wheeler, 'Introduction', p.xi.

28 Birkett and Wheeler, 'Introduction', p.x.

29 Debbie Lisle, *The Global Politics of Contemporary Travel Writing* (Cambridge: Cambridge University Press, 2006), p.95. Further page references will be given in the text.

30 Bohls, *Women Travel Writers*, p.17.

31 Sara Wheeler, 'A traveller's tale: And the boys came too', *The Guardian*, Family Section, pp.1–2, 10 October 2009.

32 See Lila Marz Harper, *Solitary Travelers: Nineteenth-century Women's Travel Narratives and the Scientific Vocation* (Madison, NJ: Fairleigh Dickinson University Press, 2001) and my colleague Carl Thompson's ongoing work on Maria Graham.

33 Sidonie Smith, *Moving Lives: Twentieth-Century Women's Travel Writing* (Minneapolis: University of Minnesota Press, 2001), p.x.

34 Smith, *Moving Lives*, p.xi.

35 Ghose, *Women Travellers*, p.12.

36 Sara Wheeler, *Terra Incognita: Travels in Antarctica* [1996] (London: Vintage, 1997), p.196.

37 Wheeler, *Terra Incognita*, p.6.

38 Sara Wheeler, *Cherry: A Life of Cherry Apsley-Garrard* (London: Jonathan Cape, 2001).

39 Anne Morrow Lindbergh, *North to the Orient* (London: Chatto & Windus, 1935), p.31.

40 Annie Caulfield, *Travel Writing: A Practical Guide* (Ramsbury: The Crowood Press, 2007), p. 20.

41 Ian Littlewood, *Sultry Climates: Travel and Sex since the Grand Tour* (London: John Murray, 2001), p.24.

42 Christopher Isherwood, *Christopher and His Kind, 1929–1939* (London: Eyre Methuen, 1977), p.10.

43 Isherwood, *Christopher and His Kind*, p.233.

44 Isherwood, *Christopher and His Kind*, pp.234–5.
45 See also Duncan Fallowell's work, especially *One Hot Summer in St. Petersburg* (1994).
46 White, *States of Desire*, p.16. Further page references to this work will be given parenthetically.
47 Rebecca Brown, 'Foreword', to Lucy Jane Bledsoe, ed., *Lesbian Travels: A Literary Companion* (San Francisco: Whereabouts Press, 1998), p.viii (pp.vii-ix).
48 Brown, 'Foreword', p.ix.
49 Brown, 'Foreword', p.ix.
50 Lucy Jane Bledsoe, 'Preface', in Bledsoe, ed., *Lesbian Travels*, pp.xi-xii (pp.xi-xiii).
51 Bledsoe, 'Preface', p.xii.
52 Donna Allegra, 'Dancing Home a Stranger', in Bledsoe, ed., *Lesbian Travels*, p.154 (pp.138–55), ellipses in original.
53 Allegra, 'Dancing Home a Stranger', p.154.
54 Allegra, 'Dancing Home a Stranger', p.155.
55 Brown, 'Foreword', p.ix.
56 Edmund White, *The Flâneur: A Stroll through the Paradoxes of Paris* [2008] (London: Bloomsbury, 2010), pp.145–6.
57 White, *The Flâneur*, p.147.
58 Lucy Jane Bledsoe, 'Preface', in Lucy Jane Bledsoe, ed., *Gay Travels: A Literary Companion* (San Francisco: Whereabouts Press, 1998), p.xi (pp.xi-xiii).
59 Bledsoe, ed., *Gay Travels*, p.xi.
60 Bledsoe, ed., *Gay Travels*, pp.xi-xii.
61 Bledsoe, ed., *Gay Travels*, p.xi.
62 Bledsoe, ed., *Gay Travels*, p.xi.
63 Geoffrey Moorhouse, 'The Inward Journey, the Outward Passage: A Literary Balancing Act', *Studies in Travel Writing* 3 (1999), 21 (17–25).
64 Paul Theroux, 'Being a Man' [1983], in *Sunrise with Seamonsters* [1985] (London: Penguin, 1986), p.309 (pp.309–12).
65 Theroux, 'Being a Man', p.310.
66 Theroux, 'Being a Man', p.310.
67 Littlewood, *Sultry Climates*, p.129.
68 Littlewood, *Sultry Climates*, p.139.
69 Littlewood, *Sultry Climates*, p.143.
70 Ian Littlewood, *Sultry Climates*, p.5.
71 See, for example, Robert Aldrich, *The Seduction of the Mediterranean: Writing, Art, and Homosexual Fantasy* (London: Routledge, 1993).
72 Littlewood, *Sultry Climates*, p.125.

Chapter 10 Writing travel

1 Paul Theroux, 'Discovering Dingle' [1976]', in *Sunrise with Seamonsters* [1985] (London: Penguin, 1986), p. 140 (pp.140–5).

2 Peter Bishop, 'The Geography of Hope and Despair: Peter Matthiessen's *The Snow Leopard*', *Critique* 26, 4 (1985), 204 (203–16).

3 Francis Bacon, 'Of Travel', in *Bacon's Essays* with annotations by Richard Whately (New York: C. S. Francis and Co., 1857), pp.178–9 (pp.178–80).

4 Nabil Matar, ed. and trans., *In the Lands of the Christians: Arabic Travel Writing in the Seventeenth Century* (New York: Routledge, 2003), p.xxi.

5 Cynthia Dial, *Travel Writing* (Abingdon: Hodder and Stoughton, 2001), p.4.

6 Dial, *Travel Writing*, p.6.

7 Dial, *Travel Writing*, p.5.

8 Dial, *Travel Writing*, p.108.

9 Dial, *Travel Writing*, p.110.

10 Dial, *Travel Writing*, p.111.

11 Dial, *Travel Writing*, p.117.

12 Jonathan Raban, personal communication 12 April 2012. This corrects the typographical error 'fictia' in Michael Shapiro, ed., *A Sense of Place: Great Travel Writers Talk about their Craft, Lives, and Inspiration* (Palo Alto, CA: Travelers' Tales, 2004), p.56. Further references to the interview with Shapiro will be given parenthetically.

13 Theroux, 'Discovering Dingle', p.140.

14 Carl Thompson, *The Suffering Traveller and the Romantic Imagination* (Oxford: Clarendon Press, 2007), p.10.

15 Richard Harding Davis, *Three Gringos in Venezuela and Central America* (New York: Harper and Brothers, 1896), p.205.

16 Davis, *Three Gringos*, pp.205–6.

17 Davis, *Three Gringos*, p.206.

18 Bill Bryson, *Notes from a Small Island* [1992] (London: Black Swan, 1998), p.233. Further page references will be given parenthetically.

19 Tim Youngs, 'Interview with Gary Younge', *Studies in Travel Writing* 6 (2002), 101 (96–107).

20 Tim Youngs, 'Interview with William Dalrymple', *Studies in Travel Writing* 9, 1 (March 2005), 38 (37–63).

21 Youngs, 'Interview with William Dalrymple', 42.

22 William Dalrymple, *City of Djinns: A Year in Delhi* [1993] (London: Flamingo, 1994), p.3.

23 Peter Hulme and Tim Youngs, *Talking about Travel Writing: A Conversation between Peter Hulme and Tim Youngs* (Leicester: The English Association, 2007), p.3.

24 Youngs, 'Interview with William Dalrymple', 38–9.

25 Youngs, 'Interview with William Dalrymple', 38.

26 Peter Hulme, 'Travelling to write (1940–2000)', in Peter Hulme and Tim Youngs, eds., *The Cambridge Companion to Travel Writing* (Cambridge: Cambridge University Press, 2002), p.90 (pp.87–101).

27 Youngs, 'Interview with William Dalrymple', 40.

28 Tim Youngs, 'Interview with Robyn Davidson', *Studies in Travel Writing* 9, 1 (March 2005), 21–36, quotation at 27.

29 Youngs, 'Interview with Robyn Davidson', 25.
30 Youngs, 'Interview with Robyn Davidson', 27.
31 Borm, 'Defining Travel', p.13. Borm adds that 'it therefore seems appropriate to consider the terms *the literature of travel*, or simply *travel literature*, as synonyms of *travel writing*' (p.13).
32 Amanda Lohrey on cover of Stephen Muecke, *No Road (bitumen all the way)* (South Fremantle: Fremantle Arts Centre Press, 1997).
33 Back cover blurb of *No Road*.
34 Stephen Muecke, 'Gulaga Story', *Studies in Travel Writing* 11, 1 (2007), 83 (83–91). Reprinted in Stephen Muecke, *Joe in the Andamans and other fictocritical stories* (Sydney: Local Consumption Publications, 2008), pp.38–48.
35 Muecke, 'Gulaga Story', 86.
36 For more on Muecke see Tim Youngs, 'Making it Move: The Aboriginal in the Whitefella's Artifact', in Julia Kuehn and Paul Smethurst, eds., *Travel Writing, Form, and Empire: The Poetics and Politics of Mobility* (New York: Routledge, 2009), pp.148–66.
37 V. S. Naipaul, *India: A Million Mutinies Now* (London: Heinemann, 1990), p.493. Further page references will be given parenthetically.
38 Dial, *Travel Writing*, p.47.
39 Shapiro, ed., *A Sense of Place*, pp.59–60.
40 Colleen J. McElroy, *Over the Lip of the World: Among the Storytellers of Madagascar* (Seattle: University of Washington Press, 1999), p.7.
41 Paul Theroux, *The Old Patagonian Express: By Train through the Americas* [1979] (London: Penguin Books, 1980), p.11. Further page references will be given parenthetically.

Chapter 11 Reading travel writing

1 Jonathan Raban, 'The Journey and the Book', in *For Love and Money: Writing, Reading, Travelling, 1969–1987* (London: Collins Harvill, 1987), p.258 (pp.253–60).
2 Peter Hulme, *Colonial Encounters: Europe and the Native Caribbean 1492–1797* [1986] (London: Routledge, 1992), Mary Louise Pratt, *Imperial Eyes: Travel Writing and Transculturation* (London: Routledge, 1992), Sara Mills, *Discourses of Difference: An Analysis of Women's Travel Writing and Colonialism* (London: Routledge, 1991).
3 Edward W. Said, *Orientalism* [1978] (Harmondsworth: Penguin, 1985), p.5.
4 Said, *Orientalism*, p.7.
5 Edward W. Said, *Orientalism* (Harmondsworth: Penguin Books, 1978), p.21.
6 Johannes Fabian, *Time and the Other: How Anthropology Makes its Object* (New York: Columbia University Press, 1983), p.95.
7 Aijaz Ahmad, *In Theory: Classes, Nations, Literatures* (London: Verso, 1994), p.185.
8 Ahmad, *In Theory*, p.93. These complaints are echoed by those who argue that studies of literary travel writing ignore the realities of travel for the majority of

people, to which a contentious answer would be that the subject of literary studies is different from that of the social sciences.

9 Dennis Porter, *Haunted Journeys: Desire and Transgression in European Travel Writing* (Princeton, NJ: Princeton University Press, 1991), p.21.

10 Caren Kaplan, *Questions of Travel: Postmodern Discourses of Displacement* (Durham, NC: Duke University Press, 1996), p.103.

11 George E. Marcus and Michael J. Fischer, *Anthropology as Cultural Critique: An Experimental Moment in the Human Sciences* (Chicago: Chicago University Press, 1986), p.8.

12 Fredric Jameson, *The Political Unconscious: Narrative as a Socially Symbolic Act* (London: Methuen, 1981), p.20.

13 Alasdair Pettinger, '"Trains and Boats and Planes": Some Reflections on Travel Writing and Public Transport', in Jean-Yves Le Disez and Jan Borm, eds., *Seuils et Traverses: Enjeux de l'écriture du voyage* 2 vols. (Brest: Université de Bretagne Occidentale; Université de Versailles-Saint-Quentin-en-Yvelines, 2002), vol. 2, p.107 (pp.107–115). Pettinger's short essay considers extracts from five texts in which the 'we' of communal travelling does appear, 'signalling a shared experience or condition which pushes against the genre's individualistic ethos' and which, even if suppressed, is 'worth paying attention to' (p.115).

14 Patrick Holland and Graham Huggan, *Tourists with Typewriters: Critical Reflections on Contemporary Travel Writing* (Ann Arbor: University of Michigan Press, 1998), p.8.

15 Raban, 'The Journey and the Book', p.258.

16 See Mary Baine Campbell, 'Travel and its Theory', in Peter Hulme and Tim Youngs, eds., *The Cambridge Companion to Travel Writing* (Cambridge: Cambridge University Press, 2002), pp.261–78.

17 Barbara Korte, *English Travel Writing from Pilgrimages to Postcolonial Explorations*, Catherine Matthias, trans. (Basingstoke: Macmillan, 2000), p.6.

18 See, for example, Diana Knight, *Barthes and Utopia: Space, Travel, Writing* (Oxford: Clarendon Press, 1997); Margarita D. Marinova, *Transnational Russian-American Travel Writing* (New York: Routledge, 2011).

19 D. B. and Alison Quinn, 'The Editing of Richard Hakluyt's "Discourse of Western Planting"', in Germaine Warkentin, *Critical Issues in Editing Exploration Texts: Papers given at the twenty-eighth annual Conference on Editorial Problems 6–7 November 1992* (Toronto: University of Toronto Press, 1995), p.65 (pp.53–66).

20 David Henige, 'Tractable Texts: Modern Editing and the Columbian Writings', in Germaine Warkentin, ed., *Critical Issues in Editing Exploration Texts: Papers given at the twenty-eighth Annual Conference on Editorial Problems, University of Toronto, 6–7 November 1992* (University of Toronto Press, 1995), p.31 (pp.1–35).

21 Henige, 'Tractable Texts', p.10.

22 Susan Morgan, *Place Matters: Gendered Geography in Victorian Women's Travel Books about Southeast Asia* (New Brunswick, NJ.: Rutgers University Press, 1996), p.9.

23 Holland and Huggan, *Tourists with Typewriters*, p.68.

24 Michael Cronin, *Across the Lines: Travel, Language, Translation* (Cork: Cork University Press, 2010), p.2.
25 Cronin, *Across the Lines*, p.4.
26 Charles Forsdick, 'Introduction: contemporary travel writing in French: tradition, innovation, boundaries', *Studies in Travel Writing* 13, 4 (December 2009), 287 (287–91).
27 Nabil Matar, ed. and trans., *In the Lands of the Christians: Arabic Travel Writing in the Seventeenth Century* (New York: Routledge, 2003), p.xxxii.
28 Cronin, *Across the Lines*, p.4. See also p.2.
29 Loredana Polezzi, 'Translation, Travel, Migration', *Translation, Travel, Migration*, ed. Loredana Polezzi. Special issue of *The Translator* 12, 2 (2006), 171 (169–88). See also Loredana Polezzi, *Translating Travel: Contemporary Italian Travel Writing in English Translation* (Aldershot: Ashgate, 2001).
30 Polezzi, 'Translation, Travel, Migration', 179–80.
31 Polezzi, 'Translation, Travel, Migration', 180.
32 Polezzi, 'Translation, Travel, Migration', 180–1.
33 Polezzi, 'Translation, Travel, Migration', 177.
34 Polezzi, 'Translation, Travel, Migration', 179.
35 Roy C. Bridges, 'Nineteenth-Century East African Travel Records with an Appendix on "Armchair Geographers" and Cartography', *Paideuma* 33 (1987), 180 (179–96).
36 I made this point also in Tim Youngs, *Travellers in Africa: British Travelogues 1850–1900* (Manchester: Manchester University Press, 1994), pp.5–6.
37 Leila Koivunen, *Visualizing Africa in Nineteenth-Century British Travel Accounts* (New York: Routledge, 2009), p.7. See also I. S. MacLaren, 'In consideration of the evolution of explorers and travellers into authors; a model', *Studies in Travel Writing* 15, 3 (September 2011), 221–41.
38 Koivunen, *Visualizing Africa*, p.233, n39.
39 Jeremy Black, *The British Abroad: The Grand Tour in the Eighteenth Century* (Stroud: Sutton, 1992), p.xi.
40 Black, *The British Abroad*, p. xii.
41 Black, *The British Abroad*, p. xiii.
42 Koivunen, *Visualizing Africa*, p.5.
43 Koivunen, *Visualizing Africa*, p.7.
44 Koivunen, *Visualizing Africa*, p.7.
45 Korte, *English Travel Writing*, p.5.
46 Holland and Huggan, *Tourists with Typewriters*, p.11.
47 Holland and Huggan, *Tourists with Typewriters*, p.19.
48 Steve Clark, ed., 'Introduction', *Travel Writing and Empire: Postcolonial Theory in Transit* (London: Zed Books, 1999), pp.1–28, quotation at p.2.
49 Holland and Huggan, *Tourists with Typewriters*, p.24.
50 Holland and Huggan, *Tourists with Typewriters*, p.67.
51 Anne Morrow Lindbergh, *North to the Orient* (London: Chatto & Windus, 1935), pp.32–3.

Chapter 12 The way ahead: Travel writing in the twenty-first century

1 Annie Caulfield, *Travel Writing: A Practical Guide* (Ramsbury: The Crowood Press, 2007), p.23.
2 Jan Morris, 'A war hero and a writer of grace: Paddy was the ideal scholarly Englishman', *The Observer*, 12 June 2011, p.30.
3 W. Fraser Rae, *The Business of Travel: A Fifty Years' Record of Progress* (London: Thomas Cook and Son, 1891), p.10.
4 Jonathan Raban, 'The Journey and the Book' [1982], in *For Love and Money: Writing, Reading, Travelling, 1969–1987* (London: Collins Harvill, 1987), p.257 (pp.253–60).
5 Sidonie Smith, *Moving Lives: Twentieth-Century Women's Travel Writing* (Minneapolis: University of Minnesota Press, 2001), p.203.
6 Smith, *Moving Lives*, p.203.
7 Smith, *Moving Lives*, p.204.
8 Sue Thomas, *Hello World: travels in virtuality* (York: Raw Nerve Books, 2004), p.9.
9 Michael Cronin, *Across the Lines: Travel, Language, Translation* (Cork: Cork University Press, 2010), p.5.
10 Thomas, *Hello World*, p.51. Further page references will be given parenthetically.
11 Martin Dodge and Rob Kitchin, *Mapping Cyberspace* (London: Routledge, 2001), p.32. Quoted in Thomas, *Hello World*, p.70.
12 There are exceptions, including Krim Benterrak, Stephen Muecke and Paddy Roe, *Reading the Country* (1984) and the fascinating volume recording the 1935 Soviet *Chelyuskin* expedition in which the more than 100 people on the vessel of that name spent two months on an icefloe after their ship had been crushed and sunk by ice. The book, edited by Schmidt, presents brief chapters giving the accounts of many of the people involved. The effect is to provide multiple perspectives on the event and to build up a sense of community. See Alec Brown trans., *The Voyage of the Chelyuskin*, by Members of the Expedition (New York: The Macmillan Company, 1935).
13 www.travellerspoint.com/blog.cfm, last accessed 28 July 2011.
14 www.travelblog.org/ and www.travelpod.com, last accessed 3 February 2012.
15 See, for example, gutenberg.net.au/explorers.html, ebooks.adelaide.edu.au/t/travel/, southseas.nla.gov.au/index_voyaging.html and lewisandclarkjournals.unl.edu/, all last accessed 16 January 2012.
16 Smith, *Moving Lives*, pp.204–5.
17 Smith, *Moving Lives*, p.205.
18 Smith, *Moving Lives*, p.207.
19 Smith, *Moving Lives*, pp.205–6.
20 Smith, *Moving Lives*, p.207.
21 Smith, *Moving Lives*, p.207.
22 Debbie Lisle, *The Global Politics of Contemporary Travel Writing* (Cambridge: Cambridge University Press, 2006), p.70.

23 Patrick Holland and Graham Huggan, *Tourists with Typewriters: Critical Reflections on Contemporary Travel Writing* (Ann Arbor: University of Michigan Press, 1998), p.197.
24 Holland and Huggan, *Tourists with Typewriters*, p.198.
25 Rhett Butler, 'How to travel ethically: An interview with writer and responsible tourism expert Jeff Greenwald', news.mongabay.com/2006/1127-interview_greenwald.html, accessed 5 February 2012.
26 Butler, 'How to travel ethically'.
27 George Monbiot, *Heat: How to Stop the Planet Burning* (London: Penguin, 2006), 188. Quoted in Martin Padget, 'The Politics of Investigative Travel Writing: An Interview with George Monbiot', *Studies in Travel Writing* 15, 2 (2011), 189–209.
28 Lisle, *The Global Politics*, p.76.
29 Lisle, *The Global Politics*, p.83.
30 David Callahan, 'Consuming and erasing Portugal in the Lonely Planet guide to East Timor', *Postcolonial Studies* 14, 1 (2011), 98 (95–109).
31 Holland and Huggan, *Tourists with Typewriters*, p.viii.
32 Peter Hulme, 'In the Wake of Columbus: Frederick Ober's Ambulant Gloss', *Literature & History* 3rd series 6, 2 (Autumn 1997), 18–36; Maria Lindgren Leavenworth, *The Second Journey: Travelling in Literary Footsteps* 2nd, revised ed. (Umeå: Umeå University, 2010). A fresh example of the footsteps genre appeared while this book was in press. Robert MacFarlane's *The Old Ways: A Journey on Foot* (London: Hamish Hamilton, 2012) has the author following ancient routes in and beyond Britain,
33 Leavenworth, *The Second Journey*, p.192.
34 For example, Roy Bridges' edition of 'Jacob Wainwright's Diary of the Transportation of Dr Livingstone's Body to the Coast, May 1873 to February 1874' in Herbert K. Beals et al, eds., *Four Travel Journals / The Americas, Antarctica and Africa / 1775–1874* (London: Hakluyt Society, 2007).
35 See, for example, www.virtualmigrants.com/, accessed 4 February 2012.
36 Corinne Fowler, *Chasing Tales: travel writing, journalism and the history of ideas about Afghanistan* (Amsterdam: Rodopi, 2007).
37 Peter Carey, *Wrong about Japan: A Father's Journey with his Son* (Sydney: Vintage, 2004), p.70. Further page references will be given in the text.
38 www.computerworld.com/s/article/9132979/A_Twitter_first_NASA_astronaut_sends_first_tweet_from_space, accessed 12 December 2010. Massimino sent emails to Mission Control, which then uploaded them to his twitter page.
39 At livingstone.library.ucla.edu/bambarre/imageprocessing.htm accessed 16 January 2012.
40 See Justin D. Edwards and Rune Graulund, *Mobility at Large: Globalization, Textuality and Innovative Travel Writing* (Liverpool: Liverpool University Press, 2012).
41 Santiago J. Henríquez Jiménez, 'Values and Visions in Dalrymple's Travel Writing: A Sort of Interview', in Santiago J. Henríquez Jiménez, ed., *Géneros en contacto: Viajes,*

crimen, novela femenina y humor. Miscelánea de literature inglesa y nortamericana (Las Palmas de Gran Canaria: Servicio de Publicaciones de la Universidad de Las Palmas de Gran Canaria, 2004), p.183.

42 Ian Littlewood, *Sultry Climates: Travel and Sex since the Grand Tour* (London: John Murray, 2001), p.20.

43 Casey Blanton, *Travel Writing: The Self and the World* (New York: Twayne, 1997), p.29.

Select Bibliography

Primary

Auden, W. H. and Louis MacNeice. *Letters from Iceland*. London: Faber and Faber, 1937.

Bledsoe, Lucy Jane, ed. *Gay Travels: A Literary Companion*. San Francisco: Whereabouts Press, 1998.

Lesbian Travels: A Literary Companion. San Francisco: Whereabouts Press, 1998.

Brody, Hugh. *Maps and Dreams: Indians and the British Columbia Frontier* [1981]. London: Faber and Faber, 1986.

Bryson, Bill. *Notes from a Small Island* [1992]. London: Black Swan, 1998.

Byron, Robert. *The Road to Oxiana* [1937]. London: Penguin, 1992.

Carey, Peter. *Wrong about Japan: A Father's Journey with His Son*. Sydney: Vintage, 2004.

Cook, James. *The Journals*. Prepared from the original manuscripts by J. C. Beaglehole for the Hakluyt Society, 1955–67. Selected and edited by Philip Edwards. London: Penguin, 2003.

Coriat Junior [Samuel Paterson]. *Another Traveller! Or Cursory Remarks and Critical Observations Made upon a Journey through Part of the Netherlands in the Latter End of the Year 1766*, 2 vols. London: Joseph Johnson and J. Payne, 1767.

Cullin, Mitch. 'Crows in the Hair'. In Raphael Kadushin, ed., *Wonderlands: Good Gay Travel Writing*. Madison: University of Wisconsin Press, 2004, pp. 263–74.

Cummings, E. E. *Eimi*. New York: Covici, Friede, 1933.

Dalrymple, William. *City of Djinns: A Year in Delhi* [1993]. London: Flamingo, 1994.

Davidson, Robyn. *Tracks* [1980]. London: Vintage, 1992.

Davis, Richard Harding. *Three Gringos in Venezuela and Central America*. New York: Harper and Brothers, 1896.

Didion, Joan. *Salvador*. London: Chatto and Windus, 1983.

Diski, Jenny. *Skating to Antarctica*. London: Granta Books, 1997.

The Epic of Gilgamesh: An English Version with an Introduction. N. K. Sanders, ed., Harmondsworth: Penguin, 1972.

Ferlinghetti, Lawrence. *Seven Days in Nicaragua Libre*. San Francisco: City Lights Books, 1984.

Fermor, Patrick Leigh. *A Time of Gifts: On Foot to Constantinople: From the Hook of Holland to the Middle Danube* [1977]. London: John Murray, 2004.

Gilpin, William. *Observations on the River Wye, and Several Parts of South Wales, &c. Relative Chiefly to Picturesque Beauty: Made in the Summer of the Year 1770* [1782]. 4th ed. London: T. Cadell Junior and W. Davies, 1800.

Three Essays: On Picturesque Beauty; on Picturesque Travel; and on Sketching Landscape: To Which is Added a Poem, on Landscape Painting. London: R. Blamire, 1792.

Greene, Graham. *Journey Without Maps* [1936]. London: Pan, 1957.

Hakluyt, Richard. *The Principal Navigations, Voyages, Traffiques & Discoveries of the English Nation, Made by Sea or Overland to the Remote and Farthest Distant Quarters of the Earth at Any Time within the Compass of these 1600 Yeeres*. 8 vols. London: J. M. Dent and Co., [n.d.].

Hamilton, Marybeth. *In Search of the Blues: Black Voices, White Visions*. London: Jonathan Cape, 2007.

Isherwood, Christopher. *Christopher and His Kind, 1929–1939*. London: Eyre Methuen, 1977.

Iyer, Pico. *The Global Soul: Jet Lag, Shopping Malls and the Search for Home* [2000]. London: Bloomsbury, 2001.

Kadushin, Raphael. 'Introduction'. In Raphael Kadushin, ed., *Wonderlands: Good Gay Travel Writing*. Madison: University of Wisconsin Press, 2004, pp. 3–7.

ed., *Wonderlands: Good Gay Travel Writing*. Madison: University of Wisconsin Press, 2004.

Kaplan, Caren. *Questions of Travel: Postmodern Discourses of Displacement*. Durham, NC: Duke University Press, 1996.

Kerouac, Jack. *Lonesome Traveler*. New York: McGraw-Hill, 1960.

Koestenbaum, Wayne. 'Goodbye Vienna'. In Raphael Kadushin, ed., *Wonderlands: Good Gay Travel Writing*. Madison: University of Wisconsin Press, 2004, pp. 185–95.

Lawrence, D. H. *Mornings in Mexico*. London: Martin Secker, 1927.

Sea and Sardinia [1923]. Harmondsworth: Penguin, 1944.

Lewis, Wyndham. *Filibusters in Barbary*. London: Grayson and Grayson, 1932.

Lindbergh, Anne Morrow. *North to the Orient*. London: Chatto & Windus, 1935.

Lowenthal, Michael. 'When Will You Be Here Again?' In Raphael Kadushin, ed., *Wonderlands: Good Gay Travel Writing*. Madison: University of Wisconsin Press, 2004, pp.37–42.

Mandeville, John. *The Travels of Sir John Mandeville*. C. W. R. D. Moseley, trans. London: Penguin, 1983.

Matar, Nabil, ed. and trans. *In the Lands of the Christians: Arabic Travel Writing in the Seventeenth Century*. New York: Routledge, 2003.

Matthiessen, Peter. *The Snow Leopard* [1978]. London: Harvill, 1989.

McElroy, Colleen J. *Over the Lip of the World: Among the Storytellers of Madagascar*. Seattle: University of Washington Press, 1999.

Montagu, Lady Mary Wortley. *The Turkish Embassy Letters*. Introduction by Anita Desai. Edited with notes by Malcolm Jack. London: Virago, 1994.
Muecke, Stephen. 'Gulaga Story'. *Studies in Travel Writing* **11**, 1 (2007), 83–91.
Murphy, Thomas D. *British Highways and Byways from a Motor Car: Being a Record of a Five Thousand Mile Tour in England, Wales and Scotland* [1908]. 2nd ed. Boston: L. C. Page and Company, 1909.
Naipaul, V. S. *India: A Million Mutinies Now*. London: Heinemann, 1990.
Nerburn, Kent. *Neither Wolf nor Dog: On Forgotten Roads with an Indian Elder* [1994]. Novato, CA: New World Library, 2002.
Newby, Eric. *A Traveller's Life* [1982]. London: Picador, 1983.
Parkes, Fanny. *Wanderings of a Pilgrim in Search of the Picturesque, during four and twenty years in the East; with revelations of Life in the Zenāna*. 2 vols. London: Pelham Richardson, 1850.
Phillips, Caryl. *The European Tribe* [1987]. London: Faber and Faber, 1988.
Polo, Marco. *The Travels of Marco Polo the Venetian*. Introduction by John Masefield. London: J. M. Dent, 1908.
Ralegh, Sir Walter. *The Discoverie of the Large, Rich and Bewtiful Empyre of Guiana*. Transcribed, annotated and introduced by Neil L. Whitehead. Manchester: Manchester University Press, 1997.
Seth, Vikram. *From Heaven Lake: Travels through Sinkiang and Tibet* [1983]. London: Phoenix, 2001.
Shyam, Bhajju with Sirish Rao and Gita Wolf. *The London Jungle Book* [2004]. London: Tara Publishing in association with the Museum of London, 2005.
Smedley, Agnes. *China Fights Back: An American Woman with the Eighth Route Army*. London: Victor Gollancz, 1938.
Spoken Word, The: Travel Writers. London: British Library, 2012. Audio recording.
Stanley, Henry M. *Through the Dark Continent. Or the Sources of the Nile around the Great Lakes of Equatorial Africa and down the Livingstone River to the Atlantic Ocean* [1878]. London: Sampson Low, Marston, Searle & Rivington, 1890.
Stark, Freya. *The Valley of the Assassins and other Persian Travels* [1934]. New York: The Modern Library, 2001.
Steinbeck, John. *A Russian Journal* with photographs by Robert Capa. New York: The Viking Press, 1948.
Travels with Charley in Search of America. New York: The Viking Press, 1962.
Sterne, Laurence. *A Sentimental Journey through France and Italy* [1768]. Harmondsworth: Penguin, 1967.
Theroux, Paul. 'Discovering Dingle' [1976]. In *Sunrise with Seamonsters* [1985]. London: Penguin, 1986, pp.140–5.
'Stranger on a Train: The Pleasures of Railways' [1976]. In *Sunrise with Seamonsters* [1985]. London: Penguin, 1986, pp.126–35.
The Old Patagonian Express: By Train through the Americas [1979]. London: Penguin Books, 1980.
Thomas, Sue. *Hello World: Travels in Virtuality*. York: Raw Nerve Books, 2004.

Thompson, Carl, ed. *Romantic-Era Shipwreck Narratives: An Anthology.* Nottingham: Trent Editions, 2007.
Thompson, R. Wardlaw. *My Trip in the 'John Williams'.* London: London Missionary Society, 1900.
Thoreau, Henry David. *Walden, or Life in the Woods* [1854] *and On the Duty of Civil Disobedience* [1866]. New York: The New American Library, 1960.
Thubron, Colin. *Among the Russians* [1983]. London: Penguin, 1985.
Twain, Mark. *The Innocents Abroad, or The New Pilgrim's Progress* [1869]. New York: Airmont, 1967.
Vincent, J. E. *Through East Anglia in a Motor Car.* London: Methuen & Co., 1907.
Wheeler, Sara. *Terra Incognita: Travels in Antarctica* [1996]. London: Vintage, 1997.
White, Edmund. *States of Desire: Travels in Gay America* [1980]. London: Picador, 1986.
The Flâneur: A Stroll through the Paradoxes of Paris [2008]. London: Bloomsbury, 2010.
Wollstonecraft, Mary. *Letters Written During a Short Residence in Sweden, Norway and Denmark* [1796]. Fontwell: Centaur Press, 1970.
Wright, Richard. *Black Power: A Record of Reactions in a Land of Pathos* [1954]. New York: Harper Perennial, 1995.

Secondary

Abrams, M. H. 'Introduction: Spiritual Travellers in Western Literature'. In Bruno Magliocchetti and Anthony Verna, eds., *The Motif of the Journey in Nineteenth-Century Italian Literature.* Gainesville: University Press of Florida, 1994, pp.1–20.
Adams, Percy G. *Travelers and Travel Liars, 1660–1800.* Berkeley: University of California Press, 1962.
Banco, Lindsey Michael. *Travel and Drugs in Twentieth-Century Travel Literature.* New York: Routledge, 2010.
Barber, Giles. 'The English-Language guide book to Europe up to 1870'. In Robin Myers and Michael Harris, eds., *Journeys through the Market: Travel, Travellers and the Book Trade.* New Castle, DE: Oak Knoll Press, 1999, pp.93–106.
Batten, Charles L. Jr. *Pleasurable Instruction: Form and Convention in Eighteenth-Century Travel Literature.* Berkeley: California University Press, 1978.
Bendixen, Alfred and Judith Hamera, eds., *The Cambridge Companion to American Travel Writing.* Cambridge: Cambridge University Press, 2009.
Birkett, Dea and Sara Wheeler, 'Introduction'. In Dea Birkett and Sara Wheeler, eds., *Amazonian: The Penguin Book of Women's New Travel Writing.* London: Penguin, 1998, pp.vii–xiii.
Bishop, Peter. 'The Geography of Hope and Despair: Peter Matthiessen's *The Snow Leopard*', *Critique* **26**, 4 (1985), 203–16.

Black, Jeremy. *The British Abroad: The Grand Tour in the Eighteenth Century*. Stroud: Sutton, 1992.

'The Grand Tour'. In Robin Myers and Michael Harris, eds., *Journeys through the Market: Travel, Travellers and the Book Trade*. New Castle, DE: Oak Knoll Press, 1999, pp. 65–91.

Blanton, Casey. *Travel Writing: The Self and the World*. New York: Twayne, 1997.

Blunt, Alison. *Travel, Gender, and Imperialism: Mary Kingsley and West Africa*. New York: The Guilford Press, 1994.

Bohls, Elizabeth A. *Women Travel Writers and the Language of Aesthetics, 1716–1818*. Cambridge: Cambridge University Press, 1995.

Bohls, Elizabeth A. and Ian Duncan, eds., *Travel Writing 1700–1830: An Anthology*. Oxford: Oxford University Press, 2005.

Borm, Jan. 'Defining Travel: On the Travel Book, Travel Writing and Terminology'. In Glenn Hooper and Tim Youngs, eds., *Perspectives on Travel Writing*. Aldershot: Ashgate, 2004, pp.13–26.

Bridges, Roy C. 'Exploration and Travel outside Europe'. In Peter Hulme and Tim Youngs, eds., *The Cambridge Companion to Travel Writing*. Cambridge: Cambridge University Press, 2002, pp.53–69.

'Nineteenth-Century East African Travel Records'. *Paideuma* **33** (1987), 179–96.

Buzard, James. *The Beaten Track: European Tourism, Literature, and the Ways to 'Culture' 1800–1918*. Oxford: Clarendon Press, 1993.

Campbell, Mary Baine. *The Witness and the Other World: Exotic European Travel Writing, 400–1600*. Ithaca: Cornell University Press, 1988.

'Travel writing and its theory'. In Peter Hulme and Tim Youngs, eds., *The Cambridge Companion to Travel Writing*. Cambridge: Cambridge University Press, 2002, pp.261–78.

Carr, Helen. 'Modernism and Travel (1880–1940)'. In Peter Hulme and Tim Youngs, eds., *The Cambridge Companion to Travel Writing*. Cambridge: Cambridge University Press, 2002, pp.70–86.

Castillo, Susan and David Seed, eds., *American Travel and Empire*. Liverpool: Liverpool University Press, 2009.

Caulfield, Annie. *Travel Writing: A Practical Guide*. Ramsbury: The Crowood Press, 2007.

Chard, Chloe. *Pleasure and Guilt on the Grand Tour: Travel Writing and Imaginative Geography 1600–1830*. Manchester: Manchester University Press, 1999.

Clark, Steve, ed. 'Introduction'. *Travel Writing and Empire: Postcolonial Theory in Transit*. London: Zed Books, 1999, pp.1–28.

Clarke, Robert. '"New Age trippers": Aboriginality and Australian New Age travel books'. *Studies in Travel Writing* **13**, 1 (February 2009), 27–43.

Cronin, Michael. *Across the Lines: Travel, Language, Translation*. Cork: Cork University Press, 2010.

Dial, Cynthia. *Travel Writing*. Abingdon: Hodder and Stoughton, 2001.

Dodd, Philip. 'The Views of Travellers: Travel Writing in the 1930s'. *Prose Studies* **5**, 1 (1982), 127–38.

Donovan, Stephen. 'Tourism in Extremis: Travel and Adventure in the Congo'. In Tim Youngs, ed., *Travel Writing in the Nineteenth Century*. London: Anthem Press, 2006, pp.37–54.

Edwards, Justin and Rune Graulund. 'Introduction: Reading Postcolonial Travel Writing'. In Justin Edwards and Rune Graulund, eds., *Postcolonial Travel Writing: Critical Explorations*. Houndmills: Palgrave Macmillan, 2011, pp.1–16.

Elsner, Jaś and Joan Pau Rubiés. 'Introduction'. In Jaś Elsner and Joan Pau Rubiés, eds., *Voyages and Visions: Towards a Cultural History of Travel*. London: Reaktion, 1999, pp.1–56.

Farley, David G. *Modernist Travel Writing: Intellectuals Abroad*. Columbia: University of Missouri Press, 2010.

Fenwick, Gillian. *Traveling Genius: The Writing Life of Jan Morris*. Columbia: University of South Carolina Press, 2008.

Forsdick, Charles. 'French Representations of Niagara: From Hennepin to Butor'. In Susan Castillo and David Seed, eds., *American Travel and Empire*. Liverpool University Press, 2009, pp.56–77.

'Introduction: contemporary travel writing in French: tradition, innovation, boundaries'. *Studies in Travel Writing* **13**, 4 (December 2009), 287–91.

Frow, John. *Genre*. London: Routledge, 2006.

Fuller, Mary C. *Voyages in Print: English Travel to America, 1576–1624*. Cambridge: Cambridge University Press, 1995.

Fussell, Paul. *Abroad: British Literary Traveling between the Wars*. New York: Oxford University Press, 1980.

Genoni, Paul. 'The Pilgrim's Progress across Time: Medievalism and Modernity on the Road to Santiago'. *Studies in Travel Writing* **15**, 2 (June 2011), 157–75.

Ghose, Indira. *Women Travellers in Colonial India: The Power of the Female Gaze*. Delhi: Oxford University Press, 1998.

Gosch, Stephen S. and Peter N. Stearns. *Premodern Travel in World History*. New York: Routledge, 2008.

Hadfield, Andrew. *Literature, Travel, and Colonial Writing in the English Renaissance, 1545–1625*. Oxford: Oxford University Press, 1998.

Hagglund, Elizabeth. 'Reviews of travel in the *Monthly Review*, 1749–1758: An introductory survey with an appendix on travel-related books reviewed by the *Monthly Review*'. *Studies in Travel Writing* **2** (Spring 1998), 1–45.

Haynes, Jonathan. *The Humanist as Traveler: George Sandys's Relation of a Journey begun An. Dom. 1610*. Rutherford, NJ: Fairleigh Dickinson/ Associated University Presses, 1986.

Henige, David. 'Tractable Texts: Modern Editing and the Columbian Writings'. In Germaine Warkentin, ed., *Critical Issues in Editing Exploration Texts: Papers given at the twenty-eighth annual Conference on Editorial Problems 6–7 November 1992*. Toronto: University of Toronto Press, 1995, pp.1–35.

Henríquez Jiménez, Santiago J. 'Values and Visions in Dalrymple's Travel Writing: A Sort of Interview'. In Santiago J. Henríquez Jiménez, ed., *Géneros en contacto: Viajes, crimen, novela femenina y humor. Miscelánea de literature inglesa y nortamericana*. Las Palmas de Gran Canaria: Servicio de Publicaciones de la Universidad de Las Palmas de Gran Canaria, 2004, 179–83.

Herbert, Christopher. *Culture and Anomie: Ethnographic Imagination in the Nineteenth Century*. Chicago: University of Chicago Press, 1991.

Hetherington, Kevin. *New Age Travellers: Vanloads of Uproarious Humanity*. London: Cassell, 2000.

Hohepa, Pat. 'My Musket, My Missionary, and My Mana'. In Alex Calder, Jonathan Lamb and Bridget Orr, eds., *Voyages and Beaches: Pacific Encounters, 1769–1840*. Honolulu: University of Hawai'i Press, 1999, pp.180–201.

Holland, Patrick and Graham Huggan. *Tourists with Typewriters: Critical Reflections on Contemporary Travel Writing*. Ann Arbor: University of Michigan Press, 1998.

Howard, Donald R. *Writers and Pilgrims: Medieval Pilgrimage Narratives and their Posterity*. Berkeley: University of California Press, 1980.

Hulme, Peter. *Colonial Encounters: Europe and the Native Caribbean 1492–1797* [1986]. London: Routledge, 1992.

'In the Wake of Columbus: Frederick Ober's Ambulant Gloss'. *Literature & History* 3rd series 6, **2** (Autumn 1997), 18–36.

'Travelling to write (1940–2000)'. In Peter Hulme and Tim Youngs, eds., *The Cambridge Companion to Travel Writing*. Cambridge: Cambridge University Press, 2002, pp.87–101.

Hulme, Peter and Tim Youngs, eds., *The Cambridge Companion to Travel Writing*. Cambridge: Cambridge University Press, 2002.

Hulme, Peter and Tim Youngs. *Talking about Travel Writing: A Conversation between Peter Hulme and Tim Youngs*. Leicester: The English Association, 2007.

Humble, Noreen. 'Xenophon's *Anabasis*: Self and Other in Fourth-Century Greece'. In Patrick Crowley, Noreen Humble and Silvia Ross, eds., *Mediterranean Travels: Writing Self and Other from the Ancient World to Contemporary Society*. London: Modern Humanities Research Association and Maney Publishing, 2011, pp.14–31.

Islam, Syed Manzurul. *The Ethics of Travel: From Marco Polo to Kafka*. Manchester: Manchester University Press, 1996.

Jameson, Fredric. *The Political Unconscious: Narrative as a Socially Symbolic Act*. London: Methuen, 1981.

JanMohamed, Abdul R. 'The Economy of Manichean Allegory: The Function of Racial Difference in Colonialist Literature'. *Critical Inquiry* **12**, 1 (Autumn 1985), 59–87.

Jarvis, Robin. *Romantic Writing and Pedestrian Travel*. Basingstoke: Macmillan, 1997.

Johnston, Anna. *Missionary Writing and Empire, 1800–1860*. Cambridge: Cambridge University Press, 2003.

Kaplan, Caren. *Questions of Travel: Postmodern Discourses of Displacement* Durham, NC: Duke University Press, 1996.

Koivunen, Leila. *Visualizing Africa in Nineteenth-Century British Travel Accounts*. New York: Routledge, 2009.

Korte, Barbara. *English Travel Writing from Pilgrimages to Postcolonial Explorations*. Catherine Matthias, trans. Basingstoke: Macmillan, 2000.

Kowaleski, Michael. 'Introduction: The Modern Literature of Travel'. In Michael Kowaleski, ed., *Temperamental Journeys: Essays on the Modern Literature of Travel*. Athens, GA: University of Georgia Press, 1992, pp.1–16.

Lamb, Jonathan. *Preserving the Self in the South Seas, 1680–1840*. University of Chicago Press, 2001.

Leask, Nigel. *Curiosity and the Aesthetics of Travel Writing 1780–1840*. Oxford: Oxford University Press, 2002.

Leavenworth, Maria Lindgren. *The Second Journey: Travelling in Literary Footsteps*. 2nd, revised ed. Umeå: Umeå University, 2010.

Lisle, Debbie. *The Global Politics of Contemporary Travel Writing*. Cambridge: Cambridge University Press, 2006.

Littlewood, Ian. *Sultry Climates: Travel and Sex since the Grand Tour*. London: John Murray, 2001.

Mackenthun, Gesa. *Metaphors of Dispossession: American Beginnings and the Translation of Empire, 1492–1637*. Norman: Oklahoma University Press, 1997.

MacLaren, I. S. 'In Consideration of the Evolution of Explorers and Travellers into Authors: One Model'. *Studies in Travel Writing* **15**, 3 (September 2011), 221–41.

Mills, Sara. *Discourses of Difference: An Analysis of Women's Travel Writing and Colonialism*. London: Routledge, 1991.

Moessner, David P. *Lord of the Banquet: The Literary and Theological Significance of the Lukan Travel Narrative*. Minneapolis: Augsburg Fortress Press, 1989.

Moorhouse, Geoffrey. 'The Inward Journey, the Outward Passage: A Literary Balancing Act'. *Studies in Travel Writing* **3** (1999), 17–25.

Morgan, Susan. *Place Matters: Gendered Geography in Victorian Women's Travel Books about Southeast Asia*. New Brunswick, NJ.: Rutgers University Press, 1996.

Morris, Mary. 'Women and Journeys: Inner and Outer'. In Michael Kowaleski, ed., *Temperamental Journeys: Essays on the Modern Literature of Travel*. Athens, Ga.: University of Georgia Press, 1992, pp.25–32.

Moseley, C. W. R. D. 'Introduction'. *The Travels of Sir John Mandeville*. C.W.R.D. Moseley, trans. London: Penguin, 1983, pp.9–39.

Nicholl, Charles. *The Creature in the Map: Sir Walter Ralegh's Quest for El Dorado* [1996]. London: Vintage, 1995.

Norman, Sylva. 'Introduction'. In Mary Wollstonecraft, *Letters Written During a Short Residence in Sweden, Norway and Denmark* [1796]. Fontwell: Centaur Press, 1970, pp.v–xv.

Payne, Anthony. *Richard Hakluyt: A guide to his books and to those associated with him 1580–1625*. London: Bernard Quaritch, 2008.

Peat, Alexandra. *Travel and Modernist Literature: Sacred and Ethical Journeys*. New York: Routledge, 2011.

Pettinger, Alasdair. '"Trains and Boats and Planes": Some Reflections on Travel Writing and Public Transport'. In Jean-Yves Le Disez and Jan Borm, eds., *Seuils et Traverses: Enjeux de l'écriture du voyage*. 2 vols. Brest: Université de Bretagne Occidentale; Université de Versailles-Saint-Quentin-en-Yvelines, 2002, vol. 2, pp.107–115.

Polezzi, Loredana. *Translating Travel: Contemporary Italian Travel Writing in English Translation*. Aldershot: Ashgate, 2001.

'Translation, Travel, Migration'. *Translation, Travel, Migration*, Loredana Polezzi, ed., Special issue of *The Translator* **12**, 2 (2006), 169–88.

Porter, Dennis. *Haunted Journeys: Desire and Transgression in European Travel Writing*. Princeton: Princeton University Press, 1991.

Pratt, Mary Louise. *Imperial Eyes: Travel Writing and Transculturation*. London: Routledge, 1992.

Pretzler, Maria. *Pausanias: Travel Writing in Ancient Greece*. London: Duckworth, 2007.

Quinn, D. B. and Alison Quinn. 'The Editing of Richard Hakluyt's "Discourse of Western Planting"'. In Germaine Warkentin, *Critical Issues in Editing Exploration Texts: Papers given at the twenty-eighth annual Conference on Editorial Problems 6–7 November 1992*. Toronto: University of Toronto Press, 1995, pp.53–66.

Raban, Jonathan. 'The Journey and the Book' [1982]. In *For Love and Money: Writing, Reading, Travelling, 1969–1987*. London: Collins Harvill, 1987, pp.253–60.

Rae, W. Fraser. *The Business of Travel: A Fifty Years' Record of Progress*. London: Thomas Cook and Son, 1891.

Rao, Sirish and Gita Wolf. 'How London became a Jungle'. In Bhajju Shyam, with Sirish Rao and Gita Wolf, *The London Jungle Book* [2004]. London: Tara Publishing in association with the Museum of London, 2005, n.p.

Redford, Bruce. *Venice and the Grand Tour*. New Haven, CT: Yale University Press, 1996.

Said, Edward W. *Orientalism*. Harmondsworth: Penguin Books, 1978.

Schivelbusch, Wolfgang. *The Railway Journey: Trains and Travel in the Nineteenth Century*. Oxford: Wiley-Blackwell, 1980.

Schweizer, Bernard. *Radicals on the Road: The Politics of English Travel Writing in the 1930s*. Charlottesville: University Press of Virginia, 2001.

Sen, Simonti. *Travels to Europe: Self and Other in Bengali Travel Narratives, 1870–1910*. Hyderabad: Orient Longman, 2005.

Shapiro, Michael, ed. *A Sense of Place: Great Travel Writers Talk about their Craft, Lives, and Inspiration.* Palo Alto, CA: Travelers' Tales, 2004.
Smith, Sidonie. *Moving Lives: Twentieth-Century Women's Travel Writing.* Minneapolis: University of Minnesota Press, 2001.
Smith, Stan. 'Burbank with a Baedeker: Modernism's Grand Tours'. *Studies in Travel Writing* **8**, 1 (2004), 1–18.
Thompson, Carl. *The Suffering Traveller and the Romantic Imagination.* Oxford: Clarendon Press, 2007.
Travel Writing. London: Routledge, 2011.
Thouroude, Guillaume. 'Towards generic autonomy: The *récit de voyage* as mode, genre and form'. *Studies in Travel Writing* **13**, 4 (December 2009), 381–90.
Webb, Diana. *Medieval European Pilgrimage, c.700-c.1500.* Houndmills: Palgrave, 2002.
Winfield, Glen. 'Interview with Colleen J. McElroy'. *Studies in Travel Writing* **16**, 1 (2012), 65–77.
Wright, Ronald. *Stolen Continents: The Indian Story* [1992]. London: Pimlico, 1993.
Youngs, Tim. 'Africa/Congo: The Politics of Darkness'. In Peter Hulme and Tim Youngs, eds., *The Cambridge Companion to Travel Writing.* Cambridge: Cambridge University Press, 2002, pp.156–73.
'"A Personal Journey on a Historic Route": Gary Younge's *No Place Like Home*'. In Hagen Schulz-Forberg, ed., *Unravelling Civilization: European Travel and Travel Writing.* Brussels: Peter Lang, 2005, pp.323–39.
'Auden's travel writings'. In Stan Smith, ed., *The Cambridge Companion to W. H. Auden.* Cambridge: Cambridge University Press, 2004, pp.68–81.
'Interview with Gary Younge'. *Studies in Travel Writing* **6** (2002), 96–107.
'Interview with Robyn Davidson'. *Studies in Travel Writing* **9**, 1 (March 2005), 21–36.
'Interview with William Dalrymple'. *Studies in Travel Writing* **9**, 1 (March 2005), 37–63.
'Making it Move: The Aboriginal in the Whitefella's Artifact'. In Julia Kuehn and Paul Smethurst, eds., *Travel Writing, Form, and Empire: The Poetics and Politics of Mobility.* New York: Routledge, 2009, pp.148–66.
'Pushing against the black/white limits of maps: African American writings of travel'. *English Studies in Africa* **53**, 2 (2010), 71–85.
'The Pacifist Traveller: Kate Crane-Gartz'. In Susan Castillo and David Seed, eds., *American Travel and Empire.* Liverpool: Liverpool University Press, 2009, pp.200–16.
Travel Writing in the Nineteenth Century: Filling the Blank Spaces. London: Anthem Press, 2006.
Travellers in Africa: British Travelogues, 1850–1900. Manchester: Manchester University Press, 1994.
Zumthor, Paul and Catherine Peebles. 'The Medieval Travel Narrative'. *New Literary History*, **25**, 4 (Autumn 1994), 809–24.

INDEX

Cambridge Introductions to Literature

Authors

Margaret Atwood Heidi Macpherson
Jane Austen Janet Todd
Samuel Beckett Ronan McDonald
Walter Benjamin David Ferris
Lord Byron Richard Lansdown
Chekhov James N. Loehlin
J. M. Coetzee Dominic Head
Samuel Taylor Coleridge John Worthen
Joseph Conrad John Peters
Jacques Derrida Leslie Hill
Charles Dickens Jon Mee
Emily Dickinson Wendy Martin
George Eliot Nancy Henry
T. S. Eliot John Xiros Cooper
William Faulkner Theresa M. Towner
F. Scott Fitzgerald Kirk Curnutt
Michel Foucault Lisa Downing
Robert Frost Robert Faggen
Gabriel Garcia Marquez Gerald Martin
Nathaniel Hawthorne Leland S. Person
Zora Neale Hurston Lovalerie King
James Joyce Eric Bulson
Thomas Mann Todd Kontje
Christopher Marlowe Tom Rutter
Herman Melville Kevin J. Hayes
Milton Stephen B. Dobranski
Toni Morrison Tessa Roynon
George Orwell John Rodden and John Rossi
Sylvia Plath Jo Gill
Edgar Allan Poe Benjamin F. Fisher
Ezra Pound Ira Nadel
Marcel Proust Adam Watt
Jean Rhys Elaine Savory
Edward Said Conor McCarthy
Shakespeare Emma Smith
Shakespeare's Comedies Penny Gay
Shakespeare's History Plays Warren Chernaik
Shakespeare's Poetry Michael Schoenfeldt
Shakespeare's Tragedies Janette Dillon
Harriet Beecher Stowe Sarah Robbins
Mark Twain Peter Messent
Edith Wharton Pamela Knights
Walt Whitman M. Jimmie Killingsworth
Virginia Woolf Jane Goldman
William Wordsworth Emma Mason
W. B. Yeats David Holdeman

Topics

American Literary Realism Phillip Barrish
The American Short Story Martin Scofield
Anglo-Saxon Literature Hugh Magennis
Comedy Eric Weitz
Creative Writing David Morley

Early English Theatre Janette Dillon

The Eighteenth-Century Novel April London

Eighteenth-Century Poetry John Sitter

English Theatre, 1660–1900 Peter Thomson

Francophone Literature Patrick Corcoran

Literature and the Environment Timothy Clark

Modern British Theatre Simon Shepherd

Modern Irish Poetry Justin Quinn

Modernism Pericles Lewis

Modernist Poetry Peter Howarth

Narrative (second edition) H. Porter Abbott

The Nineteenth-Century American Novel Gregg Crane

The Novel Marina MacKay

Old Norse Sagas Margaret Clunies Ross

Poetics Michael Hurley and Michael O'Neill

Postcolonial Literatures C. L. Innes

Postmodern Fiction Bran Nicol

Romantic Poetry Michael Ferber

Russian Literature Caryl Emerson

Scenography Joslin McKinney and Philip Butterworth

The Short Story in English Adrian Hunter

Theatre Historiography Thomas Postlewait

Theatre Studies Christopher B. Balme

Tragedy Jennifer Wallace

Travel Writing Tim Youngs

Victorian Poetry Linda K. Hughes

820.932 YA2 CEN
Youngs, Tim,
The Cambridge introduction to travel writing /
CENTRAL LIBRARY
05/14
DISCARD

CPSIA information can be obtained at www.ICGtesting.com
Printed in the USA
LVOW13s1620040114

368076LV00002B/4/P